STUDIES
IN THE
SCRIPTURES

"The Path of the Just is as the Shining Light,
Which Shineth More and More
Unto the Perfect Day."

SERIES I

The Plan of the Ages

A Vindication of the Divine Character and Government:
Showing, by a Recognition and Harmonizing of
all the Scriptures, that the Permission of Evil,
Past and Present, is Educational and
Preparatory to the Ushering of Mankind Into
THE GOLDEN AGE OF PROPHECY
In Which All the Families of the Earth Will Be
Blessed with a Full Knowledge of God and a Full
Opportunity for Attaining Everlasting Life Through
the Redeemer, Who Then Will Be the Great Restorer
and Life-Giver.   Acts 3:19-21

Reprinted in 2023
ASSOCIATED BIBLE STUDENTS
P. O. Box 92
Clawson, MI USA

ISBN 978-0-9844153-0-4

To the King of Kings and Lord of Lords

IN THE INTEREST OF

HIS CONSECRATED SAINTS,

WAITING FOR THE ADOPTION,

—AND OF—

"ALL THAT IN EVERY PLACE CALL UPON THE LORD,"

"THE HOUSEHOLD OF FAITH,"

—AND OF—

THE GROANING CREATION, TRAVAILING AND WAITING FOR THE

MANIFESTATION OF THE SONS OF GOD,

THIS WORK IS DEDICATED.

"To make all see what is the fellowship of the mystery which from the beginning
of the world hath been hid in God." "Wherein He hath abounded toward
us in all wisdom and prudence, having made known unto us the
mystery of His will, according to His good pleasure which
He hath purposed in Himself; that in the dispensation
of the fulness of the times He might
gather together in one all
things, under Christ."
Eph. 3:4, 5, 9; 1:8-10

Written in 1886 by Pastor Russell

PUBLISHERS' FOREWORD

An occasional book will transcend its time and continue to speak with meaning to many generations and thus will become a timeless classic. *The Divine Plan of the Ages* has become a modern religious classic. Quietly its circulation has spiraled well past 8,000,000 and continues to rise steadily year after year. Circulation alone, however, does not convey the scope of its influence. This work contains new ideas and concepts. It presents a chain of Scriptural evidence which reveals a comprehensive view of God's majestic plan. This book enables the reader easily to distinguish the age divisions in the Bible and God's movement in each of them. Because by it so many have been helped in understanding the Bible, it is known among its enthusiastic readers today as the "key to the Scriptures."

The Divine Plan of the Ages is not a new book. It was written in 1886. Its tone and content stood in marked contrast to the preaching of that day. The churches, prepared for an enlarged witness and conquest of the world, were surprised by a massive attack from higher critics of the Bible and religion but lacked intelligent answers to these attacks. A large-scale loss of faith in the inspiration of the Bible resulted. *The Divine Plan of the Ages* helped earnest Christians stem the tide of infidelity and brought a basis of faith even to unbelievers.

The author defined with remarkable clarity the world-wide aspects of the "time of trouble." While others spoke of peace, he boldly forecast spasms of war, revolution and anarchy culminating in the collapse of world governments. Just as the "trouble" was accurately depicted, so also events of today and the future were traced beyond the darkest moments of trouble into the glories of God's "Kingdom Come."

We recommend it unreservedly as a priceless treasure—the most reliable and significant religious work of the 19th and 20th centuries. Every perceptive reader of the Bible should find it a rewarding study.

Publishers' footnotes have superior reference numbers (^{1}); all other footnotes are the author's.

THE PUBLISHERS, 1975

Publishers' footnotes have superior reference numbers (^{1}); all other footnotes are the author's.

"The Divine Plan of the Ages"

THE AUTHOR'S FOREWORD

THE AUTHOR and the publishers desire to publicly acknowledge the favor of God which has permitted them to be identified with the circulation of this Volume, and with the results—light, joy, peace, fellowship with God, to many hungry, thirsty, bewildered souls. The first edition in its present form was issued in 1886. Since then, one edition has followed another in rapid succession and in twenty different languages, until now there are nearly five million copies of it in the hands of the people all the world over.

We cannot hope that these books have all been read; but letters continually coming to hand assure us that they are working powerfully in the hearts and minds of people everywhere. Thousands write us that they have been influenced—some who totally disbelieved in the Bible as a Divine Revelation to mankind. Others write that they have been atheists or approximately so, because they had not previously known the true God and His true Plan of the Ages, and were unable to accept, appreciate or worship the characters usually held before them in the creeds.

For above five years preceding the first publication of this Volume, we had substantially the same matter in print under another name and differently presented. That book was entitled "Food for Thinking Christians." Its style was different in that it first of all attacked the error—demolished it; and then, in its place, erected the fabric of Truth. We finally learned that this was not the best way—that some became alarmed as they saw their errors falling, and failed to read far enough to get a glimpse of the beautiful structure of Truth in place of the demolished errors.

The present Volume was written from the reverse standpoint. It presents the Truth, shows its strength and beauty, and then suggests the removal of the error, as not only unnecessary, but absolutely useless and very injurious. Thus the reader of the DIVINE PLAN OF THE AGES at each step finds a strengthening of faith and a greater nearness to the Lord, and therefore a confidence that he is in the right way. After seeing the Truth, the errors are more and more seen to be absurd, worthless, injurious, and are gladly abandoned.

The great Adversary, of course, has no love for anything which opens the eyes of God's people, increases their reverence for God's Book, and breaks their reliance upon human creeds. The great Adversary, therefore, as we might have expected, is very much opposed to this book. Few realize Satan's power and cunning; few realize the meaning of the Apostle's words in respect to this Prince of Darkness who transforms himself into a minister of light, in order to fight the Truth and destroy its influence. Few realize that our wily Adversary seeks to use the best, the most energetic, the most influential of God's people to hinder the shining of the light and to keep the Divine Plan of the Ages away from the people.

Few realize that from the time creed-making began, A.D. 325, there was practically no Bible study for 1260 years. Few realize that during that time the creeds were riveted upon the minds of millions, shackling them to horrible errors, and blinding them to the Divine character of Wisdom, Justice, Love, Power. Few realize that since the Reformation—since the Bible began to come back into the hands of the people—well-meaning but deluded reformers have been blinded and handicapped by the errors of the past, and, in turn, have served to keep the people in darkness. Few realize that real Bible study, such as was practised in the early Church in the days of the Apostles, has only now come back to Bible students.

In the earliest editions of this Volume, the title, "Millennial Dawn," was used; but we found that some were deceived thereby into thinking it a novel. In order that none might be deceived, and that none might purchase under such deception, we later adopted the present serial title, "Studies in the Scriptures," which nobody can misunderstand.

Many queries have come to us as to why these books cannot be found in the bookstores. Our answer is that while the book publishers would be glad to have these books, there are certain religious zealots who will not permit their sale—threatening boycott. At first this seemed like a great disaster—as though the power of the Adversary would be permitted to hinder the dissemination of the Truth. But God graciously overruled the matter, so that today probably no other book has so large a circulation and so steady a circulation as this Volume. Those who, through prejudice, refused to read the book and fought against it, did so because they believed falsehoods, misrepresentations.

Many of these books have been burned by people who never read them, but who were influenced by misrepresentations. Just so it was during the Dark Ages in respect to the followers of Jesus, who suffered martyrdom. Yes, Jesus Himself suffered at the hands of those who did not understand Him or His teachings, as St. Peter pointedly declares: "And now, brethren, I wot that through ignorance ye did it, as did also your rulers" (Acts 3:17); "for had they known it, they would not have crucified the Lord of Glory." 1 Cor. 2:8

But if the enemies of this book have been bitter, unjust,

iii

untruthful, its friends are proportionately warm and zealous. The millions of copies in the hands of the people have nearly all been passed out through the friends of the book, who, from the love of the Truth, have given time and energy for its wide circulation. While we write these lines, we have knowledge of the fact that approximately six hundred Christian people from various walks of life have "left all" earthly business and calling and ambitions that they may glorify the Lord and bless His hungry saints by putting this little Volume into their hands. These include doctors, schoolteachers, nurses, ministers, barbers, mechanics—people from every walk of life who, touched to the heart themselves with the love of God, are anxious to pass the blessing on to other hearts and heads.

The books are sold at a small price, and these colporteurs who take them around to the public are barely able to make their expenses. They rejoice, however, all the more if sometimes they have privations and are counted worthy to suffer some inconveniences and deprivations for the sake of the Lord, the Truth and the Brethren. The good work goes on, the Message of Life in Christ passes from hand to hand. The present output of this Volume is enormous. May its blessing in future days be proportionately as great as in the past. The author and publishers cannot ask for more.

With very best wishes to all readers,

Your servant in the Lord,
CHARLES T. RUSSELL

Brooklyn, N.Y.,
October 1, 1916

iv

CONTENTS

STUDY I
EARTH'S NIGHT OF SIN TO TERMINATE
IN A MORNING OF JOY

STUDY II
THE EXISTENCE OF A SUPREME INTELLIGENT
CREATOR ESTABLISHED

STUDY III
THE BIBLE AS A DIVINE REVELATION
VIEWED IN THE LIGHT OF REASON

SCRIPTURE STUDIES

STUDY I
EARTH'S NIGHT OF SIN TO TERMINATE
IN A MORNING OF JOY

A Night of Weeping and a Morning of Joy—Two Methods of Seeking Truth—The Method Herein Pursued—Scope of the Work—A Difference between the Reverent Study of the Scriptures and the Dangerous Habit of Speculation—The Object of Prophecy—The Present Religious Condition of the World Viewed from Two Standpoints—Egyptian Darkness—A Bow of Promise—The Path of the Just Progressive—Cause of the Great Apostasy—The Reformation—The Same Cause Again Hinders Real Progress—Perfection of Knowledge Not a Thing of the Past, but of the Future.

THE TITLE of this series of Studies—"The Divine Plan of the Ages," suggests a progression in the Divine arrangement, foreknown to our God and orderly. We believe the teachings of Divine revelation can be seen to be both beautiful and harmonious from this standpoint and from no other. The period in which sin is permitted has been a dark night to humanity, never to be forgotten; but the glorious day of righteousness and divine favor, to be ushered in by Messiah, who, as the Sun of Righteousness, shall arise and shine fully and clearly into and upon all, bringing healing and blessing, will more than counterbalance the dreadful night of weeping, sighing, pain, sickness and death, in which the groaning creation has been so long. "Weeping may endure for a night, but joy cometh in the MORNING." Psa. 30:5

9

As though by instinct, the whole creation, while it groans and travails in pain, waits for, longs for and hopes for the DAY, calling it the Golden Age; yet men grope blindly, because not aware of the great Jehovah's gracious purposes. But their highest conceptions of such an age fall far short of what the reality will be. The great Creator is preparing a "feast of fat things," which will astound his creatures, and be exceedingly, abundantly beyond what they could reasonably ask or expect. And to his wondering creatures, looking at the length and breadth, the height and depth of the love of God, surpassing all expectation, he explains: "My thoughts are not your thoughts, neither are your ways my ways, saith the Lord; for as the heavens are higher than the earth, so are my ways higher than your ways, and my thoughts than your thoughts." Isa. 55:8, 9

Though in this work we shall endeavor, and we trust with success, to set before the interested and unbiased reader the plan of God as it relates to and explains the past, the present and the future of his dealings, in a way more harmonious, beautiful and reasonable than is generally understood, yet that this is the result of extraordinary wisdom or ability on the part of the writer is positively disclaimed. It is the light from the Sun of Righteousness in this dawning of the Millennial Day that reveals these things as "present truth," now due to be appreciated by the sincere—the pure in heart.

Since skepticism is rife, the very foundation of true religion, and the foundation of truth, is questioned often, even by the sincere. We have endeavored to uncover enough of the foundation upon which all faith should be built—the Word of God—to give confidence and assurance in its testimony, even to the unbeliever. And we have endeavored to do this in a manner that will appeal to and can be accepted by reason as a foundation. Then we have endeavored to build upon that foundation the teachings of Scripture, in such a manner that, so far as possible, purely human judgment may try its squares and angles by the most exacting rules of justice which it can command.

Believing that the Scriptures reveal a consistent and harmonious plan, which, when seen, must commend itself to every sanctified conscience, this work is published in the hope of assisting students of the Word of God, by suggesting lines of thought which harmonize with each other and with the inspired Word. Those who recognize the Bible as the revelation of God's plan—and such we specially address—will doubtless agree that, if inspired of God, its teachings must, when taken as a whole, reveal a plan harmonious and consistent with itself, and with the character of its Divine Author. Our object as truth-seekers should be to obtain the complete, harmonious whole of God's revealed plan; and this, as God's children, we have reason to expect, since it is promised that the spirit of truth shall guide us into all truth. John 16:13

As inquirers, we have two methods open to us. One is to seek among all the views suggested by the various sects of the church, and to take from each that element which we might consider truth—an endless task. A difficulty which we should meet by this method would be, that if our judgment were warped and twisted, or our prejudices bent in any direction— and whose are not?—these difficulties would prevent our correct selection, and we might choose the error and reject the truth. Again, if we should adopt this as our method we should lose much, because the truth is progressive, shining more and more unto the perfect day, to those who search for it and walk in the light of it, while the various creeds of the various sects are fixed and stationary, and were made so centuries ago. And each of them must contain a large proportion of error, since each in some important respects contradicts the others. This method would lead into a labyrinth of bewilderment and confusion. The other method is to divest our minds of all prejudice, and to remember that none can know more about the plans of God than he has revealed in his Word, and that it was given to the meek and lowly of heart; and, as such, earnestly and sincerely seeking its guidance and instruction only, we shall by its great Author be guided to an understanding of it, as it becomes due to be understood, by making use of the various helps divinely provided. See Eph. 4:11-16.

As an aid to this class of students, this work is specially designed. It will be noticed that its references are to Scripture only, except where secular history may be called in to prove the fulfilment of Scripture statements. The testimony of modern theologians has been given no weight, and that of the so-called Early Fathers has been omitted. Many of them have testified in harmony with thoughts herein expressed, but we believe it to be a common failing of the present and all times for men to believe certain doctrines because others did so, in whom they had confidence. This is manifestly a fruitful cause of error, for many good people have believed and taught error in all good conscience. (Acts 26:9) Truth-seekers should empty their vessels of the muddy waters of tradition and fill them at the fountain of truth—God's Word. And no religious teaching should have weight except as it guides the truth-seeker to that fountain.

For even a general and hasty examination of the whole Bible and its teaching, this work is too small; but, recognizing the haste of our day, we have endeavored to be as brief as the importance of the subjects seemed to permit.

To the interested student we would suggest that it will be useless for him merely to skim over this work, and hope to obtain the force and harmony of the plan suggested, and the Scripture evidences herein presented. We have endeavored throughout to present the various fragments of truth, not only in such language, but also in such order, as would best enable all classes of readers to grasp the subject and general plan clearly. While thorough and orderly study is necessary to the appreciation of any of the sciences, it is specially so in the science of Divine revelation. And in this work it is doubly necessary, from the fact that in addition to its being a treatise on divinely revealed truths, it is an examination of the subject from, so far as we know, an altogether different standpoint from that of any other work. We have no apology to offer for treating many subjects usually neglected by Christians—among others, the coming of our Lord, and the prophecies and symbolism of the Old and New Testaments. No system of theology should be presented, or accepted, which overlooks or omits the most prominent features of Scripture teaching. We trust, however, that a wide distinction will be recognized between the earnest, sober and reverent study of prophecy and other scriptures, in the light of accomplished historic facts, to obtain conclusions which sanctified common sense can approve, and a too common practice of general speculation, which, when applied to divine prophecy, is too apt to give loose rein to wild theory and vague fancy. Those who fall into this dangerous habit generally develop into prophets (?) instead of prophetic students.

No work is more noble and ennobling than the reverent study of the revealed purposes of God—"which things the angels desire to look into." (1 Pet. 1:12) The fact that God's wisdom provided prophecies of the future, as well as statements regarding the present and the past, is of itself a reproof by Jehovah of the foolishness of some of his children, who have excused their ignorance and neglect of the study of His Word by saying: "There is enough in the fifth chapter of Matthew to save any man." Nor should we suppose that prophecy was given merely to satisfy curiosity

concerning the future. Its object evidently is to make the
consecrated child of God acquainted with his Father's plans,
thus to enlist his interest and sympathy in the same plans, and
to enable him to regard both the present and the future from
God's standpoint. When thus interested in the Lord's work, he
may serve with the spirit and with the understanding also; not
as a servant merely, but as a child and heir. Revealing to such
what shall be, counteracts the influence of what now is. The
effect of careful study cannot be otherwise than strengthening
to faith and stimulating to holiness.

In ignorance of God's plan for the recovery of the world
from sin and its consequences, and under the false idea that
the nominal church, in its present condition, is the sole agency
for its accomplishment, the condition of the world today, after
the Gospel has been preached for nearly nineteen centuries,
is such as to awaken serious doubts in every thoughtful mind
so misinformed. And such doubts are not easily surmounted
with anything short of the truth. In fact, to every thoughtful
observer, one of two things must be apparent: either the
church has made a great mistake in supposing that in the
present age, and in her present condition, her office has been
to convert the world, or else God's plan has been a miserable
failure. Which horn of the dilemma shall we accept? Many
have accepted, and many more doubtless will accept, the latter,
and swell the ranks of infidelity, either covertly or openly. To
assist such as are honestly falling thus, is one of the objects of
this volume.

On page sixteen we present a diagram, published by the
"London Missionary Society," and afterward in the United
States by the "Women's Presbyterian Board of Missions." It
is termed "A Mute Appeal on Behalf of Foreign Missions." It
tells a sad tale of darkness and ignorance of the only name
given under heaven, or among men, whereby we must be
saved.

The Watchman—the "Y.M.C.A." journal of Chicago—published this same diagram, and commenting on it said:

"The ideas of some are very misty and indefinite in regard to the world's spiritual condition. We hear of glorious revival work at home and abroad, of fresh missionary efforts in various directions, of one country after another opening to the gospel, and of large sums being devoted to its spread: and we get the idea that adequate efforts are being made for the evangelization of the nations of the earth. It is estimated today that the world's population is 1,424,000,000, and by studying the diagram we will see that considerably more than one-half—nearly two-thirds—are still *totally heathen,* and the remainder are mostly either followers of Mohammed or members of those great apostate churches whose religion is practically a Christianized idolatry, and who can scarcely be said to hold or teach the gospel of Christ. Even as to the 116 millions of nominal Protestants, we must remember how large a proportion in Germany, England and this country have lapsed into infidelity—a darkness deeper, if possible, than even that of heathenism—and how many are blinded by superstition, or buried in extreme ignorance; so that while eight millions of Jews still reject Jesus of Nazareth, and while more than 300 millions who bear his name have apostatized from his faith, 170 millions more bow before Mohammed, and the vast remainder of mankind are to this day worshipers of stocks and stones, of their own ancestors, of dead heroes or of the devil himself; all in one way or other worshiping and serving the creature instead of the Creator, who is God over all, blessed forever. Is there not enough here to sadden the heart of thoughtful Christians?"

Truly this is a sad picture. And though the diagram represents shades of difference between Heathens, Mohammedans and Jews, all are alike in total ignorance of Christ. Some might at first suppose that this view with reference to the proportion of Christians is too dark and rather overdrawn, but we think the reverse of this. It shows nominal Christianity in the brightest colors possible. For instance,

DIAGRAM

*Exhibiting the Actual and Relative Numbers of Mankind
Classified According to Religion*

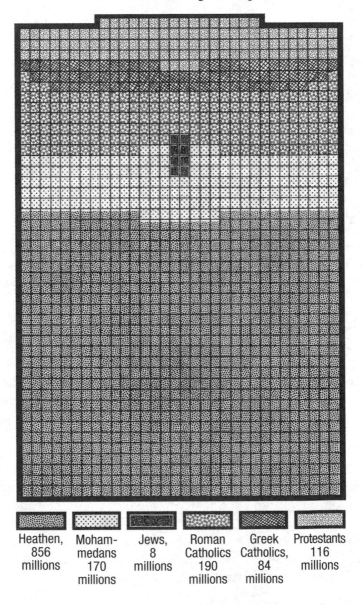

| Heathen, 856 millions | Moham-medans 170 millions | Jews, 8 millions | Roman Catholics 190 millions | Greek Catholics, 84 millions | Protestants 116 millions |

the 116,000,000 put down as Protestant is far in excess of the true number. Sixteen millions would, we believe, more nearly express the number of professing church members of *adult* years, and one million would, we fear, be far too liberal an estimate of the "little flock," the "sanctified in Christ Jesus," who "walk not after the flesh, but after the Spirit." It should be borne in mind that a large proportion of church members, always numbered in the reckoning, are young children and infants. Specially is this the case in the countries of Europe. In many of these, children are reckoned church members from earliest infancy.

But dark as this picture appears, it is not the darkest picture that fallen humanity presents. The above cut represents only the present living generations. When we consider the fact that century after century of the six thousand years past has swept away other vast multitudes, nearly all of whom were enveloped in the same ignorance and sin, how dark is the scene! Viewed from the popular standpoint, it is truly an awful picture.

The various creeds of today teach that all of these billions of humanity, ignorant of the only name under heaven by which we must be saved, are on the straight road to everlasting torment; and not only so, but that all of those 116,000,000 Protestants, except the very few saints, are sure of the same fate. No wonder, then, that those who believe such awful things of Jehovah's plans and purposes should be zealous in forwarding missionary enterprises—the wonder is that they are not frenzied by it. Really to believe thus, and to appreciate such conclusions, would rob life of every pleasure, and shroud in gloom every bright prospect of nature.

To show that we have not misstated "Orthodoxy" on the subject of the fate of the heathen, we quote from the pamphlet—"A Mute Appeal on Behalf of Foreign

Missions"—in which the diagram was published. Its concluding sentence is: "Evangelize the mighty generations abroad—the one thousand million souls who are dying in Christless despair at the rate of 100,000 a day."

But though this is the gloomy outlook from the standpoint of human creeds, the Scriptures present a brighter view, which it is the purpose of these pages to point out. Instructed by the Word, we cannot believe that God's great plan of salvation was ever intended to be, or ever will be, such a failure. It will be a relief to the perplexed child of God to notice that the Prophet Isaiah foretells this very condition of things, and its remedy, saying: "Behold, the darkness shall cover the earth, and gross darkness the people; but the Lord shall arise upon thee, and his glory shall be seen upon thee. And the Gentiles [heathen] shall come to thy light." (Isa. 60:2, 3) In this prophecy, the gross darkness is lighted by the bow of promise: "The Gentiles [the nations of earth in general] shall come to thy light."

Not only have the continued misery and darkness of the world, and the slow progress of truth, been a mystery to the Church, but the world itself has known and felt its condition. Like that which enveloped Egypt, it has been a darkness that could be felt. In evidence of this, note the spirit of the following lines, clipped from a Philadelphia journal. The doubt and gloom, intensified by the clashing creeds of the various schools, had not yet been dispelled from the writer's mind by the rays of divine truth direct from the Word of God:

"Life! great mystery! Who shall say
What need hath God of this poor clay?
Formed by his hand with potent skill—
Mind, matter, soul and stubborn will;
Born but to die: sure destiny—death.
Then where, oh! where this fleeting breath?
Not one of all the countless throng,

Who lived and died and suffered long,
Returns to tell the great design—
That future, which is yours and mine.
We plead, O God! for some new ray
Of light for guidance on our way;
Based not on faith, but clearer sight,
Dispelling these dark clouds of night;
This doubt, this dread, this trembling fear;
This thought that mars our blessings here.
This restless mind, with bolder sway,
Rejects the dogmas of the day
Taught by jarring sects and schools,
To fetter reason with their rules.
We seek to know Thee as thou art—
Our place with Thee—and then the part
We play in this stupendous plan,
Creator Infinite, and man.
Lift up this veil obscuring sight;
Command again: 'Let there be light!'
Reveal this secret of Thy throne;
We search in darkness the unknown."

To this we reply:

Life's unsealed mystery soon shall say
What joy hath God in this poor clay,
Formed by his hand with potent skill,
Stamped with his image—mind and will;
Born not to die—no, a second birth
Succeeds the sentence—"earth to earth."
For One of all the mighty host,
Who lived and died and suffered most,
Arose, and proved God's great design—
That future, therefore, yours and mine.
His Word discloses this new ray
Of light, for guidance on our way;
Based now on faith, but *sure* as sight,
Dispelling these dark clouds of night:
The doubt, the dread, the trembling fear,
The thoughts that marred our blessings here.

Now, Lord, these minds, whose bolder sway
Rejects the dogmas of today,
Taught by jarring sects and schools,
Fettering reason with their rules,
May seek, and know Thee as Thou art,
Our place with Thee, and then the part
We play in this stupendous plan,
Creator Infinite, and man.
Uplifts the veil, revealing quite
To those who walk in heaven's light
The glorious mystery of His throne
Hidden from ages, now made known.

Such a blessing is now coming to the world through the unfolding of the divine purpose and the opening of the divine Word, of which blessing and revealing this volume we trust is a part.

Those who will turn away from the mere speculations of men, and devote time to searching the Scriptures, not excluding reason, which God invites us to use (Isa. 1:18), will find that a blessed bow of promise spans the heavens. It is a mistake to suppose that those without faith, and consequent justification, should be able to apprehend clearly the truth: it is not for such. The Psalmist says, "Light [truth] is sown for the righteous."(Psa. 97:11) For the child of God a lamp is provided whose light dispels from his pathway much of the darkness. "Thy word is a lamp unto my feet, and a light unto my path." (Psa. 119:105) But it is only "the path of the just" that "is as the shining light, that shineth more and more unto the perfect day." (Prov. 4:18) Actually, there is none just, "none righteous, no, not one" (Rom. 3:10); the class referred to is "justified by faith." It is the privilege only of this class to walk in the pathway that shines more and more—to see not only the present unfoldings of God's plan, but also things to come. While it is true that the path of each individual believer is a shining one, yet the special application of this statement is to the just (justified) as a class. Patriarchs, prophets, apostles and saints of the past and present have walked in its increasing light; and the light will continue to increase beyond the present—"unto the perfect day." It is one continuous path, and the one continuous and increasing light is the Divine Record, illuminating as it becomes due.

Therefore, "Rejoice in the Lord, ye righteous," expecting the fulfilment of this promise. Many have so little faith that they do not look for more light, and, because of their unfaithfulness and unconcern, they are permitted to sit in darkness, when they might have been walking in the increasing light.

The Spirit of God, given to guide the Church into truth, will take of the things written and show them unto us; but beyond what is written we need nothing, for the Holy Scriptures are able to make wise unto salvation, through faith which is in Christ Jesus. 2 Tim. 3:15

While it is still true that "darkness covers the earth and gross darkness the people," the world is not always to remain in this condition. We are assured that "the morning cometh." (Isa. 21:12) As now God causes the natural sun to shine upon the just and the unjust, so the Sun of Righteousness will, in the Millennial day, shine for the benefit of all the world, and "bring to light the hidden things of darkness." (1 Cor. 4:5) It will dispel the noxious vapors of evil, and bring life, health, peace and joy.

Looking into the past we find that then the light shone but feebly. Dim and obscure were the promises of past ages. The promises made to Abraham and others, and typically represented in the law and ceremonies of fleshly Israel, were only shadows and gave but a vague idea of God's wonderful and gracious designs. As we reach the days of Jesus the light increases. The height of expectancy, until then, had been that God would bring a deliverer to save Israel from their enemies, and to exalt them as the chief nation of the earth, in which position of power and influence God would use them as his agency for blessing all the families of the earth. The offer given them of heirship in the kingdom of God was so different, in the conditions demanded, from what they had expected, and the prospects of the class being selected ever attaining the greatness promised were, outwardly and humanly considered, so improbable, that all but the few were thereby blinded to the message. And their blindness and hostility to it were naturally increased when, in the process of God's plan, the due time came for extending the message, and making the invitation to share in the promised Kingdom applicable to every creature under heaven who should by the exercise of faith be reckoned a child of faithful Abraham and an heir of the promise made to him.

But when the gospel which Jesus taught came to be understood after Pentecost, it was seen by the Church that the blessings for the world were to be of an enduring character, and that for the accomplishment of this purpose the Kingdom would be spiritual, and composed of Israelites indeed, a "little flock" selected from among both Jews and Gentiles to be exalted to spiritual nature and power. Hence we read that Jesus brought life and immortality to light through the gospel. (2 Tim. 1:10) And since Jesus' day yet more light shines, as he foretold it would, saying, "I have many things to say unto you, but ye cannot bear them now: howbeit when he, the Spirit of truth, is come, he will guide you into all truth . . . and he will show you things to come." John 16:12, 13

There came a time, however, after the apostles fell asleep, when the majority of the Church began to neglect the lamp, and to look to human teachers for leading: and the teachers, puffed up with pride, assumed titles and offices, and began to lord it over God's heritage. Then by degrees there came into existence a special class called "the clergy," who regarded themselves, and were regarded by others, as the proper guides to faith and practice, aside from the Word of God. Thus in time the great system of Papacy was developed by an undue respect for the teachings of fallible men and a neglect of the Word of the infallible God.

Serious indeed have been the evil results brought about by this neglect of truth. As all know, both the church and the civilized world were almost wholly enslaved by that system, and led to worship the traditions and creeds of men. From this slavery a bold and blessed strike for liberty and the Bible was made, in what is known as The Reformation. God raised up bold champions for his Word, among whom were Luther, Zwingli, Melanchthon, Wycliffe, Knox and others. These called attention to the fact that Papacy had laid aside the Bible and substituted the decrees and dogmas of the church, and pointed out a few of its erroneous teachings and practices, showing that they were built upon tradition, contrary to truth, and opposed to God's Word. These reformers and their adherents were called Protestants, because they protested against Papacy, and claimed the Word of God as the only correct rule of faith and practice. Many faithful souls in the days of the Reformation walked in the light, so far as it was then shining. But since their day Protestants have made little progress, because, instead of walking in the light, they have halted around their favorite leaders, willing to see as much as they saw but nothing more. They set boundaries to their progress in the way of truth, hedging in, with the little truth they had, a great deal of error brought along from the "mother" church. For the creeds thus formulated many years ago, the majority of Christians have a superstitious reverence, supposing that no more can be known of God's plans now than was known by the Reformers.

This mistake has been an expensive one; for, aside from the fact that but few great principles of truth were then recovered from the rubbish of error, there are special features of truth constantly becoming due, and of these Christians have been deprived by their creed fences. To illustrate: It was a truth in Noah's day, and one which required the faith of all who would walk in the light then, that a flood was coming, while Adam and others had known nothing of it. It would not be preaching truth now to preach a coming flood, but there are other dispensational truths constantly becoming due, of which, if walking in the light of the lamp, we shall know; so, if we have all the light which was due several hundred years ago, and that only, we are measurably in darkness.

God's Word is a great storehouse of food for hungry pilgrims on the shining pathway. There is milk for babes, and strong meat for those more developed (1 Pet. 2:2; Heb. 5:14); and not only so, but it contains food adapted to the different seasons and conditions; and Jesus said the faithful servant should bring forth meat *in due season* for the household of faith—"things new and old," from the storehouse. (Luke 12:42; Matt. 13:52) It would be impossible to bring forth such things from any sectarian creed or storehouse. We might bring forth some things old and good from each, but nothing new. The truth contained in the creeds of the various sects is so covered and mixed with error that its inherent beauty and real value are not discernible. The various creeds continually conflict and clash; and as each claims a Bible basis, the confusion of thought, and evident discord, are charged to God's Word. This has given rise to the common proverb: "The Bible is an old fiddle, upon which any tune can be played."

How expressive is this of the infidelity of our times, occasioned by misrepresentations of God's Word and character by human traditions, together with the growth of intelligence which will no longer bow in blind and superstitious reverence to the opinions of fellowmen, but demands a reason for the hope that is in us. The faithful student of the Word should be able always to give a reason for his hope. The Word of God alone is able to make wise, and is profitable for doctrine, instruction, etc., "that the man of God may be perfect, *thoroughly furnished.*" (1 Pet. 3:15; 2 Tim. 3:15-17) Only this one storehouse contains an exhaustless supply of things both new and old—meat in due season for the household. Surely no one who believes the Scripture statement that "the path of the just shineth more and more unto the perfect day" will claim that the perfect day came in Luther's time; and if not, we do well that we take heed to our lamp as unto "a light that shineth in a *dark place* UNTIL THE DAY DAWN." 2 Pet. 1:19

Nor is it sufficient that we find ourselves now in the path of light; we must *"walk in the light,"* continue to make progress, else the light, which does not stop, will pass on and leave us in darkness. The difficulty with many is that they sit down, and do not follow on in the path of light. Take a concordance and examine the texts under the words *sit* and *stand,* then compare these with those found under the words *walk* and *run,* and you will find a great contrast: Men *"sit* in darkness," and with "the scornful," and *stand* among the ungodly, but *"walk* in the light," and *"run* for the prize." Isa. 42:7; Psa. 1:1; Heb. 12:1

Perfection of knowledge is not a thing of the past, but of the future—the very near future, we trust; and until we recognize this fact we are unprepared to appreciate and expect fresh unfoldings of our Father's plan. True, we still go back to the words of the prophets and apostles for all knowledge of the present and the future; not, however, because they always understood God's plans and purposes better than we, but because God used them as his mouthpieces *to communicate to us,* and to all the Church throughout the Christian Age, truth relative to his plans, as fast as it becomes due. This fact is abundantly proven by the apostles. Paul tells us that God has made known to the Christian Church the mystery (secret) of his will which he had purposed in himself, and had never before revealed, though he had it recorded in dark sayings which could not be understood until due, in order that the eyes of our understanding should be opened to appreciate the *"high calling"* designed exclusively for believers of the Christian Age. (Eph. 1:9, 10, 17, 18; 3:4-6) This shows us clearly that neither the prophets nor the angels understood the meaning of the prophecies uttered. Peter says that when they inquired anxiously to know their meaning, God told them that the truths covered up in their prophecies were not for themselves, but for us of the Christian Age. And he exhorts the Church to hope for still further grace (favor, blessing) in this direction—yet more knowledge of God's plans. 1 Pet. 1:10-13

It is evident that though Jesus promised that the Church should be guided into all truth, it was to be a gradual unfolding. While the Church, in the days of the apostles, was free from many of the errors which sprang up under and in Papacy, yet we cannot suppose that the early church saw as deeply or as clearly into God's plan as it is possible to see today. It is evident, too, that the different apostles had different degrees of insight into God's plan, though *all their writings* were guided and inspired of God, as truly as were the words of the prophets. To illustrate differences of knowledge, we have but to remember the wavering course, for a time, of Peter and the other apostles, except Paul, when the gospel was beginning to go to the Gentiles. (Acts 10:28;

11:1-3; Gal. 2:11-14) Peter's uncertainty was in marked contrast with Paul's assurance, inspired by the words of the prophets, God's past dealings, and the direct revelations made to himself.

Paul evidently had more abundant revelations than any other apostle. These revelations he was not allowed to make known to the Church, nor fully and plainly even to the other apostles (2 Cor. 12:4; Gal. 2:2), yet we can see a value to the entire church in those visions and revelations given to Paul; for though he was not permitted to tell what he saw, nor to particularize all he knew of the mysteries of God relating to the "ages to come," yet what he saw gave a force, shading and depth of meaning to his words which, in the light of subsequent facts, prophetic fulfilments and the Spirit's guidance, we are able to appreciate more fully than could the early church.

As corroborative of the foregoing statement, we call to mind the last book of the Bible—Revelation, written about A.D. 96. The introductory words announce it as a special revelation of things not previously understood. This proves conclusively that up to that time, at least, God's plan had not been fully revealed. Nor has that book ever been, until now, all that its name implies—an unfolding, a REVELATION. So far as the early church was concerned, probably none understood any part of the book. Even John, who saw the visions, was probably ignorant of the significance of what he saw. He was both a prophet and an apostle; and while as an apostle he understood and taught what was then "meat in due season," as a prophet he uttered things which would supply "meat" in seasons future for the household.

During the Christian Age, some of the saints sought to understand the Church's future by examining this symbolic book, and doubtless all who read and understood even a part of its teachings were blessed as promised. (Rev. 1:3)

The book kept opening up to such, and in the days of the Reformation was an important aid to Luther in deciding that the Papacy, of which he was a conscientious minister, was indeed the "Antichrist" mentioned by the Apostle, the history of which we now see fills so large a part of that prophecy.

Thus gradually God opens up his truth and reveals the exceeding riches of his grace; and consequently much more light is due now than at any previous time in the Church's history.

> "And still new beauties shall we see,
> And still increasing light."

STUDY II
THE EXISTENCE OF A SUPREME INTELLIGENT CREATOR ESTABLISHED

EVIDENCE ASIDE FROM THE BIBLE, EXAMINED IN THE LIGHT OF REASON—AN UNTENABLE THEORY—A REASONABLE THEORY—THE CHARACTER OF GOD DEMONSTRATED—REASONABLE DEDUCTIONS.

EVEN from the standpoint of the skeptic, a reasonable and candid search into the unknown, by the light of what is known, will guide the unbiased, intelligent reasoner in the direction of the truth. Yet it is evident that without a direct revelation of the plans and purposes of God, men could only approximate the truth, and arrive at indefinite conclusions. But let us for the moment lay aside the Bible, and look at things from the standpoint of reason alone.

He who can look into the sky with a telescope, or even with his natural eye alone, and see there the immensity of creation, its symmetry, beauty, order, harmony and diversity, and yet doubt that the Creator of these is vastly his superior both in wisdom and power, or who can suppose for a moment that such order came by chance, without a Creator, has so far lost or ignored the faculty of reason as to be properly considered what the Bible terms him, a fool (one who ignores or lacks reason): "The fool hath said in his heart, There is no God." However it happened, at least that much of the Bible is true, as every reasonable mind must conclude; for it is a self-evident truth that effects must be produced by competent causes. Every plant and every flower, even, speaks volumes of testimony on this subject. Intricate in construction, exquisitely beautiful in form and texture, each speaks of a wisdom and skill above the human. How shortsighted the absurdity which boasts of human skill and ingenuity, and attributes to mere chance the regularity, uniformity and harmony of nature; which acknowledges the laws of nature, while denying that nature has an intelligent Lawgiver.

Some who deny the existence of an intelligent Creator claim that nature is the only God, and that from nature all forms of animal and vegetable developments proceeded without the ordering of intelligence, but governed, they say, by "the law of the survival of the fittest" in a process of evolution.

This theory lacks proof, for all about us we see that the various creatures are of fixed natures which do not evolve to higher natures; and though those who hold to this theory have made repeated endeavors, they have never succeeded either in blending different species or in producing a new fixed variety. No instance is known where one kind has changed to another kind.* Though there are fish that can use their fins for a moment as wings, and fly out of the water, and frogs that can sing, they have never been known to change into birds; and though there are among brutes some which bear a slight resemblance to men, the evidence is wholly lacking that man was evolved from such creatures. On the contrary, investigations prove that though different varieties of the same species may be produced, it is impossible to blend the various species, or for one to evolve from another. For the same reason the donkey and the horse, though resembling each other, cannot be claimed as related, for it is well known that their offspring is imperfect and cannot propagate either species.

---

*For the benefit of some readers we remark that changes such as the transformation of caterpillars into butterflies are not changes of nature: the caterpillar is but the larva hatched from the butterfly's egg.

Surely if unintelligent nature were the creator or evolver she would continue the process, and there would be no such thing as fixed species, since without intelligence nothing would arrive at fixed conditions. Evolution would be a fact today, and we would see about us fish becoming birds, and monkeys becoming men. This theory we conclude to be as contrary to human reason as to the Bible, when it claims that intelligent beings were created by a power lacking intelligence.

One theory regarding the creation (excepting man) by a process of evolution, to which we see no serious objection, we briefly state as follows: It assumes that the various species of the present are fixed and unchangeable so far as nature or kind is concerned, and though present natures may be developed to a much higher standard, even to perfection, these species or natures will forever be the same. This theory further assumes that none of these fixed species were originally created so, but that in the remote past they were developed from the earth, and by gradual processes of evolution from one form to another. These evolutions, under divinely established laws, in which changes of food and climate played an important part, may have continued until the fixed species, as at present seen, were established, beyond which change is impossible, the ultimate purpose of the Creator in this respect, to all appearance, having been reached. Though each of the various families of plants and animals is capable of improvement or of degradation, none of them is susceptible of change into, nor can they be produced from, other families or kinds. Though each of these may attain to the perfection of its own fixed nature, the Creator's design as to nature having been attained, further change in this respect is impossible.

It is claimed that the original plants and animals, from which present fixed varieties came, became extinct before the creation of man. Skeletons and fossils of animals and plants which do not now exist, found deep below the earth's surface, favor this theory. This view neither ignores nor rejects the Bible teaching that man was a direct and perfect creation, made in the mental and moral image of his Maker, and not a development by a process of evolution, probably common to the remainder of creation. This view would in no sense invalidate, but would support, the Bible's claim, that nature as it is today teaches that an Intelligent Being ordered it, and was its first cause. Let human reason do her best to trace known facts to reasonable and competent causes, giving due credit to nature's laws in every case; but back of all the intricate machinery of nature is the hand of its great Author, the intelligent, omnipotent God.

We claim, then, that the existence of an Intelligent Creator is a clearly demonstrated truth, the proof of which lies all around us: yea, and within us; for we are his workmanship, whose every power of mind and body speaks of a marvelous skill beyond our comprehension. And he is also the Designer and Creator of what we term nature. We claim that he ordered and established the laws of nature, the beauty and harmony of whose operation we see and admire. This one whose wisdom planned and whose power upholds and guides the universe, whose wisdom and power so immeasurably transcend our own, we instinctively worship and adore.

To realize the existence of this mighty God is but to dread his omnipotent strength, unless we can see him possessed of benevolence and goodness corresponding to his power. Of this fact we are also fully assured by the same evidence which proves his existence, power and wisdom. Not only are we forced to the conclusion that there is a God, and that his power and wisdom are immeasurably beyond our own, but we are forced by reason to the conclusion that the grandest thing created is not superior to its Creator; hence we must conclude that the greatest manifestation of benevolence and justice among men is inferior in scope to that of the Creator, even as man's wisdom and power are inferior to his. And thus we have before our mental vision the character and attributes of the great Creator. He is wise, just, loving and powerful; and the scope of his attributes is, of necessity, immeasurably wider than that of his grandest creation.

But further: having reached this reasonable conclusion relative to the existence and character of our Creator, let us inquire, What should we expect of such a being? The answer comes, that the possession of such attributes reasonably argues their exercise, their use. God's power must be used, and that in harmony with his own nature—wisely, justly and benevolently. Whatever may be the means to that end, whatever may be the operation of God's power, the final outcome must be consistent with his nature and character, and every step must be approved of his infinite wisdom.

What could be more reasonable than such exercise of power as we see manifested in the creation of countless worlds about us, and in the wonderful variety of earth? What could be more reasonable than the creation of man, endowed with reason and judgment, capable of appreciating his Creator's works, and judging of his skill—of his wisdom, justice, power and love? All this is reasonable, and all in perfect accord with facts known to us.

And now comes our final proposition. Is it not reasonable to suppose that such an infinitely wise and good being, having made a creature capable of appreciating himself and his plan, would be moved by his love and justice to supply the wants of that creature's nature, by giving him *some* REVELATION? Would it not be a reasonable supposition, that

God would supply to man information concerning the object of his existence, and his plans for his future? On the contrary, we ask, would it not be unreasonable to suppose that such a Creator would make such a creature as man, endow him with powers of reason reaching out into the future, and yet make no revelation of his plans to meet those longings? Such a course would be unreasonable, because contrary to the character which we reasonably attribute to God; contrary to the proper course of a being controlled by justice and love.

We may reason that in creating man, had Divine Wisdom decided it inexpedient to grant him a knowledge of his future destiny, and his share in his Creator's plans, then surely Divine Justice, as well as Divine Love, would have insisted that the being should be so limited in his capacity that he would not continually be tormented and perplexed with doubts, and fears, and ignorance; and as a consequence Divine Power would have been used under those limitations. The fact, then, that man has capacity for appreciating a revelation of the Divine plan, taken in connection with the conceded character of his Creator, is an abundant reason for expecting that God would grant such a revelation, in such time and manner as his wisdom approved. So, then, in view of these considerations, even if we were ignorant of the Bible, reason would lead us to expect and to be on the lookout for some such revelation as the Bible claims to be. And furthermore, noting the order and harmony of the general creation, as in grand procession the spheres and systems keep time and place, we cannot but conclude that the minor irregularities, such as earthquakes, cyclones, etc., are but indications that the working together of the various elements in this world is not at present perfect. An assurance that all will ultimately be perfect and harmonious on earth as in the heavens, with some explanation why it is not so at present, are requests which are not unreasonable for reasoning men to ask, nor for the Creator, whose wisdom, power and benevolence are demonstrated, to answer. Hence we should expect the revelation sought to include such an assurance and such an explanation.

Having established the reasonableness of expecting a revelation of God's will and plan concerning our race, we will examine in the next chapter the general character of the Bible which claims to be just such a revelation. And if it presents the character of God in perfect harmony with what reason as above considered dictates, we should conclude that it thus proves itself to be the needed and reasonably expected revelation from God, and should then accept its testimony as such. If of God, its teachings, when fully appreciated, will accord with his character, which reason assures us is perfect in wisdom, justice, love and power.

"Ye curious minds, who roam abroad,
   And trace creation's wonders o'er,
Confess the footsteps of your God,
   And bow before him, and adore.

"The heavens declare thy glory, Lord;
   In every star thy wisdom shines;
But when our eyes behold thy Word,
   We read thy name in fairer lines."

Sunshine Over All

"What folly, then," the faithless critic cries,
With sneering lip and wise, world-knowing eyes,
"While fort to fort and post to post repeat
The ceaseless challenge of the war-drum's beat,
And round the green earth, to the church-bell's chime,
The morning drum-roll of the camp keeps time,
To dream of peace amidst a world in arms;
Of swords to plowshares changed by Scriptural charms;
Of nations, drunken with the wine of blood,
Staggering to take the pledge of brotherhood,
Like tipplers answering Father Mathew's call.

* * *

"Check Bau or Kaiser with a barricade
Of 'Olive leaves' and resolutions made;
Spike guns with pointed Scripture texts, and hope
To capsize navies with a windy trope;
Still shall the glory and the pomp of war
Along their train the shouting millions draw;
Still dusky labor to the parting brave
His cap shall doff and beauty's kerchief wave;
Still shall the bard to valor tune his song;
Still hero-worship kneel before the strong;
Rosy and sleek, the sable-gowned divine,
O'er his third bottle of suggestive wine,
To plumed and sworded auditors shall prove
Their trade accordant with the law of love;
And Church for State, and State for Church shall fight,
And both agree that might alone is right."

Despite the sneers like these, O faithful few,
Who dare to hold God's Word and witness true,
Whose clear-eyed faith transcends our evil time,
And o'er the present wilderness of crime
Sees the calm future with its robes of green,
Its fleece-flecked mountains, and soft streams between,
Still keep the track which duty bids ye tread,
Though worldly wisdom shake the cautious head.
No truth from heaven descends upon our sphere
Without the greeting of the skeptic's sneer:
Denied, and mocked at, till its blessings fall
Common as dew and sunshine over all. —*Whittier*

STUDY III
THE BIBLE AS A DIVINE REVELATION
VIEWED IN THE LIGHT OF REASON

The Claims of the Bible and its Surface Evidence of Credibility—Its Antiquity and Preservation—Its Moral Influence—Motives of the Writers—General Character of the Writings—The Books of Moses—The Law of Moses—Peculiarities of the Government Instituted by Moses—It was not a System of Priestcraft—Instructions to Civil Rulers—Rich and Poor on a Common Level Before the Law—Safeguards Against Tampering With the Rights of the People—The Priesthood Not a Favored Class, How Supported, etc.—Oppression of Foreigners, Widows, Orphans and Servants Guarded Against—The Prophets of the Bible—Is There a Common Bond of Union Between the Law, the Prophets and the New Testament Writers?—Miracles Not Unreasonable—The Reasonable Conclusion.

THE Bible is the torch of civilization and liberty. Its influence for good in society has been recognized by the greatest statesmen, even though they for the most part have looked at it through the various glasses of conflicting creeds, which, while upholding the Bible, grievously misrepresent its teachings. The grand old book is unintentionally but woefully misrepresented by its friends, many of whom would lay down life on its behalf; and yet they do it more vital injury than its foes, by claiming its support to their long-revered misconceptions of its truth, received through the traditions of their fathers. Would that such would awake, re-examine their oracle, and put to confusion its enemies by disarming them of their weapons!

Since the light of nature leads us to expect a fuller revelation of God than that which nature supplies, the reasonable, thinking mind will be prepared to examine the claims of anything purporting to be a divine revelation, which

37

bears a reasonable surface evidence of the truthfulness of such claims. The Bible claims to be such a revelation from God, and it does come to us with sufficient surface evidence as to the probable correctness of its claims, and gives us a reasonable hope that closer investigation will disclose more complete and positive evidence that it is indeed the Word of God.

The Bible is the oldest book in existence; it has outlived the storms of thirty centuries. Men have endeavored by every means possible to banish it from the face of the earth: they have hidden it, burned it, made it a crime punishable with death to have it in possession, and the most bitter and relentless persecutions have been waged against those who had faith in it; but still the book lives. Today, while many of its foes slumber in death, and hundreds of volumes written to discredit it and to overthrow its influence, are long since forgotten, the Bible has found its way into every nation and language of earth, over two hundred different translations of it having been made. The fact that this book has survived so many centuries, notwithstanding such unparalleled efforts to banish and destroy it, is at least strong circumstantial evidence that the great Being whom it claims as its Author has also been its Preserver.

It is also true that the moral influence of the Bible is uniformly good. Those who become careful students of its pages are invariably elevated to a purer life. Other writings upon religion and the various sciences have done good and have ennobled and blessed mankind, to some extent; but all other books combined have failed to bring the joy, peace and blessing to the groaning creation that the Bible has brought to both the rich and the poor, to the learned and the unlearned. The Bible is not a book to be read merely: it is a book to be studied with care and thought; for God's thoughts are higher than our thoughts, and his ways than our ways. And if we would comprehend the plan and thoughts of the infinite God, we must bend all our energies to that important work. The richest treasures of truth do not always lie on the surface.

This book throughout constantly points and refers to one prominent character, Jesus of Nazareth, who, it claims, was the Son of God. From beginning to end his name, and office, and work, are made prominent. That a man called Jesus of Nazareth lived, and was somewhat noted, about the time indicated by the writers of the Bible, is a fact of history outside the Bible, and it is variously and fully corroborated. That this Jesus was crucified because he had rendered himself offensive to the Jews and their priesthood is a further fact established by history outside the evidence furnished by the New Testament writers. The writers of the New Testament (except Paul and Luke) were the personal acquaintances and disciples of Jesus of Nazareth, whose doctrines their writings set forth.

The existence of any book implies motive on the part of the writer. We therefore inquire, What motives could have inspired these men to espouse the cause of this person? He was condemned to death and crucified as a malefactor by the Jews, the most religious among them assenting to and demanding his death, as one unfit to live. And in espousing his cause, and promulgating his doctrines, these men braved contempt, deprivation and bitter persecution, risked life itself, and in some cases even suffered martyrdom. Admitting that while he lived Jesus was a remarkable person, in both his life and his teaching, what motive could there have been for any to espouse his cause after he was dead?—especially when his death was so ignominious? And if we suppose that these writers invented their narratives, and that Jesus was their imaginary or ideal hero, how absurd it would be to suppose that sane men, after claiming that he was the Son of God, that he had been begotten in a supernatural way, had supernatural powers by which he had healed lepers, restored sight to those born blind, caused the deaf to hear, and even raised the dead—how very absurd to suppose that they would wind up the story of such a character by stating that a little band of his enemies executed him as a felon, while all his friends and disciples, and among them the writers themselves, forsook him and fled in the trying moment?

The fact that profane history does not agree in some respects with these writers should not lead us to regard their records as untrue. Those who do thus conclude should assign and prove some motive on the part of these writers for making false statements. What motives could have prompted them? Could they reasonably have hoped thereby for fortune, or fame, or power, or any earthly advantage? The poverty of Jesus' friends, and the unpopularity of their hero himself with the great religionists of Judea, contradict such a thought; while the facts that he died as a malefactor, a disturber of the peace, and that he was made of no reputation, held forth no hope of enviable fame or earthly advantage to those who should attempt to re-establish his doctrine. On the contrary, if such had been the object of those who preached Jesus, would they not speedily have given it up when they found that it brought disgrace, persecution, imprisonment, stripes and even death? Reason plainly teaches that men who sacrificed home, reputation, honor and life; who lived not for present gratification; but whose central aim was to elevate their fellowmen, and who inculcated morals of the highest type, were not only possessed of a motive, but further that their motive must have been pure and their object grandly sublime. Reason further declares that the testimony of such men, actuated only by pure and good motives, is worthy of ten times the weight and consideration of ordinary writers. Nor were these men fanatics: they were men of sound and reasonable mind, and furnished in every case a reason for their faith and hope; and they were perseveringly faithful to those reasonable convictions.

And what we have here noticed is likewise applicable to the various writers of the Old Testament. They were, in the main, men notable for their fidelity to the Lord; and this history as impartially records and reproves their weaknesses and shortcomings as it commends their virtues and faithfulness. This must astonish those who presume the Bible to be a manufactured history, designed to awe men into reverence of a religious system. There is a straightforwardness about the Bible that stamps it as truth. Knaves, desirous of representing a man as great, and especially if desirous of presenting some of his writings as inspired of God, would undoubtedly paint such a one's character blameless and noble to the last degree. The fact that such a course has not been pursued in the Bible is *reasonable* evidence that it was not fraudulently gotten up to deceive.

Having, then, reason to *expect* a revelation of God's will and plan, and having found that the Bible, which claims to be that revelation, was written by men whose motives we see no reason to impugn, but which, on the contrary, we see reason to approve, let us examine the character of the writings claimed as inspired, to see whether their teachings correspond with the character we have *reasonably* imputed to God, and whether they bear internal evidence of their truthfulness.

The first five books of the New Testament and several of the Old Testament are narratives or histories of facts known to the writers and vouched for by their characters. It is manifest to all that it did not require a special revelation simply to tell the truth with reference to matters with which they were intimately and fully acquainted. Yet, since God desired to make a revelation to men, the fact that these histories of passing events have a bearing on that revelation would be a sufficient ground to make the inference a reasonable one, that God would supervise, and so arrange, that the honest writer whom he selected for the work should be brought in contact with the needful facts. The credibility of these historic portions of the Bible rests almost entirely upon the characters and motives of their writers. Good men will not utter falsehoods. A pure fountain will not give forth bitter waters. And the united testimony of these writings silences any suspicion that their authors would say or do evil, that good might follow.

It in no way invalidates the truthfulness of certain books of the Bible, such as Kings, Chronicles, Judges, etc., when we say that they are simply truthful and carefully kept histories of prominent events and persons of their times. When it is remembered that the Hebrew Scriptures contain history, as well as the law and the prophecies, and that their histories, genealogies, etc., were the more explicit in detailing circumstances because of the expectancy that the promised Messiah would come in a particular line from Abraham, we see a reason for the recording of certain facts of history considered indelicate in the light of this twentieth century. For instance, a clear record of the origin of the nations of the Moabites and of the Ammonites, and of their relationship to Abraham and the Israelites, was probably the necessity in the historian's mind for a full history of their nativity. (Gen. 19:36-38) Likewise, a very detailed account of Judah's children is given, of whom came David, the king, through whom the genealogy of Mary, Jesus' mother, as well as that of Joseph, her husband (Luke 3:23, 31, 33, 34; Matt. 1:2-16), is traced back to Abraham. Doubtless the necessity of thoroughly establishing the pedigree was the more important, since of this tribe (Gen. 49:10) was to come the ruling King of Israel, as well as the promised Messiah, and hence the minutiae of detail not given in other instances. Gen. 38

There may be similar or different reasons for other historic facts recorded in the Bible, of which by and by we may see the utility, which, were it not a history, but simply a treatise on morals, might without detriment be omitted; though no one can reasonably say that the Bible anywhere countenances impurity. It is well, furthermore, to remember that the same facts may be more or less delicately stated in any language; and that while the translators of the Bible were, rightly, too conscientious to omit any of the record, yet they lived in a day less particular in the choice of refined expressions than ours; and the same may be surmised of the early Bible times and habits of expression. Certainly the most fastidious can find no objection on this score to any expression of the New Testament.

The Books of Moses and the
Laws Therein Promulgated

The first five books of the Bible are known as the Five Books of Moses, though they nowhere mention his name as their author. That they were written by Moses, or under his supervision, is a reasonable inference; the account of his death and burial being properly added by his secretary. The omission of the positive statement that these books were written by Moses is no proof against the thought; for had another written them to deceive and commit a fraud, he would surely have claimed that they were written by the great leader and statesman of Israel, in order to make good his imposition. (See Deut. 31:9-27.) Of one thing we are certain, Moses did lead out of Egypt the Hebrew nation. He did organize them as a nation under the laws set forth in these books; and the Hebrew nation, by common consent, for over three thousand years, has claimed these books as a gift to them from Moses, and has held them so sacred that a jot or tittle must not be altered—thus giving assurance of the purity of the text.

These writings of Moses contain the only credible history extant of the epoch which it traverses. Chinese history affects to begin at creation, telling how God went out on the water in a skiff, and, taking in his hand a lump of earth, cast it into the water. That lump of earth, it claims, became this world, etc. But the entire story is so devoid of reason that the merest child of intelligence would not be deceived by it. On the contrary, the account given in Genesis starts with the reasonable assumption that a God, a Creator, an intelligent First Cause, already existed. It treats not of God's having a beginning, but of his work and of its beginning and its systematic orderly progress—"In the beginning God created the heavens and the earth." Then stepping over the origin of the earth without detail or explanation, the narrative of the six days [epochs] of preparing it for man proceeds. That account is substantially corroborated by the accumulating light of science for four thousand years; hence it is far more reasonable to accept the claim that its author, Moses, was divinely inspired, than to assume that the intelligence of one man was superior to the combined intelligence and research of the rest of the race in three thousand years since, aided by modern implements and millions of money.

Look next at the system of laws laid down in these writings. They certainly were without an equal, either in their day or since, until this twentieth century; and the laws of this century are based upon the principles laid down in the Mosaic Law, and framed in the main by men who acknowledged the Mosaic Law as of divine origin.

The Decalogue is a brief synopsis of the whole law. Those Ten Commandments enjoin a code of worship and morals that must strike every student as remarkable; and if never before known, and now found among the ruins and relics of Greece, or Rome, or Babylon (nations which have risen and fallen again, long since those laws were given), they would be regarded as marvelous if not supernatural. But familiarity with them and their claims has begotten measurable indifference, so that their real greatness is unnoticed except by the few. True, those commandments do not teach of Christ; but they were given, not to Christians, but to Hebrews; not to teach faith in a ransom, but to convince men of their sinful state, and need of a ransom. And the substance of those commandments was grandly epitomized by the illustrious founder of Christianity, in the words: "Thou shalt love the Lord thy God with all thy heart, and with all thy soul, and with all thy mind, and with all thy strength"; and "Thou shalt love thy neighbor as thyself." Mark 12:30, 31

The government instituted by Moses differed from all others, ancient and modern, in that it claimed to be that of the Creator himself, and the people were held accountable to him; their laws and institutions, civil and religious, claimed to emanate from God, and, as we shall presently see, were in perfect harmony with what reason teaches us to be God's character. The Tabernacle, in the center of the camp, had in its "Most Holy" apartment a manifestation of Jehovah's presence as their King, whence by supernatural means they received instruction for the proper administration of their affairs as a nation. An order of priests was established, which had complete charge of the Tabernacle, and through them alone access and communion with Jehovah was permitted. The first thought of some in this connection would perhaps be: "Ah! there we have the object of their organization: with them, as with other nations, the priests ruled the people, imposing upon their credulity and exciting their fears for their own honor and profit." But hold, friend; let us not too hastily assume anything. Where there is such good opportunity for testing this matter by the facts, it would not be reasonable to jump to conclusions without the facts. The unanswerable evidences are contrary to such suppositions. The rights and the privileges of the priests were limited; they were given no civil power whatever, and wholly lacked opportunity for using their office to impose upon the rights or consciences of the people; and this arrangement was made by Moses, a member of the priestly line.

As God's representative in bringing Israel out of Egyptian bondage, the force of circumstances had centralized the government in his hand, and made the meek Moses an autocrat in power and authority, though from the meekness of his disposition he was in fact the overworked servant of the people, whose very life was being exhausted by the onerous cares of his position. At this juncture a civil government was established, which was virtually a democracy. Let us not be misunderstood: Regarded as unbelievers would esteem it, Israel's government was a democracy, but regarded in the light of its own claims, it was a theocracy, i.e., a divine government; for the laws given by God, through Moses, permitted of no amendments: they must neither add to nor take from their code of laws. Thus seen, Israel's government was different from any other civil government, either before or since. "The Lord said unto Moses, Gather unto me seventy men of the elders of Israel, whom thou knowest to be elders of the people and officers over them; and bring them unto the Tabernacle of the congregation, that they may stand there with thee. And I will come down and talk with thee there, and I will take of the spirit which is upon thee and will put it upon them, and they shall bear the burden of the people with thee, that thou bear it not alone." (Num. 11:16, 17. See also verses 24 to 30 for an example of true and guileless statesmanship and meekness.) Moses, rehearsing this matter, says: "So I took the chief of your tribes, wise men, and known [of influence], and made them heads over you: captains over thousands, and captains over hundreds, and captains over fifties, and captains over tens, and officers among your tribes." Deut. 1:15; Exod. 18:13-26

Thus it appears that this distinguished lawgiver, so far from seeking to perpetuate or increase his own power by placing the government of the people under the control of his direct relatives, of the priestly tribe, to use their religious authority to fetter the rights and liberties of the people, on the contrary introduced to the people a form of government calculated to cultivate the spirit of liberty. The histories of other nations and rulers show no parallel to this. In every case the ruler has sought his own aggrandizement and greater power. Even in instances where such have aided in establishing republics, it has appeared from subsequent events that they did it through policy, to obtain favor with the people, and to perpetuate their own power. Circumstanced as Moses was, any ambitious man, governed by policy and attempting to perpetuate a fraud upon the people, would have worked for greater centralization of power in himself and his family; especially as this would have seemed an easy task from the religious authority being already in that tribe, and from the claim of this nation to be governed by God, from the Tabernacle. Nor is it supposable that a man capable of forming such laws, and of ruling such a people, would be so dull of comprehension as not to see what the tendency of his course would be. So completely was the government of the people put into their own hands, that though it was stipulated that the weightier cases which those governors could not decide were to be brought unto Moses, yet they themselves were the judges as to what cases went before Moses: "The cause which is too hard for you, bring it unto me, and I will hear it." Deut. 1:17

Thus seen, Israel was a republic whose officers acted under a divine commission. And to the confusion of those who ignorantly claim that the Bible sanctions an established empire rule over the people, instead of "a government of the people by the people," be it noted that this republican form of civil government continued for over four hundred years. And it was then changed for that of a kingdom at the request of "The Elders," without the Lord's approval, who said to Samuel, then acting as a sort of informal president, "Hearken unto the voice of the people in all that they shall say unto thee, for they have not rejected thee, but they have rejected Me, that I should not reign over them." At God's instance Samuel explained to the people how their rights and liberties would be disregarded, and how they would become servants by such a change; yet they had become infatuated with the popular idea, illustrated all around them in other nations. (1 Sam. 8:6-22) In considering this account of their *desire* for a king, who is not impressed with the thought that Moses could have firmly established himself at the head of a great empire without difficulty?

While Israel as a whole constituted one nation, yet the tribal division was ever recognized after Jacob's death. Each family, or tribe, by common consent, elected or recognized certain members as its representatives, or chiefs. This custom was continued even through their long slavery in Egypt. These were called chiefs or elders, and it was to these that Moses delivered the honor and power of civil government; whereas, had he desired to centralize power in himself and his own family, these would have been the last men to honor with power and office.

The instructions given those appointed to civil rulership as from God are a model of simplicity and purity. Moses declares to the people, in the hearing of these judges: "I charged your judges at that time, saying, Hear the causes between your brethren, and judge righteously between every man and his brother, and the stranger [foreigner] that is with him. Ye shall not respect persons in judgment; but ye shall hear the small as well as the great; ye shall not be afraid of the face of man, for the judgment is God's; and the cause that is too hard for you, bring it unto me, and I will hear it." (Deut. 1:16, 17) Such hard cases were, after Moses' death, brought directly to the Lord through the High Priest, the answer being Yes or No, by the Urim and Thummim.

In view of these *facts,* what shall we say of the theory which suggests that these books were written by knavish priests to secure to themselves influence and power over the people? Would such men for such a purpose forge records destructive to the very aims they sought to advance—records which prove conclusively that the great Chief of Israel, and one of their own tribe, at the instance of God, cut off the priesthood from civil power by placing that power in the hands of the people? Does any one consider such a conclusion reasonable?

Again, it is worthy of note that the laws of the most advanced civilization, in this twentieth century, do not more carefully provide that rich and poor shall stand on a common level in accountability before the civil law. Absolutely no distinction was made by Moses' laws. And as for the protection of the people from the dangers incident to some becoming very poor and others excessively wealthy and powerful, no other national law has ever been enacted which so carefully guarded this point. Moses' law provided for a restitution every fiftieth year—their Jubilee year. This law, by preventing the absolute alienation of property, thereby prevented its accumulation in the hands of a few. (Lev. 25:9, 13-23, 27-30) In fact, they were taught to consider themselves brethren, and to act accordingly; to assist each other without compensation, and to take no usury of one another. See Exod. 22:25; Lev. 25:36, 37; Num. 26:52-56.

All the laws were made public, thus preventing designing men from successfully tampering with the rights of the people. The laws were exposed in such a manner that any who chose might copy them; and, in order that the poorest and most unlearned might not be ignorant of them, it was made the duty of the priests to read them to the people at their septennial festivals. (Deut. 31:10-13) Is it reasonable to suppose that such laws and arrangements were designed by bad men, or by men scheming to defraud the people of their liberties and happiness? Such an assumption would be unreasonable.

In its regard for the rights and interests of foreigners, and of enemies, the Mosaic law was thirty-two centuries ahead of its times—if indeed the laws of the most civilized of today equal it in fairness and benevolence. We read:

"Ye shall have one manner of law as well for the stranger [foreigner] as for one of your own country; for I am the Lord your God." Exod. 12:49; Lev. 24:22

"And if a stranger sojourn with thee in your land, ye shall not vex him; but the stranger that dwelleth with you shall be unto you as one born among you, and thou shalt love him as thyself; for ye were strangers in the land of Egypt." Lev. 19:33, 34

"If thou meet thine *enemy's* ox or his ass going astray, thou shalt surely bring it back to him again. If thou see the ass of him that *hateth thee* lying under his burden, wouldst thou cease to leave thy business and help him? Thou shalt surely leave it, to join with [assist] him." Exod. 23:4, 5, margin

Even the dumb animals were not forgotten. Cruelty to these as well as to human beings was prohibited strictly. An ox must not be muzzled while threshing the grain; for the good reason that any laborer is worthy of his food. Even the ox and the ass must not plow together, because so unequal in strength and tread: it would be cruelty. Their rest was also provided for. Deut. 25:4; 22:10; Exod. 23:12

The priesthood may be claimed by some to have been a selfish institution, because the tribe of Levites was supported by the annual tenth, or tithe, of the individual produce of their brethren of the other tribes. This fact, stated thus, is an unfair presentation too common to skeptics, who, possibly ignorantly, thereby misrepresent one of the most remarkable evidences of God's part in the organization of that system, and that it was not the work of a selfish and scheming priesthood. Indeed, it is not infrequently misrepresented by a modern priesthood, which urges a similar system now, using that as a precedent, without mentioning the condition of things upon which it was founded, or its method of payment.

It was, in fact, founded upon the strictest equity. When Israel came into possession of the land of Canaan, the Levites certainly had as much right to a share of the land as the other tribes; yet, by God's express command, they got none of it, except certain cities or villages for residence, scattered among the various tribes, whom they were to serve in religious things. Nine times is this prohibition given, before the division of the land. Instead of the land, some equivalent should surely be provided them, and the *tithe* was therefore this reasonable and just provision. Nor is this all: the tithe, though, as we have seen, a just debt, was not enforced as a tax, but was to be paid as a voluntary contribution. And no threat bound them to make those contributions: all depended upon their conscientiousness. The only exhortations to the people on the subject are as follows:

"Take heed to thyself that thou forsake not the Levite as long as thou livest upon the earth." (Deut. 12:19) "And the Levite that is within thy gates, thou shalt not forsake him; for he hath no part nor inheritance with thee" [in the land]. Deut. 14:27

Is it, we ask, reasonable to suppose that this order of things would have been thus arranged by selfish and ambitious priests?—an arrangement to disinherit themselves and to make them dependent for support upon their brethren? Does not reason teach us to the contrary?

In harmony with this, and equally inexplicable on any other grounds than those claimed—that God is the author of those laws—is the fact that no special provision was made for honoring the priesthood. In nothing would imposters be more careful than to provide reverence and respect for themselves, and severest penalties and curses upon those who misused them. But nothing of the kind appears: no special honor, or reverence, or immunity from violence or insult, is provided. The common law, which made no distinction between classes, and was no respecter of persons, was their only protection. This is the more remarkable because the treatment of servants, and strangers, and the aged, was the subject of special legislation. For instance: Thou shalt not vex nor oppress a *stranger, or widow, or fatherless child;* for if they cry at all unto me [to God] I will surely hear their cry; and my wrath shall wax hot, and I will kill you with the sword, and your wives shall be widows and your children fatherless. (Exod. 22:21-24; 23:9; Lev. 19:33, 34) "Thou shalt not oppress an *hired servant* that is poor and needy, whether he be of thy brethren, or of strangers that are in thy land, within thy gates. At his day thou shalt give him his hire, neither shall the sun go down upon it, for he is poor, and setteth his heart upon it; lest he cry against thee unto the Lord and it be sin unto thee." (Lev. 19:13; Deut. 24:14, 15; Exod. 21:26, 27) "Thou shalt rise up before the hoary head and honor the face of the old man." (Lev. 19:32. See also Lev. 19:14.) All this, yet nothing special for Priests, or Levites, or their tithes.

The sanitary arrangements of the law, so needful to a poor and long-oppressed people, together with the arrangements and limitations respecting clean and unclean animals which might or might not be eaten, are remarkable, and would, with other features, be of interest if space permitted their examination, as showing that law to have been abreast with, if not in advance of, the latest conclusions of medical science on the subject. The law of Moses had also a typical character, which we must leave for future consideration; but even our hasty glance has furnished overwhelming evidence that this law, which constitutes the very framework of the entire system of revealed religion, which the remainder of the Bible elaborates, is truly a marvelous display of wisdom and justice, especially when its date is taken into consideration.

In the light of reason, all must admit that it bears no evidence of being the work of wicked, designing men, but that it corresponds exactly with what nature teaches to be the character of God. It gives evidence of his Wisdom, Justice and Love. And further, the evidently pious and noble lawgiver, Moses, denies that the laws were his own, and attributes them to God. (Exod. 24:12; Deut. 9:9-11; Exod. 26:30;

Lev. 1:1) In view of his general character, and his commands to the people not to bear false witness, and to avoid hypocrisy and lying, is it reasonable to suppose that such a man bore false witness and palmed off his own views and laws for those of God? It should be remembered also that we are examining the present copies of the Bible, and that therefore the integrity for which it is so marked applies equally to the successors of Moses; for though bad men were among those successors, who did seek their own and not the people's good, it is evident that they did not tamper with the Sacred Writings, which are pure to this day.

The Prophets of the Bible

Glance now at the general character of the prophets of the Bible and their testimonies. A rather remarkable fact is that the prophets, with few exceptions, were not of the priestly class; and that in their day their prophecies were generally repugnant to the degenerating and time-serving priesthood, as well as to the idolatrously inclined people. The burden of their messages from God to the people was generally reproof for sin, coupled with warnings of coming punishments, intertwined with which we find occasional promises of future blessings, after they should be cleansed from sin and should return to favor with the Lord. Their experiences, for the most part, were far from enviable: they were generally reviled, many of them being imprisoned and put to violent deaths. See 1 Kings 18:4, 10, 17, 18; 19:10; Jer. 38:6; Heb. 11:32-38. In some instances it was years after their death before their true character as God's prophets was recognized. But we speak thus of the prophetic writers whose utterances claim to be the direct inspiration of Jehovah. It is well in this connection that we should remember that in the giving of the law to Israel there was no priestly intervention: it was given by God to the people by the hand of Moses. (Exod. 19:17-25; Deut. 5:1-5) And, furthermore, it was made the duty of every man seeing a violation of the law to reprove the sinner. (Lev. 19:17) Thus all had the authority to teach and reprove; but since, as in our own day, the majority were absorbed in the cares of business, and became indifferent and irreligious, the few comparatively fulfilled this requirement by reproving sin and exhorting to godliness; and these preachers are termed "prophets" in both the Old and New Testaments. The term prophet, as generally used, signifies *public expounder,* and the public teachers of idolatry were also so called; for instance, "the prophets of Baal," etc. See 1 Cor. 14:1-6; 2 Pet. 2:1; Matt. 7:15; 14:5; Neh. 6:7; 1 Kings 18:40; Titus 1:12.

Prophesying, in the ordinary sense of teaching, afterward became popular with a certain class, and degenerated into Phariseeism—teaching, instead of God's commandments, the traditions of the ancients, thereby opposing the truth and becoming false prophets, or false teachers. Matt. 15:2-9

Out of the large class called prophets, Jehovah at various times made choice of some whom he specially commissioned to deliver messages, relating sometimes to things then at hand, at other times to future events. It is to the writings of this class, who spoke and wrote as they were moved by the holy Spirit, that we are now giving attention. They might with propriety be designated

Divinely Commissioned Prophets or Seers.

When it is remembered that these prophets were mainly laymen, drawing no support from the tithes of the priestly tribe, and when, added to this, is the fact that they were frequently not only the reprovers of kings and judges, but also of priests (though they reproved not the office, but the personal sins of the men who filled it), it becomes evident that we could not reasonably decide that these prophets were parties to any league of priests, or others, to fabricate falsehood in the name of God. Reason in the light of facts contradicts such a suspicion.

If, then, we find no reason to impeach the motives of the various writers of the Bible, but find that the spirit of its various parts is righteousness and truth, let us next proceed to inquire whether there exists any link, or bond of union, between the records of Moses, those of the other prophets, and those of the New Testament writers. If we shall find one common line of thought interwoven throughout the Law and the Prophets and the New Testament writings, which cover a period of fifteen hundred years, this, taken in connection with the character of the writers, will be a good reason for admitting their claim—that they are divinely inspired—particularly if the theme common to all of them is a grand and noble one, comporting well with what sanctified common sense teaches regarding the character and attributes of God.

This we do find: One plan, spirit, aim and purpose pervades the entire book. Its opening pages record the creation and fall of man; its closing pages tell of man's recovery from that fall; and its intervening pages show the successive steps of the plan of God for the accomplishment of this purpose. The harmony, yet contrast, of the first three and the last three chapters of the Bible is striking. The one describes the first creation, the other the renewed or restored creation, with sin and its penal-curse removed; the one shows Satan and evil entering the world to deceive and destroy, the other shows his work undone, the destroyed ones restored, evil extinguished and Satan destroyed; the one shows the dominion lost by Adam, the other shows it restored and forever established by Christ, and God's will done in earth as in heaven; the one shows sin the producing cause of degradation, shame and death, the other shows the reward of righteousness to be glory, honor and life.

Though written by many pens, at various times, under different circumstances, the Bible is not merely a collection of moral precepts, wise maxims and words of comfort. It is more: it is a reasonable, philosophical and harmonious statement of the causes of present evil in the world, its only remedy and the final results as seen by divine wisdom, which saw the end of the plan from before its beginning, marking as well the pathway of God's people, and upholding and strengthening them with exceeding great and precious promises to be realized in due time.

The teaching of Genesis, that man was tried in a state of original perfection in one representative, that he failed, and that the present imperfection, sickness and death are the results, but that God has not forsaken him, and will ultimately recover him through a redeemer, born of a woman (Gen. 3:15), is kept up and elaborated all the way through. The necessity of the death of a redeemer as a sacrifice for sins, and of his righteousness as a covering for our sin, is pointed out in the clothing of skins for Adam and Eve; in the acceptance of Abel's offerings; in Isaac on the altar; in the death of the various sacrifices by which the patriarchs had access to God, and of those instituted under the law and perpetuated throughout the Jewish age. The prophets, though credited with understanding but slightly the significance of some of their utterances (1 Pet. 1:12), mention the laying of the sins upon a person instead of a dumb animal, and in prophetic vision they see him who is to redeem and to deliver the race led "as a lamb to the slaughter," that "the chastisement of our peace was upon him," and that "by his stripes we are healed." They pictured him as "despised and rejected of men, a man of sorrows and acquainted

with grief," and declared that "The Lord hath laid on him
the iniquity of us all." (Isa. 53:3-6) They told where this
deliverer would be born (Micah 5:2), and when he should
die, assuring us that it would be "not for himself." (Dan.
9:26) They mention various peculiarities concerning
him—that he would be "righteous," and free from
"deceit," "violence," or any just cause of death (Isa. 53:8,
9, 11); that he would be betrayed for thirty pieces of silver
(Zech. 11:12); that he would be numbered among
transgressors in his death (Isa. 53:12); that not a bone of
him should be broken (Psa. 34:20; John 19:36); and that
though he should die and be buried, his flesh would not
corrupt, neither would he remain in the grave. Psa. 16:10;
Acts 2:31

The New Testament writers clearly and forcibly, yet
simply, record the fulfilment of all these predictions in
Jesus of Nazareth, and by logical reasonings show that
such a *ransom price* as he gave was needful, as already
predicted in the Law and the Prophets, before the sins of
the world could be blotted out. (Isa. 1:18) They trace the
entire plan in a most logical and forcible manner,
appealing neither to the prejudices nor to the passions of
their hearers, but to their enlightened reason alone,
furnishing some of the most remarkably close and cogent
reasoning to be found anywhere on any subject. See Rom.
5:17-19, and onward to the 12th chapter.

Moses, in the Law, pointed not alone to a sacrifice, but
also to a blotting out of sins and a blessing of the people
under this great deliverer, whose power and authority he
declares shall vastly exceed his own, though it should be
"like unto" it. (Deut. 18:15, 19) The promised deliverer is
to bless not only Israel, but through Israel "all the families
of the earth." (Gen. 12:3; 18:18; 22:18; 26:4) And
notwithstanding the prejudices of the Jewish people to the

contrary, the prophets continue the same strain, declaring that Messiah shall be also "for a light to lighten the Gentiles" (Isa. 49:6; Luke 2:32); that the Gentiles should come to him "from the ends of the earth" (Jer. 16:19); that his name "shall be great among the Gentiles" (Mal. 1:11); and that "the glory of the Lord shall be revealed and all flesh shall see it together." Isa. 40:5. See also Isa. 42:1-7.

The New Testament writers claim a divine anointing which enabled them to realize the fulfilment of the prophecies concerning the sacrifice of Christ. They, though prejudiced as Jews to think of every blessing as limited to their own people (Acts 11:1-18), were enabled to see that while their nation would be blessed, all the families of the earth should be blessed also, with and through them. They saw also that, before the blessing of either Israel or the world, a selection would be made of a "little flock" from both Jews and Gentiles, who, being tried, would be found worthy to be made joint-heirs of the glory and honor of the Great Deliverer, and sharers with him of the honor of blessing Israel and all the nations. Rom. 8:17

These writers point out the harmony of this view with what is written in the Law and the Prophets; and the grandeur and breadth of the plan they present more than meets the most exalted conception of what it purports to be—"Good tidings of great joy, which shall be unto all people."

The thought of Messiah as a ruler of not only Israel, but also of the world, suggested in the books of Moses, is the theme of all the prophets. The thought of the kingdom was uppermost also in the teaching of the apostles; and Jesus taught that we should pray, "Thy Kingdom come," and promised those a share in it who would first suffer for the truth, and thus prove themselves worthy.

This hope of the coming glorious kingdom gave all the faithful ones courage to endure persecution and to suffer reproach, deprivation and loss, even unto death. And in the grand allegorical prophecy which closes the New Testament, the worthy "Lamb that was slain" (Rev. 5:12), the worthy "overcomers" whom he will make kings and priests in his kingdom, and the trials and obstacles which they must overcome to be worthy to share that kingdom, are all faithfully portrayed. Then are introduced symbolic representations of the blessings to accrue to the world under that Millennial reign, when Satan shall be bound and Adamic death and sorrow wiped out, and when all the nations of earth shall walk in the light of the heavenly kingdom—the new Jerusalem.

The Bible, from first to last, holds out a doctrine found nowhere else, and in opposition to the theories of all the heathen religions—that a future life for the dead will come through a RESURRECTION OF THE DEAD. All the inspired writers expressed their confidence in a redeemer, and one declares that "in the morning," when God shall call them from the tomb, and they shall come forth, the wicked shall no longer hold the rulership of earth; for "The upright shall have dominion over them, in the morning." (Psa. 49:14) The resurrection of the dead is taught by the prophets; and the writers of the New Testament base all their hopes of future life and blessing upon it. Paul expresses it thus: "If there be no resurrection of the dead, then is Christ not risen; and if Christ be not risen, then is our preaching vain and your faith is also vain; . . . then they which are fallen asleep in Christ are *perished*. But now is Christ risen from the dead, and become the firstfruits of them that slept; . . . for as in Adam all die, even so in Christ shall all be made alive." 1 Cor. 15:13-22

Like a watch, whose many wheels might at first seem superfluous, but whose slowest moving wheels are essential, so the Bible, composed of many parts, and prepared by many pens, is one complete and harmonious whole. Not a single part is superfluous, and though some parts take a more active and prominent place than others, all are useful and necessary. It is becoming popular among the so-called "advanced thinkers" and "great theologians" of the present day to treat lightly, or to ignore if they do not deny, many of the "miracles" of the Old Testament, calling them "old wives' fables." Of these are the accounts of Jonah and the great fish, Noah and the ark, Eve and the serpent, the standing still of the sun at the command of Joshua, and Balaam's speaking ass. Seemingly these wise men overlook the fact that the Bible is so interwoven and united in its various parts that to tear from it these miracles, or to discredit them, is to destroy or discredit the whole. For if the original accounts are false, those who repeated them were either falsifiers or dupes, and in either case it would be impossible for us to accept their testimony as divinely inspired. To eliminate from the Bible the miracles mentioned would invalidate the testimony of its principal writers, besides that of our Lord Jesus. The story of the fall is attested by Paul (Rom. 5:17); also Eve's beguilement by the serpent (2 Cor. 11:3; 1 Tim. 2:14). See also our Lord's reference to the latter in Rev. 12:9 and 20:2. The standing of the sun at the overthrow of the Amorites, as an evidence of the Lord's power, was evidently typical of the power to be displayed in the future, in "the day of the Lord," at the hand of him whom Joshua typified. This is attested by three prophets. (Isa. 28:21; Habak. 2:1-3, 13, 14 and 3:2-11; Zech. 14:1, 6, 7) The account of the speaking ass is confirmed by Jude (verse 11), and by Peter (2 Pet. 2:16). And the great teacher, Jesus, confirms the narratives of Jonah and the great fish and of Noah and the flood. (Matt. 12:40; 24:38, 39; Luke 17:26. See also 1 Pet. 3:20.) Really these are no greater miracles than those performed by Jesus and the apostles, such as the turning of water into wine, the healing of diseases, etc.; and as a miracle, the awakening of the dead is most wonderful of all.

These miracles, not common to our experience, find parallels about us every day, which, being more common, are passed by unnoticed. The reproduction of living organisms, either animal or vegetable, is *beyond our comprehension*, as well as beyond our power—hence miraculous. We can see the exercise of life principle, but can neither understand nor produce it. We plant two seeds side by side; the conditions, air, water, and soil, are alike; they *grow*, we cannot tell *how*, nor can the wisest philosopher explain this miracle. These seeds develop organisms of opposite tendencies; one creeps, the other stands erect; form, flower, coloring, everything differs, though the conditions were the same. Such miracles grow common to us, and we cease to remember them as such as we leave the wonderment of childhood; yet they manifest a power as much beyond our own, and beyond our limited intelligence, as the few miracles recorded in the Bible for special purposes, and as intended illustrations of omnipotence, and of the ability of the great Creator to overcome every obstacle and to accomplish all his will, even to our promised resurrection from the dead, the extermination of evil, and the ultimate reign of everlasting righteousness.

Here we rest the case. Every step has been tested by reason. We have found that there is a God, a supreme, intelligent Creator, in whom wisdom, justice, love and power exist in perfect harmony. We have found it reasonable to expect a revelation of his plans to his creatures capable of appreciating and having an interest in them. We have found the Bible, claiming to be that revelation, worthy of consideration. We have examined its writers, and their possible objects, in the light of what they taught; we have been astonished; and our *reason* has told us that such wisdom, combined with such purity of motive, was not the cunning device of crafty men for selfish ends. Reason has urged that it is far more probable that such righteous and benevolent sentiments and laws must be of God and not of men, and has insisted that they could not be the work of knavish priests. We have seen the harmony of testimony concerning Jesus, his ransom-sacrifice, and the resurrection and blessing of all as the outcome, in his glorious kingdom to come; and reason has told us that a scheme so grand and comprehensive, beyond all we could otherwise have reason to expect, yet built upon such reasonable deductions, must be the plan of God for which we seek. It cannot be the mere device of men, for even when revealed, it is almost too grand to be believed by men.

When Columbus discovered the Orinoco river, some one said he had found an island. He replied: "No such river as that flows from an island. That mighty torrent must drain the waters of a continent." So the depth and power and wisdom and scope of the Bible's testimony convince us that not man, but the Almighty God, is the author of its plans and revelations. We have taken but a hasty glance at the surface claims of the Scriptures to be of divine origin, and have found them reasonable. Succeeding chapters will unfold the various parts of the plan of God, and will, we trust, give ample evidence to every candid mind that the Bible is a divinely inspired revelation, and that the length and breadth and height and depth of the plan it unfolds gloriously reflect the divine character, hitherto but dimly comprehended, but now more clearly seen in the light of the dawning Millennial Day.

Truth Most Precious

Great truths are dearly bought. The common truth,
 Such as men give and take from day to day,
Comes in the common walk of easy life,
 Blown by the careless wind across our way.

Great truths are dearly won; not found by chance,
 Nor wafted on the breath of summer dream;
But grasped in the great struggle of the soul,
 Hard buffeting with adverse wind and stream.

Sometimes, 'mid conflict, turmoil, fear and grief,
 When the strong hand of God, put forth in might,
Ploughs up the subsoil of the stagnant heart,
 It brings some buried truth-seeds to the light.

Not in the general mart, 'mid corn and wine;
 Not in the merchandise of gold and gems;
Not in the world's gay hall of midnight mirth,
 Nor 'mid the blaze of regal diadems;

Not in the general clash of human creeds,
 Nor in the merchandise 'twixt church and world,
Is truth's fair treasure found, 'mongst tares and weeds;
 Nor her fair banner in their midst unfurled.

Truth springs like harvest from the well-ploughed fields,
 Rewarding patient toil, and faith and zeal.
To those thus seeking her, she ever yields
 Her richest treasures for their lasting weal.

STUDY IV

THE EPOCHS AND DISPENSATIONS MARKED IN THE DEVELOPMENT OF THE DIVINE PLAN

God's Plan Definite and Systematic—Three Great Epochs of the World's History—Their Distinctive Features—"The Earth Abideth Forever"—The World to Come, the New Heavens and Earth—Subdivisions of These Great Epochs—The Important Features of God's Plan thus Brought to View—Order Recognized Discloses Harmony—Rightly Dividing the Word of Truth.

AS SOME ignorantly misjudge the skill and wisdom of a great architect and builder by his unfinished work, so also many in their ignorance now misjudge God by his unfinished work; but by and by, when the rough scaffolding of evil, which has been permitted for man's discipline, and which shall finally be overruled for his good, has been removed, and the rubbish cleared away, God's *finished work* will universally declare his infinite wisdom and power; and his plans will be seen to be in harmony with his glorious character.

Since God tells us that he has a definitely fixed purpose, and that all his purposes shall be accomplished, it behooves us, as his children, to inquire diligently what those plans are, that we may be found in harmony with them. Notice how emphatically Jehovah affirms the fixedness of his purpose: "Jehovah of hosts hath sworn, saying, Surely as I have thought, so shall it come to pass; and as I have purposed, so shall it be." "The Lord of hosts hath purposed, and who shall disannul it?" "I am God, and there is none else; I am God, and there is none like me, . . . My counsel shall stand,

65

and I will do all my pleasure: . . . Yea, I have spoken it, I will also bring it to pass; I have purposed it, I will also do it." (Isa. 14:24-27; 46:9-11) Therefore, however haphazard or mysterious God's dealings with men may appear, those who believe this testimony of his Word must acknowledge that his original and unalterable plan has been, and still is, progressing systematically to completion.

While the mass of mankind, groping in the darkness of ignorance, must await the actual developments of God's plan, before they can realize the glorious character of the Divine Architect, it is the privilege of the child of God to see by faith and the light of his lamp the foretold glories of the future, and thereby to appreciate the otherwise mysterious dealings of the past and the present. Therefore, as interested sons of God, and heirs of a promised inheritance, we apply to our Father's Word, that we may understand his purposes from the plans and specifications therein given. There we learn that the plan of God, with reference to man, spans three great periods of time, beginning with man's creation and reaching into the illimitable future. Peter and Paul designate these periods "three worlds," which we represent in the following diagram.

Great Epochs Called "Worlds"

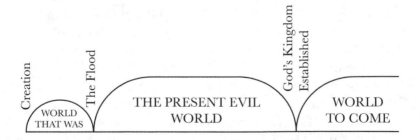

These three great epochs represent three distinct manifestations of divine providence. The first, from creation to the flood, was under the ministration of angels, and is called by Peter "THE WORLD THAT WAS." 2 Pet. 3:6

The second great epoch, from the flood to the establishment of the kingdom of God, is under the limited control of Satan, "the prince of this world," and is therefore called "THIS PRESENT EVIL WORLD." Gal. 1:4; 2 Pet. 3:7

The third is to be a "world without end" (Isa. 45:17) under divine administration, the kingdom of God, and is called "THE WORLD TO COME—wherein dwelleth righteousness." Heb. 2:5; 2 Pet. 3:13

The first of these periods, or "worlds," under the ministration of angels, was a failure; the second, under the rule of Satan, the usurper, has been indeed an "evil world"; but the third will be an era of righteousness and of blessing to all the families of the earth.

The last two of these "worlds" are most particularly mentioned, and the statements relative to them are in strong contrast. The present, or second period, is called "the present evil world," not because there is nothing good in it, but because in it evil is permitted to predominate. "Now we call the proud happy; yea, they that work wickedness are set up; yea, they that tempt God are even delivered." (Mal. 3:15) The third world or epoch is mentioned as "THE WORLD TO COME—*wherein dwelleth righteousness,*" not because there will be no evil in it, but because evil will not predominate. The blotting out of evil will be gradual, requiring all of the first thousand years. Evil will not rule then; it will not prosper; it will no longer be the wicked that will flourish; but "the righteous shall flourish" (Psa. 72:7), the "obedient shall eat the good of the land" (Isa. 1:19), and "the evil doer shall be cut off." Psa. 37:9

Thus seen, the next dispensation is to be so dissimilar as to be the very reverse of the present one in almost every particular. Our Lord's words show why there is to be a difference between the present and the future dispensations. It is because he will be the prince or ruler of the world to come, that in it righteousness and truth will prosper; while, because Satan is the prince (ruler) of the present evil world, evil prospers and the wicked flourish. It is because, as Jesus said, the prince of this world "hath nothing in me"—and consequently no interest in his followers except to oppose, tempt, annoy and buffet them (John 14:30; 2 Cor. 12:7)—that in this present evil world or epoch, whosoever will live godly shall suffer persecution, while the wicked flourish like a green bay tree. 2 Tim. 3:12; Psa. 37:35

Jesus said, "My kingdom is not of this world," and until the era or "world to come" *does come*, Christ's kingdom will not control the earth. And for this we are taught to hope and pray, "Thy kingdom come, thy will be done on earth." Satan is the "ruler of the darkness of this world," and therefore "darkness covers the earth and gross darkness the people." He now rules and works in the hearts of the children of disobedience. Eph. 2:2; 6:12

There must be some very important part of the great Architect's plan for man's salvation not yet fully developed—else the new prince and the new dispensation would have been long ago introduced. Why it was postponed for an appointed time, and also the manner of the change from the present dominion of evil under Satan to that of righteousness under Christ, are points of interest which will be more fully shown hereafter. Suffice it now to say, that the kingdoms of this world, now subject to Satan, are at the proper time to become the kingdoms of our Lord and of his Christ. (Rev. 11:15) The context shows that the transfer will be accomplished by a general time of trouble. In reference to it Jesus said, "No man can enter into a strong man's house and spoil his goods, except he will first bind the strong man, and then he will spoil his house." (Mark 3:22-27) Thus we are taught that Satan must first be bound, restrained and deposed, before Christ's reign of righteousness and peace can be established. This binding of Satan is accordingly shown to be the first work of the new dispensation. Rev. 20:2

It should be remembered that this earth is the basis of all these "worlds" and dispensations, and that though ages pass and dispensations change, still the earth continues—"The earth abideth forever." (Eccl. 1:4) Carrying out the same figure, Peter calls each of these periods a separate heavens and earth. Here the word *heavens* symbolizes the higher or spiritual controlling powers, and *earth* symbolizes human government and social arrangements. Thus the first heavens and earth, or the order and arrangement of things then existing, having served their purpose, ended at the flood. But the physical heavens (sky and atmosphere), and the physical earth, did not pass away: they remained. So likewise the present world (heavens and earth) will pass away with a great noise, fire and melting—confusion, trouble and dissolution. The strong man (Satan), being bound, will struggle to retain his power. The present order or arrangement of government and society, not that of the physical sky and earth, will pass away. The present *heavens* (powers of spiritual control) must give place to the "new heavens"—Christ's spiritual control. The present *earth* (human society as now organized under Satan's control) must (symbolically) melt and be dissolved, in the beginning of the "Day of the Lord," which "shall burn as an oven." (Mal. 4:1) It will be succeeded by "a new earth," i.e., society reorganized in harmony with earth's new Prince—Christ. Righteousness, peace and love will rule among men when present arrangements have given place to the new and better kingdom, the basis of which will be the strictest justice.

Paul was given a glimpse of the next dispensation, or, as he calls it, "the world to come." He says he was "caught away" (physically or mentally, or both, he could not tell, things were so real to his view) down the stream of time to the new condition of things, the "new heaven," hence the "third heaven." He thus saw things as they will be under the spiritual control of Christ, things which he might not disclose. (2 Cor. 12:2-4) Doubtless these were the same things which John afterward saw, and was permitted to express to the Church in *symbols,* which may only be understood as they become due. John, in the revelation given to him by our Lord on the Isle of Patmos, was in vision carried down through this Christian Age and its changing scenes of church and state, to the end of the present evil world, or epoch, and there in prophetic visions he saw Satan bound, Christ reigning, and the new heaven and the new earth established; for the former heaven and earth were passed away. Rev. 21:1

Ages or Dispensations

We now notice the ages into which these great epochs are subdivided, as illustrated in the diagram below.

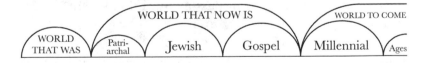

The first of these great epochs ("worlds") was not subdivided: God's method of dealing with men did not vary during all that time—from Adam's fall to the flood. God had given man his law, written in his very nature; but after he had sinned he left him measurably to his own course, which was downward, "evil, and that continually," that thus man might realize his folly, and that the wisdom of God in commanding absolute obedience might be made manifest. That dispensation ended with a flood, which took away all but faithful Noah and his family. Thus the first dispensation not only manifested the disastrous effects of sin, but showed that the tendency of sin is downward to greater degradation and misery, and proves the necessity of Jehovah's interposition, if the recovery of "that which was lost"—man's first estate—is ever to be accomplished.

The second epoch, or "world that now is," includes three ages, each a step in the plan of God for the overthrow of evil. Each step is higher than that preceding it, and carries the plan forward and nearer to completion.

The third great epoch—"the world to come"—future from the second advent of Christ, comprises the Millennial Age, or "times of restitution"; and following it are other "ages to come," the particulars of which are not revealed. Present revelations treat of man's recovery from sin, and not of the eternity of glory to follow.

The first age in the "world that now is" we call the PATRIARCHAL AGE, or dispensation, because during that period God's dealings and favors were with a few individuals only, the remainder of mankind being almost ignored. Such favored ones were the patriarchs Noah, Abraham, Isaac and Jacob. Each of these in turn seems to have been God's favored one. At the death of Jacob, that age or order of dealing ended. At Jacob's death, his descendants were first called "the twelve tribes of Israel," and were together recognized of God as his "peculiar people"; and through typical sacrifices they were typically "a holy nation," separated from other nations for a particular purpose, and therefore to enjoy certain special favors. The time allotted to this feature of the divine plan, beginning here and ending at the death of Christ, we designate the JEWISH AGE, or the Law dispensation. During that age God specially blessed that nation. He gave them his law; he made a special covenant with them; he gave them the Tabernacle, whose shekinah glory in the Most Holy represented Jehovah's presence with them as their Leader and King. To them he sent the prophets, and finally his Son. Jesus performed his miracles and taught in their midst, and would neither go to others himself, nor permit his disciples to go to the surrounding nations. He sent them out, saying, "Go not into the way of the Gentiles, and into any city of the Samaritans enter ye not; but go rather to the lost sheep of the house of Israel." (Matt. 10:5,6) And again he said, "I am not sent but unto the lost sheep of the house of Israel." (Matt. 15:24) That this national favor ended with their rejection and crucifixion of Jesus is shown by Jesus' words, when, five days before his crucifixion, he declared, "Your house is left unto you desolate." Matt. 23:38

There, at Jesus' death, a new age began—the CHRISTIAN AGE or GOSPEL DISPENSATION, wherein should be heralded good tidings of justification, not to the Jew only, but to all nations; for Jesus Christ, by the grace of God, tasted death for every man. During this Gospel age also there is a class called to special favor, to whom special promises are made; namely, those who by faith accept Christ Jesus as their Redeemer and Lord, following in his footsteps. The gospel proclamation has gone hither and thither through the earth for nearly nineteen hundred years, so that it can now be said that it has been preached more or less in *every nation*. It has not converted nations—it was not designed to do so in this age; but it has selected here and there some, in all a "little flock," as Jesus had foretold (Luke 12:32), to whom it is the Father's good pleasure to give the Kingdom in an age to follow this.

With this age the "present evil world" ends; and mark well that while God has been thus permitting the predominance and reign of evil, to the seeming detriment of his cause, nevertheless his deep designs have been steadily progressing according to a fixed and definite plan, and in the exact order of the seasons which he has appointed. In the end of this age, and the dawn of its successor, the Millennial age, Satan is to be bound and his power overthrown, preparatory to the establishment of Christ's kingdom and the beginning of "the world to come, wherein dwelleth righteousness."

Millennium, signifying a thousand years, is by common consent used as the name for the period mentioned in Rev. 20:4—the thousand years of Christ's reign, the first age in the "world to come." During the Millennial age, there will be a restitution of all things lost by the fall of Adam (Acts 3:19-21), and before its close all tears shall have been wiped away. Beyond its boundary, in the ages of blessedness to follow, there shall be no more death, neither sorrow nor crying; neither shall there be any more pain. The former things will have passed away. (Rev. 21:4) God's revelations particularize no further, and there we stop.

We have here only glanced at the mere outline of this plan of the ages. The more we examine it, the more we will find in it perfect harmony, beauty and order. Each age has its part to accomplish, necessary to the complete development of God's plan as a whole. The plan is a progressive one, gradually unfolding from age to age, upward and onward to the grand consummation of the original design of the Divine Architect, "who worketh all things after the counsel of his own will." (Eph. 1:11) Not one of these great periods is an hour too long or too short for the accomplishment of its object. God is a wise economist of both time and means, though his resources are infinite; and no power, however malicious, for a moment retards or thwarts his purposes. All things, evil as well as good, under divine supervision and overruling, are working together for the accomplishment of his will.

To an uninstructed and undisciplined mind, which can see only a little of the intricate machinery of God's plan, it appears like anarchy, confusion and failure, just as the whole, or even a part, of an intricate machine would appear to a child. To its immature and untutored mind it is incomprehensible, and the opposite motions of its wheels and belts are but confusion. But maturity and investigation will show that the seeming confusion is beautiful harmony, working good results. The machine, however, was as truly a success before the child understood its operation as after. So, while God's plan is, and has been for ages, in successful operation, man has been receiving the necessary discipline, not only to enable him to understand its intricate workings, but also to experience its blessed results.

As we pursue our study of the divine plan, it is essential that we keep in memory these ages and their respective peculiarities and objects; for in *no one* of them can the plan be seen, *but in all of them,* even as a link is not a chain, but several links united form a chain. We obtain correct ideas of the whole plan by noting the distinctive features of each part, and thus we are enabled to divide rightly the Word of truth.

A statement of the Word which belongs to one epoch, or dispensation, should not be applied to another, as things stated of one age are not always true of another. For instance, it would be an untruth to say of the present time that the knowledge of the Lord fills the whole earth, or that there is no need to say to your neighbor, Know the Lord.

(Isa. 11:9; Jer. 31:34) This is not true in this age, and it cannot be true until the Lord, having come again, has established his kingdom; for throughout this age there have been many seducing deceptions, and we are told that even in the very end of the age—"*In the last days* . . . evil men and seducers shall wax worse and worse, deceiving and being deceived." (2 Tim. 3:1, 13) It will be as the result of Messiah's reign during the Millennial age that knowledge and righteousness shall cover the earth as the waters cover the sea.

A similar mistake, and a very common one, is to suppose that God's kingdom is now established and ruling over the earth, and that his will is now done among the nations. This is manifestly far from the truth, for the kingdoms of this world are supported and enriched through oppression, injustice and deceit, to as great an extent as the increasing intelligence of the people will permit. Satan, the present "prince of this world," must yet be displaced, and these kingdoms, now under his control, must become the kingdoms of our Lord and of his Anointed, when he shall take unto himself his great power, and reign.

By the light now due to the household of faith, we discern that system and order which mark the stately steppings of our God through the ages past, and we are forcibly reminded of the beautiful lines of Cowper, inspired by a living faith, which trusted where it could not trace the Almighty Jehovah:

He Will Make It Plain

"God moves in a mysterious way,
His wonders to perform:
He plants his footsteps in the sea,
And rides upon the storm.

"Deep in unfathomable mines
  Of never-failing skill,
He treasures up his bright designs,
  And works his sovereign will.

"Ye fearful saints, fresh courage take;
  The clouds ye so much dread
Are big with mercy, and shall break
  In blessings on your head.

"Judge not the Lord by feeble sense,
  But trust him for his grace.
Behind a frowning providence
  He hides a smiling face.

"His purposes will ripen fast,
  Unfolding every hour.
The bud may have a bitter taste,
  But sweet will be the flower.

"Blind unbelief is sure to err,
  And scan his work in vain.
God is his own interpreter,
  And he will make it plain."

"I know not the way that's before me,
  The joys or the griefs it may bring;
What clouds are o'erhanging the future,
  What flowers by the wayside may spring.
But there's One who will journey beside me,
  Nor in weal nor in woe will forsake;
And this is my solace and comfort,
  'He knoweth the way that I take.'"

STUDY V

"THE MYSTERY HID FROM AGES AND FROM GENERATIONS, BUT NOW MADE MANIFEST TO HIS SAINTS"–COL. 1:26

THE GLIMMERING LIGHT OF THE FIRST PROMISE—THE PROMISE TO ABRAHAM—HOPE DEFERRED—THE MYSTERY BEGINS TO UNRAVEL AT PENTECOST—WHAT THE MYSTERY IS—WHY SO LONG KEPT A MYSTERY—STILL A MYSTERY TO THE WORLD—IN DUE TIME TO BE MADE MANIFEST TO ALL—WHEN THE MYSTERY WILL BE FINISHED.

WHILE mankind was under the discipline of evil, and unable to understand its necessity, God repeatedly expressed his purpose to restore and bless them through a coming deliverer. But who that deliverer should be was a mystery for four thousand years, and it only began to be clearly revealed after the resurrection of Christ, in the beginning of the Christian or Gospel age.

Looking back to the time when life and Edenic happiness were forfeited by our first parents, we see them under the just penalty of sin filled with sorrow, and without a ray of hope, except that drawn from the obscure statement that the seed of the woman should bruise the serpent's head. Though in the light of subsequent developments this is full of significance to us, to them it was but a faint and glimmering light. Nearly two thousand years rolled by with no evidence of a fulfilment.

About two thousand years after, God called Abraham, and promised that his seed should bless all the families of the earth. This looked as though God still held to his previously expressed purpose, and was now about to fulfil it.

Time sped on: the promised land of Canaan was not yet in
his possession; they had yet no offspring, and Abraham and
Sarah were growing old. Abraham reasoned that he must
help God to fulfil his promise; so Ishmael was born. But his
assistance was not needed, for in *due time* Isaac, the child of
hope and promise, was born. Then it seemed that the
promised ruler and blesser of nations had come. But no:
years rolled by, and seemingly God's promise had failed; for
Isaac died, and his heir, Jacob, also. But the faith of a few
still held firmly to the promise, and was sustained by God;
for "the covenant which he made with Abraham" was
assured by God's "oath unto Isaac, and confirmed to Jacob
. . . and to Israel for an everlasting covenant." 1 Chron.
16:16, 17

When at the time of Jacob's death his descendants were
first called the TWELVE TRIBES OF ISRAEL, and recognized
of God as a "chosen nation" (Gen. 49:28; Deut. 26:5), the
expectation that this nation as a whole, as the promised seed
of Abraham, should possess Canaan, and rule and bless the
world, seemed to be on the eve of realization; for already,
under the favor of Egypt, they were becoming a strong
nation. But hope was almost blasted and the promise almost
forgotten when the Egyptians, having gained control of
them, held them as slaves for a long period.

Truly God's promises were shrouded in mystery, and his
ways seemed past finding out. However, in due time came
Moses, a great deliverer, by whose hand God led them out
of bondage, working mighty miracles on their behalf. Before
entering Canaan this great deliverer died; but as the Lord's
mouthpiece he declared, "A prophet shall the Lord your
God raise up unto you of your brethren, like unto me."
(Deut. 18:15; Acts 3:22) This gave a further insight into
God's plan, showing that not only would their nation, as a
whole, be associated in some way with the future work of

ruling and blessing, but that one to be selected from among them would lead to victory and to the fulfilment of the promise. Then Joshua, whose name signifies deliverer, or savior, became their leader, and under him they won great victories, and actually entered the land promised in the covenant. Surely then it seemed that the true leader had come, and that the promise was about to have complete fulfilment.

But Joshua died, and they made no headway as a nation until David, and then Solomon, were given them as kings. There they reached the very zenith of their glory; but soon, instead of seeing the promise accomplished, they were shorn of their power, and became tributary to other nations. Some held fast the promise of God, however, and still looked for the great deliverer of whom Moses, Joshua, David and Solomon were only types.

About the time when Jesus was born, all men were in expectation of the Messiah, the coming king of Israel and, through Israel, of the world. But Israel's hope of the glory and honor of their coming king, inspired as it was by the types and prophecies of his greatness and power, caused them to overlook another set of types and prophecies, which pointed to a work of suffering and death, as a ransom for sinners, necessary before the blessing could come. This was prefigured in the Passover before they were delivered from Egypt, in the slaying of the animals at the giving of the law covenant (Heb. 9:11-20; 10:8-18), and in the Atonement sacrifices performed year by year continually by the priesthood. They overlooked, too, the statement of the prophets, "who testified beforehand the *sufferings* of Christ, and the glory that *should follow.*" (1 Peter 1:11) Hence, when Jesus came as a sacrifice, they did not recognize him; they knew not the time of their visitation. (Luke 19:44) Even his immediate followers were sorely perplexed when Jesus died; and sadly they said, "We trusted it had been he which should have redeemed Israel." (Luke 24:21) Apparently, their confidence in him had been misplaced. They failed to see that the death of their leader was a surety for the New Covenant under which the blessings were to come, a partial fulfilment of the covenant of promise. However, when they found that he had risen from the tomb, their withered hopes again began to revive (1 Peter 1:3), and when he was about to leave them, they asked concerning their long-cherished and oft-deferred hope, saying, "Lord, wilt thou at this time restore again the kingdom to Israel?" That their hopes were in the main correct, though they might not know the time when they would be fulfilled, is evident from our Lord's reply: "It is not for you to know the times and seasons which the Father hath put in his own power." Acts 1:6, 7

What turn has God's plan now taken? must have been the query of his disciples when Jesus had ascended; for we must remember that our Lord's teachings concerning the Kingdom were principally in parables and dark sayings. He had said to them, "I have yet many things to say unto you, but ye cannot bear them now; howbeit, when he, the Spirit of truth, is come, he will guide you into all truth." "He shall teach you all things, and bring all things to your remembrance, whatsoever I have said unto you." (John 16:12, 13; 14:26) So they could not understand before the Pentecostal blessing came.

Even then, it was some time before they got a clear, full understanding of the work being done, and its relation to the original covenant. (Acts 11:9; Gal. 2:2, 12, 14) However, it would seem that even before they fully and clearly understood, they were used as the mouthpieces of God, and their inspired words were probably clearer and deeper expressions of truth than they themselves fully comprehended.

For instance, read James' discourse in which he says: "Simeon hath declared how God at the first did visit the Gentiles to take out of them a people for his name [a bride]. And to this agree the words of the prophets, as it is written, 'After this [after this people from the Gentiles has been taken out] I will return, and will build again the tabernacle of David [the earthly dominion] which is fallen down, and I will build again the ruins thereof, and I will set it up.'" Acts 15:14-16

James began to read in God's providence, in the sending of the Gospel through Peter to the first Gentile convert and through Paul to Gentiles in general, that during this age believing Jews and Gentiles were to be alike favored. He then looked up the prophecies and found it so written; and that after the work of this Gospel age is completed, then the promises to fleshly Israel will be fulfilled. Gradually the great mystery, so long hidden, began to be understood by a few— the saints, the special "friends" of God.

Paul declares (Col. 1:27) that this mystery which hath been hid from ages and from generations, now made manifest to his saints, is

"Christ in You, the Hope of Glory."

This is the great mystery of God which has been hidden from all previous ages, and is still hidden from all except a special class—the saints, or consecrated believers. But what is meant by "Christ in you?" We have learned that Jesus was anointed with the holy Spirit (Acts 10:38), and thus we recognize him to be the Christ—the anointed—for the word *Christ* signifies *anointed*. And the Apostle John says that *the anointing* which *we* (consecrated believers) have received *abideth in us.* (1 John 2:27) Thus the saints of this Gospel age are an anointed company—anointed to be kings and priests unto God (2 Cor. 1:21; 1 Peter 2:9); and together with

Jesus, their chief and Lord, they constitute Jehovah's Anointed—the Christ.

In harmony with this teaching of John, that we also are *anointed,* Paul assures us that this mystery which has been kept secret in ages past, but which is now made known to the saints, is that *the Christ* (the Anointed) is "not one member, but many," just as the human body is one, and has many members; but as all the members of the body, being many, are one body, so also is the Anointed—the Christ. (1 Cor. 12:12-28) Jesus is anointed to be the Head or Lord over the Church, which is his body (or his bride, as expressed in another figure—Eph. 5:25-30), and unitedly they constitute the *promised "Seed"*—the Great Deliverer: "If ye be Christ's, then are ye Abraham's *seed,* and *heirs* according to the promise." Gal. 3:29

The Apostle carefully guards the Church against any presumptive claims, saying of Jesus that "God hath put all things under his feet, and gave him to be the head over all things to the Church, which is his body," "that in all things he might have *the pre-eminence."* (Eph. 1:22; Col. 1:18) Yet, under the figure of the human body, he beautifully and forcibly shows our intimate relationship. This same oneness Jesus also taught, saying, "I am the vine, ye are the branches." John 15:5

Our oneness with the Lord Jesus, as members of the Christ, the anointed company, is well illustrated by the figure of the pyramid.

The top-stone is a perfect pyramid of itself. Other stones may be built up under it, and, if in harmony with all the characteristic lines of the top-stone, the whole mass will be a perfect pyramid. How beautifully this illustrates our position as members of "the Seed"—"the Christ." Joined to and perfectly in harmony with our Head, we, as living stones, are perfect; separated from him, we are nothing.

Jesus, the perfect one, has been highly exalted, and now we present ourselves to him that we may be formed and shaped according to his example, and that we may be built up as a building of God. In an ordinary building there is no *chief* corner-stone; but in our building there is one chief corner-stone, the "top-stone," as it is written: "Behold, I lay in Zion a chief corner-stone, elect, precious"—"to whom coming as unto a living stone . . . ye also as lively [living] stones are built up a spiritual house, a holy priesthood, to offer up *sacrifices acceptable to God by Jesus Christ." (1 Pet. 2:4-6) And very soon, we trust, the union between Jesus, the "Head," and "the Church, which is his body," will be complete.

And, dearly beloved, many blows and much polishing must we endure—much transforming must we undergo, and much conforming to his example, under the direction of the great Master-builder; and in order to have the ability and ideality of the builder displayed in us, we will need to see that we have no cross-grained will of our own to oppose or thwart the accomplishment of His will in us; we must be very childlike and humble—"clothed with humility; for God resisteth the proud, and giveth grace to the humble."

---

*Sinaitic MS. omits *spiritual* before sacrifices.

Let us humble ourselves, therefore, under the mighty hand of God, that he may exalt us in due time (1 Peter 5:5, 6), as he has exalted our Head and Forerunner. Phil. 2:8, 9

This is indeed a wonderful message, and, as we come to the Word of God to inquire concerning our great high calling, we find the prophets all eloquent in proclaiming the grace [favor or blessing] that is come unto us (1 Peter 1:10); while types, and parables, and hitherto dark sayings, now become luminous, shedding their light on the "narrow way" in which the anointed [Christ] company is called to run for the prize now disclosed to view. This was truly a mystery never before thought of—that God intends to raise up not only a deliverer, but a deliverer composed of many members. This is the *"high calling"* to which the consecrated believers of the Gospel age are privileged to attain. Jesus did not attempt to unfold it to the disciples while natural men, but waited until at Pentecost they were anointed—begotten to the new nature. From Paul's explanation we know that none but "new creatures" can now appreciate or understand this high calling. He says: "We speak the wisdom of God in a *mystery,* even the hidden wisdom [plan] which God ordained before the world unto our glory; which none of the princes [chief ones] of this world knew; . . . as it is written, 'Eye hath not seen, nor ear heard, neither have entered into the heart of man, the things which God hath prepared for them that love him'; but God hath revealed them unto us by his Spirit." 1 Cor. 2:6-14

In his letter to the Galatians, Paul opens up the entire mystery, and shows how the Abrahamic covenant is to be fulfilled. He shows that the Law given to Israel did not interfere with the original covenant (Gal. 3:15-18), and that the seed of Abraham which is to bless all nations is Christ. (Verse 16) Then, carrying out the idea already alluded to, that the Christ includes all anointed of the Spirit, he says: "For as many of you as have been baptized *into Christ* have put on Christ; . . . and if ye be Christ's then are YE [together with Jesus] *Abraham's seed,* and heirs, according to the promise" made to Abraham. (Verses 27, 29) Following up the same line of reasoning, he shows (Gal. 4) that Abraham was a type of Jehovah, Sarah a type of the covenant or promise, and Isaac a type of Christ (head and body); and then adds, "We, brethren, as Isaac was, are the children of promise." (Verse 28) Thus the plan of God was hidden in types until the Gospel age began the development of the Christ.

There has existed a necessity for keeping this mystery hidden, else it would not have been so kept. It was necessary, because to have revealed the plan in full to mankind would have been to frustrate it. Had men known, they would not have crucified either the Lord of glory or the Church which is his body. (1 Cor. 2:8) Not only would the death of Christ, as the price of man's redemption, have been interfered with, had not the plan been kept a mystery from the world, but the trial of the faith of the Church, as sharers in the sufferings of Christ, would thereby have been prevented also; for "The world knoweth us not [as his joint-heirs] because [for the same reason that] it knew him not." 1 John 3:1

Not only is the plan of God, and the Christ which is the very embodiment of that plan, a great mystery to the world, but the peculiar course in which this little flock is called to walk marks its members as "peculiar people." It was a mystery to the world that a person of so much ability as Jesus of Nazareth should spend his time and talent as he did, whereas, if he had turned his attention to politics, law, merchandise or popular religion, he might have become great and respected. In the opinion of men he foolishly wasted his life, and they said, "He hath a devil and is mad." His life and teachings were mysteries to them. They could not understand him.

The apostles and their companions were likewise mysteries in the world, in leaving their business prospects, etc., to preach forgiveness of sins through the death of the despised and crucified Jesus. Paul forsook a high station and social influence to labor with his hands, and to preach Christ, and the invisible crown for all believers who should walk in his footsteps. This was so mysterious that some said, "Paul, thou art beside thyself: much learning doth make thee mad." And all who so follow in the Master's footsteps are, like Paul, counted fools for Christ's sake.

But God's plan will not always be shrouded in mystery: the dawn of the Millennial Day brings the fuller light of God to men, and "the knowledge of the Lord shall fill the whole earth." The Sun of Righteousness, which shall arise with healing in his wings, dispelling the darkness of ignorance, is the Christ in Millennial glory—not the Head alone, but also the members of his body; for it is written: If we suffer with him, we shall also be glorified together. "When Christ, who is our life, shall appear, then shall we also appear *with him in glory*"; and "Then shall the righteous shine forth *as the sun* in the kingdom of their Father." Rom. 8:17; 2 Tim. 2:11, 12; Col. 3:4; Matt. 13:43

Now, to all except those begotten to a new mind, by receiving "the mind of Christ," the promises which we believe, and the hopes which we cherish, seem visionary, and too improbable to be received or acted upon. In the age to come, when God shall "pour out his spirit upon all flesh," as during the present age he pours it upon his "servants and handmaids," then indeed all will understand and appreciate the promises now being grasped by the "little flock";

and they will rejoice in the obedience and exaltation of the Church, saying, "Let us be glad, and rejoice, and give honor to God, for the marriage of the Lamb is come, and his wife hath made herself ready." (Rev. 19:7) They will rejoice in the glorification of the Church, through which blessings will then be flowing to them; and while they will realize that the "exceeding great and precious promises" inherited by the Anointed (head and body) are not for them, but are fulfilled upon us, they will be blessed by the lesson illustrated in the Church; and while they run for the blessings *then held out to them,* they will profit by the example of the Church, and glorify God on her behalf. But this knowledge will not bring covetousness; for under the new order of things their calling to perfect human nature will fully satisfy them, and will seem more desirable to them than a change of nature.

Then the "mystery" will have ended; for the world will have come to see that it was the spirit of God in Christ, and the spirit of Christ in us—God manifested in the flesh—which they had hitherto misunderstood. Then they will see that we were not mad, nor fools; but that we chose the better part when we ran for the riches, honors and crown, unseen by them, but eternal.

In point of time, the mystery of God will be finished during the period of the sounding of the seventh [symbolic] trumpet. (Rev. 10:7) This applies to the mystery in both senses in which it is used: the mystery or secret features of God's *plan* will then be made known and will be clearly seen; and also the "mystery of God," the Church, the embodiment of that plan. Both will then be finished. The secret, hidden plan will have sought out the full, complete number of the members of the body of Christ, and hence it, the BODY OF CHRIST, will be finished. The plan will cease to be a mystery, because there will be no further object in perpetuating its secrecy. The greatness of the mystery, so long kept secret, and hidden in promises, types and figures, and the wonderful grace bestowed on those called to fellowship in this mystery (Eph. 3:9), suggest to us that the work to follow its completion, for which for six thousand years Jehovah has kept mankind in expectation and hope, must be an immense work, a grand work, worthy of such great preparations. What may we not expect in blessings upon the world, when the veil of mystery is withdrawn and the showers of blessing descend! It is this for which the whole creation groans and travails in pain together until now, *waiting* for the completion of this mystery— for the manifestation of the Sons of God, the promised "Seed," in whom they shall all be blessed. Rom. 8:19, 21, 22

A Lord's Day Offering

"I offer Thee:
Every heart's throb, they are Thine;
Every human tie of mine;
Every joy and every pain;
Every act of mind or brain—
　　My blessed God!
Every hope and every fear;
Every smile and every tear;
Every song and hymn,
　　'Laudamus Te.'

"Take them all, my blessed Lord,
Bind them with thy secret cord;
Glorify thyself in me,
　　Adored One!
Multiply them by thy Word;
Strengthen, bless, increase, my Lord
　　Of perfect love!
　　Thou First and Last!"

STUDY VI
OUR LORD'S RETURN—ITS OBJECT, THE RESTITUTION OF ALL THINGS

Our Lord's Second Advent Personal and Pre-Millennial—Its Relationship to the First Advent—The Selection of the Church and the Conversion of the World—Election and Free Grace—Prisoners of Hope—Prophetic Testimony Regarding Restitution—Our Lord's Return Manifestly the Hope of the Church and the World.

"AND He shall send Jesus Christ, which [who] before was preached unto you; whom the heaven must retain until the times of restitution of all things, which God hath spoken by the mouth of all his holy prophets since the world began." Acts 3:20, 21

That our Lord intended his disciples to understand that for some purpose, in some manner, and at some time, he would come again, is, we presume, admitted and believed by all familiar with the Scriptures. True, Jesus said, "Lo, I am with you alway, even unto the end of the age" (Matt. 28:20), and by his spirit and by his Word he has been with the Church continually, guiding, directing, comforting and sustaining his saints, and cheering them in the midst of all their afflictions. But though the Church has been blessedly conscious of the Lord's knowledge of all her ways and of his constant care and love, yet she longs for his promised personal return; for, when he said, "If I go, I will come again" (John 14:3), he certainly referred to a *second personal coming.*

Some think he referred to the descent of the holy Spirit at Pentecost; others, to the destruction of Jerusalem, etc.; but these apparently overlook the fact that in the last book

89

of the Bible, written some sixty years after Pentecost, and twenty-six years after Jerusalem's destruction, he that was dead and is alive speaks of the event as yet future, saying: "Behold, I come quickly, and my reward is with me." And the inspired John replies, "Even so, come, Lord Jesus." Rev. 22:12, 20

Quite a number think that when sinners are converted that forms a part of the coming of Christ, and that so he will continue coming until all the world is converted. Then, say they, he will have fully come.

These evidently forget the testimony of the Scriptures on the subject, which declares the reverse of their expectation: that at the time of our Lord's second coming the world will be far from converted to God; that "In the last days perilous times shall come, for men shall be lovers of pleasure more than lovers of God" (2 Tim. 3:1-4); that "Evil men and seducers shall wax worse and worse, deceiving, and being deceived." (Verse 13) They forget the Master's special warning to his little flock: "Take heed to yourselves lest that day come upon *you* unawares, for as *a snare* shall it come on all them [not taking heed] that dwell on the face of the whole earth." (Luke 21:34, 35) Again, we may rest assured that when it is said, "All kindreds of the earth shall wail because of him," when they see him coming (Rev. 1:7), no reference is made to the conversion of sinners. Do all men wail because of the conversion of sinners? On the contrary, if this passage refers, as almost all admit, to Christ's presence on earth, it teaches that all on earth will not love his appearing, as they certainly would do if all were converted.

Some expect an actual coming and presence of the Lord, but *set the time* of the event a long way off, claiming that through the efforts of the Church in its present condition the world must be converted, and thus the Millennial age be introduced. They claim that when the world has been converted, and Satan bound, and the knowledge of the Lord caused to fill the whole earth, and when the nations learn war no more, then the work of the Church in her present condition will be ended; and that when she has accomplished this great and difficult task, the Lord will come to wind up earthly affairs, reward believers and condemn sinners.

Some scriptures, taken disconnectedly, seem to favor this view; but when God's Word and plan are viewed as a whole, these will all be found to favor the opposite view, viz.: that Christ comes before the conversion of the world, and reigns for the purpose of converting the world; that the Church is now being tried, and that the reward promised the overcomers is that after being glorified they shall share with the Lord Jesus in that reign, which is God's appointed means of blessing the world and causing the knowledge of the Lord to come to every creature. Such are the Lord's special promises: "To him that overcometh will I grant to sit with me in my throne." (Rev. 3:21) "And they lived and reigned with Christ a thousand years." Rev. 20:4

There are two texts chiefly relied upon by those who claim that the Lord will not come until after the Millennium, to which we would here call attention. One is, "This gospel of the Kingdom shall be preached in all the world for a witness unto all nations; and then shall the end come." (Matt. 24:14) They claim this as having reference to the conversion of the world before the end of the Gospel age. But *witnessing* to the world does not imply the conversion of the world. The text says nothing about how the testimony will be received. This witness has already been given. In 1861 the reports of the Bible Societies showed that the Gospel had been published in every language of earth, though not all of earth's millions had received it. No, not one half of the sixteen hundred millions living have ever heard the name of Jesus. Yet the condition of the text is fulfilled: the gospel has been preached in all the world for a *witness*—to every *nation*.

The Apostle (Acts 15:14) tells that the *main object* of the gospel in the present age is "to take out a people" for Christ's name—the overcoming Church, which, at his second advent, will be united to him and receive his name. The witnessing to the world during this age is a secondary object.

The other text is, "Sit thou at my right hand, until I make thine enemies thy footstool." (Psa. 110:1) The vague, indefinite idea regarding this text seems to be that Christ sits on a material throne somewhere in the heavens until the work of subduing all things is accomplished for him through the Church, and that then he comes to reign. This is a misconception. The throne of God referred to is not a material one, but refers to his supreme authority and rulership; and the Lord Jesus has been exalted to a share in that rulership. Paul declares, "God hath highly exalted him [Jesus] and given him a name above every name." He hath given him *authority* above every other, next to the Father. If Christ sits upon a material throne until his enemies are made his footstool [all subdued], then of course he cannot come until all things are subdued. But if "right hand" in this text refers, not to a fixed locality and bench, but, as we claim, to power, authority, rulership, it follows that the text under consideration would in no wise conflict with the other scripture which teaches that he comes to "subdue all things unto himself" (Phil. 3:21), by virtue of the power vested in him. To illustrate: Emperor William is on the throne of Germany, we say, yet we do not refer to the royal bench, and as a matter of fact he seldom occupies it. When we say that he is on the throne, we mean that he rules Germany. Right hand signifies the chief place, position of excellence or favor, next to the chief ruler. Thus Prince Bismarck was exalted or seated at the right hand of power, by the German Emperor; and Joseph was at the right hand of Pharaoh in the kingdom of Egypt—not literally, but after the customary figure of speech. Jesus' words to Caiaphas agree with this thought: "Hereafter shall ye see the Son of Man sitting on *the right hand of power,* and coming in the clouds of heaven." (Matt. 26:64) He will be on the right hand when coming, and will remain on the right hand during the Millennial age, and forever.

A further examination of God's revealed plans will give a broader view of the object of both the first and second advents; and we should remember that both events stand related as parts of one plan. The specific work of the first advent was to *redeem* men; and that of the second is to *restore,* and bless, and liberate the redeemed. Having given his life a ransom for all, our Savior ascended to present that sacrifice to the Father, thus making reconciliation for man's iniquity. He tarries and permits "the prince of this world" to continue the rule of evil, until after the selection of "the Bride, the Lamb's wife," who, to be accounted *worthy* of such honor, must overcome the influences of the present evil world. Then the work of giving to the world of mankind the great blessings secured to them by his sacrifice will be due to commence, and he will come forth to bless all the families of the earth.

True, the restoring and blessing could have commenced at once, when the ransom price was paid by the Redeemer, and then the coming of Messiah would have been but one event, the reign and blessing beginning at once, as the apostles at first expected. (Acts 1:6) But God had provided "some better thing for us"—the Christian Church (Heb. 11:40); hence it is in our interest that the reign of Christ is separated from the sufferings of the Head by these nineteen centuries.

This period between the first and second advents, between the ransom for all and the blessing of all, is for the trial and selection of the Church, which is the body of Christ; otherwise there would have been only the one advent, and the work which will be done during the period of his second presence, in the Millennium, would have followed the resurrection of Jesus. Or, instead of saying that the work of the second advent would have followed at once the work of the first, let us say rather that had Jehovah not purposed the selection of the "little flock," "the body of Christ," the first advent would not have taken place when it did, but would have occurred at the time of the second advent, and there would have been but the one. For God has evidently designed the *permission* of evil for six thousand years, as well as that the cleansing and restitution of all shall be accomplished during the seventh thousand.

Thus seen, the coming of Jesus, as the sacrifice and ransom for sinners, was just long enough in advance of the blessing and restoring time to allow for the selection of his "little flock" of "joint-heirs." This will account to some for the apparent delay on God's part in giving the blessings promised, and provided for, in the ransom. The blessings will come in due time, as at first planned, though, for a glorious purpose, the price was provided longer beforehand than men would have expected.

The Apostle informs us that Jesus has been absent from earth—in the heaven—during all the intervening time from his ascension to the beginning of the times of restitution, or the Millennial age—"whom the heaven must retain *until* the times of restitution of all things," etc. (Acts 3:21) Since the Scriptures thus teach that the object of our Lord's second advent is the restitution of all things, and that at the time of his appearing the nations are so far from being converted as to be angry (Rev. 11:18) and in opposition, it must be admitted either that the Church will fail to accomplish her mission, and that the plan of God will be thus far frustrated, or else, as we claim and have shown, that the conversion of the world in the present age was not expected of the Church, but that her mission has been to preach the Gospel in all the world *for a witness,* and to prepare herself under divine direction for her great future work. God has not yet by any means exhausted his power for the world's conversion. Nay, more: he has not yet *even attempted* the world's conversion.

This may seem a strange statement to some, but let such reflect that if God has attempted such a work he has signally failed; for, as we have seen, only a small fraction of earth's billions have ever intelligently heard of the *only name* whereby they must be saved. We have only forcibly stated the views and teachings of some of the leading sects—Baptists, Presbyterians and others—viz., that God is electing or selecting out of the world a "little flock," a Church. They believe that God will do no more than choose this Church, while we find the Scriptures teaching a further step in the divine plan—a RESTITUTION for the world, to be accomplished through the elect Church, when completed and glorified. The "little flock," the overcomers, of this Gospel age, are only the body of "The Seed" in or by whom all the families of the earth are to be blessed.

Those who claim that Jehovah has been trying for six thousand years to convert the world, and failing all the time, must find it difficult to reconcile such views with the Bible assurance that all God's purposes shall be accomplished, and that his Word shall not return unto him void, but shall prosper in *the thing whereto it was sent.* (Isa. 55:11) The fact that the world has not yet been converted, and that the knowledge of the Lord has not yet filled the earth, is a proof that it has not yet been *sent* on that mission.

This brings us to the two lines of thought which have divided Christians for centuries, namely, Election and Free Grace. That both of these doctrines, notwithstanding their apparent oppositeness, have Scriptural support, no Bible student will deny. This fact should lead us at once to surmise that in some way both must be true; but in no way can they be reconciled except by observing heaven's law, *order,* and "rightly dividing the word of truth" on this subject. This order, as represented in the plan of the ages, if observed, will clearly show us that while an Election has been in progress during the present and past ages, what is by way of distinction designated Free Grace is God's gracious provision for the world in general during the Millennial age. If the distinctive features of the epochs and dispensations outlined in a preceding chapter be kept in mind, and all the passages relating to Election and Free Grace be examined and located, it will be found that all those which treat of Election apply to the present and past ages, while those which teach Free Grace are fully applicable to the next age.

However, Election, as taught in the Bible, is not the arbitrary coercion, or fatalism, usually believed and taught by its advocates, but a selection according to fitness and adaptability to the end God has in view, during the period appointed for that purpose.

The doctrine of Free Grace, advocated by Arminians, is also a much grander display of God's abounding favor than its most earnest advocates have ever taught. God's grace or favor in Christ is ever free, in the sense of being unmerited; but since the fall of man into sin, to the present time, certain of God's favors have been restricted to special individuals, nations and classes, while in the next age all the world will be invited to share the favors then offered, on the conditions then made known to all, and whosoever will may come and drink at life's fountain freely. Rev. 22:17

Glancing backward, we notice the selection or election of Abraham and certain of his offspring as the channels through which the promised Seed, the blesser of all the families of the earth, should come. (Gal. 3:29) We note also the selection of Israel from among all nations, as the one in whom, typically, God illustrated how the great work for the world should be accomplished—their deliverance from Egypt, their Canaan, their covenants, their laws, their sacrifices for sins, for the blotting out of guilt and for the sprinkling of the people, and their priesthood for the accomplishment of all this, being a miniature and typical representation of the real priesthood and sacrifices for the purifying of the world of mankind. God, speaking to the people, said, "You only have I known of all the families of the earth." (Amos 3:2) This people alone was recognized until Christ came; yes, and afterwards, for his ministry was confined to them, and he would not permit his disciples to go to others—saying, as he sent them out, "Go not into the way of the Gentiles, and into any city of the Samaritans enter ye not." Why so, Lord? Because, he explains, "I am not sent but to the lost sheep of the house of Israel." (Matt. 10:5, 6; 15:24) All his time was devoted to them until his death, and there was done his first work for the world, the first display of his free and all-abounding grace, which in "due time" shall indeed be a blessing to all.

This, God's grandest gift, was not limited to nation or class. It was not for Israel only, but for all the world; for Jesus Christ, by the grace of God, tasted death for *every man.* Heb. 2:9

And now also, in the Gospel age, a certain sort of election obtains. Some parts of the world are more favored with the gospel (which is free to all who hear) than others. Glance at a map of the world and see how small is the portion enlightened or blessed in any appreciable degree by the gospel of Christ. Contrast yourself, with your privileges and knowledge, with the millions in heathen darkness today, who never heard the call, and who consequently were not called. When the called-out company (called to be sons of God, heirs of God, and joint-heirs with Jesus Christ our Lord—who have made their calling and election sure) is complete, then the plan of God for the *world's* salvation will be only beginning.

Not until it is selected, developed, and exalted to power, will *the Seed* bruise the serpent's head. "The God of peace shall bruise Satan under your feet *shortly.*" (Rom. 16:20; Gen. 3:15) The Gospel age makes ready the chaste virgin, the faithful Church, for the coming Bridegroom. And in the end of the age, when she is made "ready" (Rev. 19:7), the Bridegroom comes, and they that are ready go in with him to the marriage—the second Adam and the second Eve become one, and then the glorious work of restitution begins. In the next dispensation, the new heaven and the new earth, the Church will be no longer the espoused virgin, but the Bride; and then shall "The Spirit and the Bride say, Come! And let him that heareth say, Come! And let him that is athirst come. And whosoever will, let him take the water of life freely." Rev. 22:17

The Gospel age, so far from closing the Church's mission, is only a necessary preparation for the great future work. For this promised and coming blessing, the whole creation groaneth and travaileth in pain together until now, waiting for the *manifestation* of the sons of God. (Rom. 8:22, 19) And it is a blessed fact that free grace in fullest measure, not merely for the living but for those who have died as well, is provided in our Father's plan as the blessed opportunity of the coming age.

Some who can see something of the blessings due at the second advent, and who appreciate in some measure the fact that the Lord comes to bestow the grand blessing purchased by his death, fail to see this last proposition, viz.: that those in their graves have as much interest in that glorious reign of Messiah as those who at that time will be less completely under the bondage of corruption—death. But as surely as Jesus died for *all,* they all must have the blessings and opportunities which he purchased with his own precious blood. Hence we should expect blessings in the Millennial age upon all those in their graves as well as upon those not in them; and of this we will find abundant proof, as we look further into the Lord's testimony on the subject. It is because of God's plan for their release that those in the tomb are called *"prisoners of hope."*

It is estimated that about one hundred and forty-three billions of human beings have lived on the earth in the six thousand years since Adam's creation. Of these, the very broadest estimate that could be made with reason would be that less than one billion were saints of God. This broad estimate would leave the immense aggregate of one hundred and forty-two billions (142,000,000,000) who went down into death without faith and hope in the *only name* given under heaven or among men whereby we must be saved. Indeed, the vast majority of these never knew or heard of Jesus, and could not believe in him of whom they had not heard.

What, we ask, has become of this vast multitude, of which figures give a wholly inadequate idea? What is, and is to be, their condition? Did God make no provision for these, whose condition and circumstances he must have foreseen? Or did he, from the foundation of the world, make a wretched and merciless provision for their hopeless, eternal torment, as many of his children claim? Or has he yet in store for them, in the heights and depths and lengths and breadths of his plan, an opportunity for all to come to the knowledge of that *only name,* and, by becoming obedient to the conditions, to enjoy everlasting life?

To these questions, which every thinking Christian asks himself, and yearns to see answered truthfully, and in harmony with the character of Jehovah, comes a variety of answers:

Atheism answers, They are eternally dead: there is no hereafter: they will never live again.

Calvinism answers, They were not elected to be saved. God foreordained and predestined them to be lost—to go to hell—and they are there now, writhing in agony, where they will ever remain, without hope.

Arminianism answers, We believe that God excuses many of them on account of ignorance. Those who did the best they knew how will be sure of being a part of the "Church of the First-born," even though they never heard of Jesus.

To this last view the majority of Christians of all denominations assent (notwithstanding the creeds of some to the contrary), from a feeling that any other view would be irreconcilable with justice on God's part. But do the Scriptures support this last view? Do they teach that ignorance is a ground of salvation? No; the only ground of salvation mentioned in the Scriptures is *faith* in Christ as our Redeemer and Lord. "By grace are ye saved, *through faith.*" (Eph. 2:8) Justification by faith is the underlying principle of the whole system of Christianity. When asked, What must I do to be saved? the apostles answered, Believe on the Lord Jesus Christ. "There is *none other* name under heaven given among men whereby we must be saved"

(Acts 4:12); and "Whosoever shall call upon the name of the Lord shall be saved." Rom. 10:13

But Paul reasons that a man must hear the gospel before he can believe, saying, "How then shall they call on him in whom they have not believed? and how shall they believe in him of whom they have not heard?" Rom. 10:14

Some claim that Paul teaches that *ignorance* will save men, when he says that "The Gentiles, which have not the law, are a law unto themselves." (Rom. 2:14) They gather from this that the law which their conscience furnishes is sufficient to justify them. But such persons misunderstand Paul. His argument is that the whole world is guilty before God (Rom. 3:19); that the Gentiles, who had not the written law, were *condemned*, not justified, by the light of conscience, which, whether it excused them or accused them, proved that they were short of perfection and unworthy of life, even as the Jews who had the written law were *condemned* by it; "For by the law is the knowledge of sin." (Rom. 3:20) The law given to the Jew revealed his weakness, and was intended to show him that he was unable to justify himself before God; for "By the deeds of the Law there shall no flesh be justified in his [God's] sight." The written law *condemned the Jews*, and the Gentiles had light enough of conscience to *condemn them;* and thus every mouth is stopped from claiming the right of life, and all the world stands guilty before God.

Remembering the statement of James (2:10), that whosoever shall keep the whole law, except to offend in one point, is guilty, and cannot claim any blessing promised by the Law Covenant, we realize that indeed "there is none righteous; no, not one." (Rom. 3:10) And thus the Scriptures close every door of hope save one, showing that not one of the condemned is able to secure eternal life by meritorious works, and that it is equally useless to plead ignorance as a ground of salvation. Ignorance cannot entitle any one to the *reward* of faith and obedience.

Many Christians, unwilling to believe that so many millions of ignorant infants and heathen will be eternally lost (which they have been taught means to be sent to a place of eternal and hopeless torment), insist, notwithstanding these Bible statements, that God will not condemn the ignorant. We admire their liberality of heart and their appreciation of God's goodness, but urge them not to be too hasty about discarding or ignoring Bible statements. God has a blessing for all, in a better way than through ignorance.

But do these act in accordance with their stated belief? No: though they profess to believe that the ignorant will be saved on account of their ignorance, they continue to send missionaries to the heathen at the cost of thousands of valuable lives and millions of money. If they all, or even half of them, would be saved through ignorance, it is doing them a positive injury to send missionaries to teach them of Christ; for only about one in a thousand believes, when the missionaries do go to them. If this idea be correct, it would be much better to let them remain in ignorance; for then a much larger proportion would be saved. Continuing the same line of argument, might we not reason that if God had left *all men* in ignorance, *all* would have been saved? If so, the coming and death of Jesus were useless, the preaching and suffering of apostles and saints were vain, and the so-called gospel, instead of being good news, is very bad news. The sending of missionaries to the heathen by those who believe the Calvinistic or fatalistic view of election, that the eternal destiny of each individual was unalterably fixed before he had an existence, is even more absurd and unreasonable.

But the Bible, which is full of the missionary spirit, does not teach that there are several ways of salvation—one way by faith, another by works, and another by ignorance. Neither does it teach the God-dishonoring doctrine of fatalism. While it shows every other door of hope closed against the race, it throws wide open the one, only door, and proclaims that whosoever will may enter into life; and it shows that all who do not now see or appreciate the blessed privilege of entering shall in due time be brought to a full knowledge and appreciation. The *only way,* by which any and all of the condemned race may come to God, is not by meritorious works, neither by ignorance, but by faith in the precious blood of Christ, which taketh away the sin of the world. (1 Peter 1:19; John 1:29) This is the Gospel, the good tidings of great joy, "which *shall be* unto ALL PEOPLE."

Suppose we now look at these things just as God tells us of them, and leave the clearing of his character to himself. Let us inquire, What has become of the one hundred and forty-two billions?

Whatever may have become of them, we may be sure they are not now in a condition of suffering; because, not only do the Scriptures teach that full and complete reward is not given to the Church until Christ comes, when he shall reward every man (Matt. 16:27), but that the unjust are to receive their punishment then also. Whatever may be their present condition, it cannot be their full reward; for Peter says, "The Lord knoweth how to reserve the unjust unto the day of judgment to be punished" (2 Peter 2:9); and he will do so.

But the thought that so many of our fellow creatures should at any time be lost from lack of having had the knowledge which is necessary to salvation would be sad indeed to all who have a spark of love or pity. Then, too, there are numerous scriptures which it seems impossible to harmonize with all this. Let us see: In the light of the past and the present as the only opportunities, laying aside all hope through a restitution in the coming age, how shall we understand the statements, "God is love," and "God so loved the world that he gave his only begotten Son, that whosoever believeth in him should not perish"? (1 John 4:8; John 3:16) Would it not seem that if God loved the world so much he might have made provision, not only that believers might be saved, but also that all might hear in order to believe?

Again, when we read, "That was the true light that lighteth every man that cometh into the world" (John 1:9), our observation says, Not so; every man has not been enlightened; we cannot see that our Lord has lighted more than a few of earth's billions. Even in this comparatively enlightened day, millions of heathen give no evidence of such enlightenment; neither did the Sodomites, nor multitudes of others in past ages.

We read that Jesus Christ, by the grace of God, tasted death *"for every man."* (Heb. 2:9) But if he tasted death for the one hundred and forty-three billions, and from any cause that sacrifice becomes efficacious to only one billion, was not the redemption comparatively a failure? And in that case, is not the Apostle's statement too broad? When again we read, "Behold, I bring you good tidings of great joy, which shall be to ALL PEOPLE" (Luke 2:10), and, looking about us, see that it is only to a "little flock" that it has been good tidings, and not to all people, we would be compelled to wonder whether the angels had not overstated the goodness and breadth of their message, and overrated the importance of the work to be accomplished by the Messiah whom they announced.

Another statement is, "There is one God, and one Mediator between God and men, the man Christ Jesus, who gave himself a ransom for all." (1 Tim. 2:5, 6) A ransom for all?

Then why should not all involved have some benefit from Christ's death? Why should not *all* come to a knowledge of the truth, that they may believe?

Without the key, how dark, how inconsistent, these statements appear; but when we find the key to God's plan, these texts all declare with one voice, "God is love." This key is found in the latter part of the text last quoted—"Who gave himself a ransom for all, TO BE TESTIFIED IN DUE TIME." God has a due time for everything. He could have testified it to these in their past lifetime; but since he did not, it proves that their due time must be future. For those who will be of the Church, the bride of Christ, and share the kingdom honors, the present is the "due time" to hear; and whosoever now has an ear to hear, let him hear and heed, and he will be blessed accordingly. Though Jesus paid our ransom before we were born, it was not our "due time" to hear of it for long years afterward, and only the appreciation of it brought responsibility; and this, only to the extent of our ability and appreciation. The same principle applies to all: in God's due time it will be testified to all, and all will then have opportunity to believe and to be blessed by it.

The prevailing opinion is that death ends all probation; but there is no scripture which so teaches; and all the above, and many more scriptures, would be meaningless, or worse, if death ends all hope for the ignorant masses of the world. The one scripture quoted to prove this generally entertained view is, "Where the tree falleth, there it shall be." (Eccl. 11:3) If this has any relation to man's future, it indicates that whatever his condition when he enters the tomb, no change takes place until he is awakened out of it. And this is the uniform teaching of all scriptures bearing on the subject, as will be shown in succeeding chapters. Since God does not propose to save men on account of ignorance, but "will have *all men* to come unto the knowledge of the truth" (1 Tim. 2:4); and since the masses of mankind have died in ignorance; and since "there is no work, nor device, nor knowledge, nor wisdom, in the grave" (Eccl. 9:10); therefore God has prepared for the awakening of the dead, in order to knowledge, faith and salvation. Hence his plan is, that "as all in Adam die, even so all in Christ shall be made alive, but each one in his own order"—the Gospel Church, the Bride, the body of Christ, first; afterward, during the Millennial age, all who shall become his during that thousand years of his *presence* (mistranslated *coming*), the Lord's due time for all to know him, from the least to the greatest. 1 Cor. 15:22

As death came by the first Adam, so life comes by Christ, the second Adam. Everything that mankind lost through being in the first Adam is to be restored to those who believe into the second Adam. When awakened, with the advantage of experience with evil, which Adam lacked, those who thankfully accept the redemption as God's gift may continue to live everlastingly on the original condition of obedience. Perfect obedience will be required, and perfect ability to obey will be given, under the righteous reign of the Prince of Peace. Here is the salvation offered to the world.

Let us now consider another text which is generally ignored except by Universalists; for, although we are not Universalists, we claim the right to use, and believe, and rejoice in, every testimony of God's Word. It reads, "We trust in the living God, who is the Savior of *all men,* specially of *those that believe.*" (1 Tim. 4:10) God will save all men, but will not specially ("to the uttermost") save any except those who come unto him through Christ. God's arbitrary salvation of all men is not such as will conflict with their freedom of will, or their liberty of choice, to give them life against their wills: "I have set before you, this day, life and death; *choose* life, that ye may live."

Simeon contrasted these two salvations, saying, "Mine eyes have seen thy salvation, . . . *a light to lighten the nations,* and *the glory of thy people,* Israel[ites indeed]." This is in harmony with the declaration of the Apostle, that the fact that Jesus Christ, the Mediator, gave himself a ransom for all is to be *testified to all* IN DUE TIME. This is that which shall come to all men, regardless of faith or will on their part. This *good tidings* of a Savior shall be to *all* people (Luke 2:10,11), but the special salvation from sin and death will come only to *his* people (Matt. 1:21)—those who believe into him—for we read that the wrath of God continues to abide on the unbeliever. John 3:36

We see, then, that the general salvation, which will come to every individual, consists of light from the true light, and an opportunity to choose life; and, as the great majority of the race is in the tomb, it will be necessary to bring them forth from the grave in order to testify to them the good tidings of a Savior; also that the special salvation which believers now enjoy in hope (Rom. 8:24), and the reality of which will, in the Millennial age, be revealed, also, to those who "believe in that day," is a *full* release from the thraldom of sin, and the corruption of death, into the glorious liberty of children of God. But attainment to all these blessings will depend upon hearty compliance with the laws of Christ's Kingdom—the rapidity of the attainment to perfection indicating the degree of love for the King and for his law of love. If any, enlightened by the Truth, and brought to a knowledge of the love of God, and restored (either actually or reckonedly) to human perfection, become "fearful," and "draw back" (Heb. 10:38, 39), they, with the unbelievers (Rev. 21:8), will be destroyed from among the people. (Acts 3:23) This is the second death.

Thus we see that all these hitherto difficult texts are explained by the statement—"to be testified in due time." *In due time,* that true light shall lighten every man that has come into the world. *In due time,* it shall be "good tidings of great joy to all people." And in no other way can these scriptures be used without wresting. Paul carries out this line of argument with emphasis in Rom. 5:18, 19. He reasons that, as all men were condemned to death because of Adam's transgression, so also, Christ's righteousness, and obedience even unto death, have become a ground of justification; and that, as all lost life in the first Adam, so all, aside from personal demerit, may receive life by accepting the second Adam.

Peter tells us that this restitution is spoken of by the mouth of all the holy prophets. (Acts 3:19-21) They do all teach it. Ezekiel says of the valley of dry bones, "These bones are the whole house of Israel." And God says to Israel, "Behold, O my people, I will open your graves, and cause you to come up out of your graves, and bring you into the land of Israel. And ye shall know that I am the Lord, when I . . . shall put my spirit in you, and I shall place you in your own land; then shall ye know that I the Lord have spoken it, and performed it, saith the Lord." Ezek. 37:11-14

To this Paul's words agree (Rom. 11:25, 26)— "Blindness in part is happened to Israel until the fulness of the Gentiles [the elect company, the bride of Christ] be come in; and so all Israel shall be saved," or brought back from their cast-off condition; for "God hath not cast away his people which he foreknew." (Verse 2) They were cast off from his favor while the bride of Christ was being selected, but will be reinstated when that work is accomplished. (Verses 28-33) The prophets are full of statements of how God will plant them again, and they shall be no more plucked up. "Thus saith the Lord, the God of Israel, . . . I will set mine eyes upon them for good, and I will bring them again to this land; and I will build them and not pull them down, and I will plant them and not pluck them up. And I will give them an heart to know me, that I am the Lord; and they shall be my people, and I will be their God, for they shall return unto me with their whole heart." (Jer. 24:5-7; 31:28; Jer. 32:40-42; 33:6-16) These cannot merely refer to restorations from former captivities in Babylon, Syria, etc., for they have since been plucked up.

Furthermore, the Lord says, "In those days, they shall say no more, The fathers have eaten a sour grape, and the children's teeth are set on edge, but every one [who dies] shall die for his own iniquity." (Jer. 31:29, 30) This is not the case now. Each does not now die for his own sin, but for Adam's sin—"In Adam all die." He ate the sour grape of sin, and our fathers continued to eat them, entailing further sickness and misery upon their children, thus hastening the penalty, death. The day in which "every man [who dies] shall die for his own sin," only, is the Millennial or Restitution day.

Though many of the prophecies and promises of future blessing seem to apply to Israel only, it must be remembered that they were a typical people, and hence the promises made to them, while sometimes having a special application to themselves, generally have also a wider application to the whole world of mankind which that nation typified. While Israel as a nation was typical of the whole world, its priesthood was typical of the elect "little flock," the head and body of Christ, the "Royal Priesthood"; and the sacrifices, cleansings and atonements made for Israel typified the "better sacrifices," fuller cleansings and real atonement "for the sins of the whole world," of which they are a part.

And not only so, but God mentions by name other nations and promises their restoration. As a forcible illustration we mention the Sodomites. Surely, if we shall find the restitution of the Sodomites clearly taught, we may feel satisfied of the truth of this glorious doctrine of Restitution for all mankind, spoken by the mouth of all the holy prophets. And why should not the Sodomites have an opportunity to reach perfection and everlasting life as well as Israel, or as any of us? True, they were not righteous, but neither was Israel, nor were we who now hear the gospel. "There is none righteous; no, not one," aside from the imputed righteousness of Christ, who died for all. Our Lord's own words tell us that although God rained down fire from heaven and destroyed them all because of their wickedness, yet the Sodomites were not so great sinners in his sight as were the Jews, who had more knowledge. (Gen. 19:24; Luke 17:29) Unto the Jews of Capernaum he said, "If the mighty works which have been done in thee had been done in Sodom, it would have remained until this day." Matt. 11:23

Thus our Lord teaches that the Sodomites did not have a full opportunity; and he guarantees them such opportunity when he adds (verse 24), "But I say unto you, that it shall be more tolerable for the land of Sodom, in the day of judgment, than for thee." The character of the Day of Judgment and its work will be shown in succeeding pages. Here we merely call attention to the fact that it will be a *tolerable* time for Capernaum, and yet *more tolerable* for Sodom; because, though neither had yet had *full* knowledge, nor all the blessings designed to come through the "Seed," yet Capernaum had sinned against more light.

And if Capernaum and all Israel are to be remembered and blessed under the "New Covenant," sealed by the blood of Jesus, why should not the Sodomites also be blessed among "*all* the families of the earth"? They assuredly will be. And let it be remembered that since God "rained down fire from heaven and *destroyed them all*" many centuries before Jesus' day, when their restoration is spoken of, it implies their awakening, their coming from the tomb.

Let us now examine the prophecy of Ezekiel 16:48-63. Read it carefully. God here speaks of Israel, and compares her with her neighbor, Samaria, and also with the Sodomites, of whom he says, "I took them away as I *saw good.*" Neither Jesus nor the Prophet offers any explanation of the seeming inequality of God's dealings in destroying Sodom and permitting others more guilty than Sodom to go unpunished. That will all be made clear when, in "due time," his great designs are made manifest. The Prophet simply states that God "saw good" to do so, and Jesus adds that it will be more tolerable for them in the day of judgment than for others more guilty. But upon the supposition that death ends all probation, and that thereafter none may have opportunity to come to a knowledge of the truth and to obey it, we may well inquire, Why did God see good to take away these people without giving them a chance of salvation through the knowledge of the only name whereby they can be saved? The answer is, because it was not yet their *due time.* In "due time" they will be awakened from death and brought to a knowledge of the truth, and thus blessed together with all the families of the earth, by the promised "Seed." They will then be on trial for everlasting life.

With this thought, and with no other, can we understand the dealings of the God of love with those Amalekites and other nations whom he not only permitted but commanded Israel to destroy, saying, "Go, smite Amalek and utterly destroy all that they have, and spare them not; but slay both man and woman, infant and suckling, ox and sheep, camel and ass." (1 Sam. 15:3) This apparently reckless destruction of life seems irreconcilable with the character of love attributed to God, and with the teaching of Jesus, "Love your enemies," etc., until we come to recognize the systematic order of God's plan, the "due time" for the accomplishment of every feature of it, and the fact that every member of the human race has a place in it.

We can now see that those Amalekites, Sodomites and others were set forth as examples of God's just indignation, and of his determination to destroy finally and utterly evildoers: examples which will be of service not only to others, but also to themselves, when their day of judgment or trial comes. Those people might just as well die in that way as from disease and plague. It mattered little to them, as they were merely learning to know evil, that when on trial, in due time, they might learn righteousness, and be able to discriminate and choose the good and have life.

But let us examine the prophecy further. After comparing Israel with Sodom and Samaria, and pronouncing Israel the most blameworthy (Ezek. 16:48-54), the Lord says, "When I shall bring again their captivity, the captivity of Sodom and her daughters, and the captivity of Samaria and her daughters, then will I bring again the captivity of thy captives in the midst of them." The captivity referred to can be no other than their captivity in death; for those mentioned were then dead. In death all are captives; and Christ comes to open the doors of the grave, and to set at liberty the captives. (Isa. 61:1; Zech. 9:11) In verse 55 this is called a "return to their former estate"—a restitution.

Some, who are willing enough to accept of God's mercy through Christ in the forgiveness of their own trespasses and weaknesses under greater light and knowledge, cannot conceive of the same favor being applicable under the New Covenant to others; though they seem to admit the Apostle's statement that Jesus Christ, by the favor of God, tasted death for every man. Some of these suggest that the Lord must, in this prophecy, be speaking ironically to the Jews, implying that he would just as willingly bring back the Sodomites as them, but had no intention of restoring either. But let us see how the succeeding verses agree with this idea. The Lord says, "Nevertheless, I *will* remember my covenant with thee in the days of thy youth, and *I will* establish unto thee an everlasting covenant. *Then, thou shalt remember* thy ways and be ashamed, when thou shalt receive thy sisters. . . . And I *will* establish my covenant with thee, and thou shalt know that I am the Lord; that thou mayest remember and be confounded, and never open thy mouth any more because of thy shame, when I am pacified toward thee for all that thou hast done, SAITH THE LORD GOD." When a promise is thus signed by the Great Jehovah, all who have set to their seal that God is true may rejoice in its certainty with confidence; especially those who realize that these New Covenant blessings have been confirmed of God in Christ, whose precious blood is to seal the covenant.

To this Paul adds his testimony, saying, "And so all Israel [living and dead] shall be saved [recovered from blindness], as it is written, 'There shall come out of Zion the Deliverer, and shall turn away ungodliness from Jacob. For this is my covenant unto them when I shall take away their sins.'. . . They are beloved for the fathers' sakes; because the gracious gifts and callings of God are not things to be repented of." Rom. 11:26-29

We need not wonder that Jews, Sodomites, Samaritans, and all mankind, will be ashamed and confounded when in his own "due time" God shows forth the riches of his favor. Yea, many of those who are now God's children will be confounded and amazed when they see how *God so loved* THE WORLD, and how much his thoughts and plans were above their own.

Christian people generally believe that God's blessings are all and only for the selected Church, but now we begin to see that God's plan is wider than we had supposed, and that though he has given the Church "exceeding great and precious promises," he has also made bountiful provision for the world which he so loved as to redeem. The Jews made a very similar mistake in supposing that all the promises of God were to and for them alone; but when the "due time" came and the Gentiles were favored, the remnant of Israel, whose hearts were large enough to rejoice in this wider evidence of God's grace, shared that increased favor, while the rest were blinded by prejudice and human tradition. Let those of the Church who now see the dawning light of the Millennial age, with its gracious advantages for all the world, take heed lest they be found in opposition to the advancing light, and so for a time be blinded to its glory and blessings.

How different is this glorious plan of God for the selection of a few now, in order to the blessing of the many hereafter, from the distortions of these truths, as represented by the two opposing views—Calvinism and Arminianism. The former both denies the Bible doctrine of Free Grace and miserably distorts the glorious doctrine of Election; the latter denies the doctrine of Election and fails to comprehend the blessed fulness of God's Free Grace.

Calvinism says: God is all-wise; he knew the end from the beginning; and as all his purposes shall be accomplished, he never could have intended to save any but a few, the Church. These he elected and foreordained to be eternally saved; all others were equally foreordained and elected to go to eternal torment; for "Known unto God are all his works from the beginning of the world."

This view has its good features. It recognizes God's omniscience. This would be our ideal of a *great* God, were it not that two essential qualities of greatness are lacking, namely, love and justice, neither of which is exemplified in bringing into the world one hundred and forty-two billions of creatures doomed to eternal torture before they were born, and mocked with protestations of his love. Since God is love, and justice is the foundation of his throne, such cannot be his character.

Arminianism says: Yes, God is love; and in bringing humanity into the world he meant them no harm—only good. But Satan succeeded in tempting the first pair, and thus sin entered into the world, and death by sin. And ever since, God has been doing all he can to deliver man from his enemy, even to the giving of his Son. And though now, six thousand years after, the gospel has reached only a very small proportion of mankind, yet we do hope and trust that within six thousand years more, through the energy and liberality of the church, God will so far have remedied the evil introduced by Satan that all then living may at least know of his love, and have an opportunity to believe and be saved.

While this view presents God as a being full of loving and benevolent designs for his creatures, it implies that he lacks ability and foreknowledge adequate to the accomplishment of his benevolent designs: that he is deficient in wisdom and power. From this view it would appear that while God was engaged in arranging and devising for the good of his newly-created children, Satan slipped in and by one master-stroke upset all God's plans to such an extent that, even by exhausting all his power, God must spend twelve thousand years to reinstate righteousness, even to such a degree that the remainder of the race who still live will have an opportunity to choose good as readily as evil. But the one hundred and forty-two billions of the past six thousand years, and as many more of the next, are, according to this view, lost to all eternity, in spite of God's love for them, because Satan interfered with his plans. Thus Satan would get thousands into eternal torment to one that God saves to glory.

This view must exalt men's ideas of the wisdom and power of Satan, and lower their estimation of these attributes in God, of whom the Psalmist to the contrary declares that, "He spake and it was done; he commanded and it stood fast." But no: God was not surprised nor overtaken by the adversary; neither has Satan in any measure thwarted his plans. God is, and always has been, perfect master of the situation, and in the end it will be seen that all has been working together to the accomplishment of his purposes.

While the doctrines of election and free grace, as taught by Calvinism and Arminianism, could never be harmonized with each other, with reason, or with the Bible, yet these two glorious Bible doctrines are perfectly harmonious and beautiful, seen from the standpoint of the plan of the ages.

Seeing, then, that so many of the great and glorious features of God's plan for human salvation from sin and death lie in the future, and that the second advent of our Lord Jesus is the designed first step in the accomplishment of those long promised and long expected blessings, shall we not even more earnestly long for the time of his second advent than the less informed Jew looked and longed for his first advent? Seeing that the time of evil, injustice and death is to be brought to an end by the dominion of power which he will then exercise, and that righteousness, truth and peace are to be universal, who should not rejoice to see his day? And who that is now suffering with Christ, inspired by the precious promise that "if we suffer with him we shall also reign with him," will not lift up his head and rejoice at any evidence of the approach of the Master, knowing thereby that our deliverance and our glorification with him draw nigh? Surely all in sympathy with his mission of blessing and his spirit of love will hail every evidence of his coming as the approach of the "great joy which shall be to all people."

STUDY VII
THE PERMISSION OF EVIL AND ITS
RELATION TO GOD'S PLAN

WHY EVIL WAS PERMITTED—RIGHT AND WRONG AS PRINCIPLES—THE
MORAL SENSE—GOD PERMITTED EVIL, AND WILL OVERRULE IT FOR
GOOD—GOD NOT THE AUTHOR OF SIN—ADAM'S TRIAL NOT A FARCE—
HIS TEMPTATION SEVERE—HE SINNED WILFULLY—THE PENALTY OF SIN NOT
UNJUST, NOR TOO SEVERE—THE WISDOM, LOVE AND JUSTICE DISPLAYED IN
CONDEMNING ALL IN ADAM—GOD'S LAW UNIVERSAL.

EVIL is that which produces unhappiness; anything which
either directly or remotely causes suffering of any kind—
Webster. This subject, therefore, not only inquires regarding
human ailments, sorrows, pains, weaknesses and death, but
goes back of all these to consider their primary cause—sin—
and its remedy. Since sin is the cause of evil, its removal is the
only method of permanently curing the malady.

No difficulty, perhaps, more frequently presents itself to
the inquiring mind than the questions, Why did God permit
the present reign of evil? Why did he permit Satan to present
the temptation to our first parents, after having created them
perfect and upright? Or why did he allow the forbidden tree
to have a place among the good? Despite all attempts to turn
it aside, the question will obtrude itself—Could not God have
prevented all possibility of man's fall?

The difficulty undoubtedly arises from a failure to
comprehend the plan of God. God could have prevented the
entrance of sin, but the fact that he did not should be
sufficient proof to us that its present permission is designed
ultimately to work out some greater good. God's plans, seen

117

in their completeness, will prove the wisdom of the course pursued. Some inquire, Could not God, with whom all things are possible, have interfered in season to prevent the full accomplishment of Satan's design? Doubtless he could; but such interference would have prevented the accomplishment of his own purposes. His purpose was to make manifest the perfection, majesty and righteous authority of his law, and to prove both to men and to angels the evil consequences resulting from its violation. Besides, in their very nature, some things are impossible even with God, as the Scriptures state. It is "impossible for God to lie."(Heb. 6:18) "He cannot deny himself." (2 Tim. 2:13) He cannot do wrong, and therefore he could not choose any but the wisest and best plan for introducing his creatures into life, even though our short-sighted vision might for a time fail to discern the hidden springs of infinite wisdom.

The Scriptures declare that all things were created for the Lord's pleasure (Rev. 4:11)—without doubt, for the pleasure of dispensing his blessings, and of exercising the attributes of his glorious being. And though, in the working out of his benevolent designs, he permits evil and evildoers for a time to play an active part, yet it is not for evil's sake, nor because he is in league with sin; for he declares that he is "not a God that hath pleasure in wickedness." (Psa. 5:4) Though opposed to evil in every sense, God *permits* (i.e., does not hinder) it for a time, because his wisdom sees a way in which it may be made a lasting and valuable lesson to his creatures.

It is a self-evident truth that for every right principle there is a corresponding wrong principle; as, for instance, truth and falsity, love and hatred, justice and injustice. We distinguish these opposite principles as *right* and *wrong*, by their effects when put in action. That principle the result of which, when active, is beneficial and productive of ultimate order, harmony and happiness, we call a *right* principle; and the opposite, which is productive of discord, unhappiness and destruction, we call a *wrong* principle. The results of these principles in action we call *good* and *evil;* and the intelligent being, capable of discerning the right principle from the wrong, and voluntarily governed by the one or the other, we call virtuous or sinful.

This faculty of discerning between right and wrong principles is called *the moral sense,* or *conscience.* It is by this moral sense which God has given to man that we are able to judge of God and to recognize that he is good. It is to this moral sense that God always appeals to prove his righteousness or justice; and by the same moral sense Adam could discern sin, or unrighteousness, to be *evil,* even before he knew all its consequences. The lower orders of God's creatures are not endowed with this moral sense. A dog has some intelligence, but not to this degree, though he may learn that certain actions bring the approval and reward of his master, and certain others his disapproval. He might steal or take life, but would not be termed a sinner; or he might protect property and life, but would not be called virtuous—because he is ignorant of the moral quality of his actions.

God could have made mankind devoid of ability to discern between right and wrong, or able only to discern and to do right; but to have made him so would have been to make merely a living machine, and certainly not a mental image of his Creator. Or he might have made man perfect and a free agent, as he did, and have guarded him from Satan's temptation. In that case, man's experience being limited to good, he would have been continually liable to suggestions of evil from without, or to ambitions from within, which would have made the everlasting future uncertain, and an outbreak of disobedience and disorder might always have been a possibility; besides which, good would never have been so highly appreciated except by its contrast with evil.

God first made his creatures acquainted with good, surrounding them with it in Eden; and afterward, as a penalty for disobedience, he gave them a severe knowledge of evil. Expelled from Eden and deprived of fellowship with himself, God let them experience sickness, pain and death, that they might thus forever know evil and the inexpediency and exceeding sinfulness of sin.

By a comparison of results they came to an appreciation and proper estimate of both; "And the Lord said, Behold, the man is become as one of us, to know good and evil." (Gen. 3:22) In this their posterity share, except that they first obtain their knowledge of evil, and cannot fully realize what good is until they experience it in the Millennium, as a result of their redemption by him who will then be their Judge and King.

The moral sense, or judgment of right and wrong, and the liberty to use it, which Adam possessed, were important features of his likeness to God. The law of right and wrong was written in his natural constitution. It was a part of his nature, just as it is a part of the divine nature. But let us not forget that this image or likeness of God, this originally law-inscribed nature of man, has lost much of its clear outline through the erasing, degrading influence of sin; hence it is not now what it was in the first man. Ability to love implies ability to hate; hence we may reason that the Creator could not make man in his own likeness, with power to love and to do right, without the corresponding ability to hate and to do wrong. This liberty of choice, termed free moral agency, or free will, is a part of man's original endowment; and this, together with the full measure of his mental and moral faculties, constituted him an image of his Creator. Today, after six thousand years of degradation, so much of the original likeness has been erased by sin that we are not free, being bound, to a greater or less extent, by sin and its entailments, so that sin is now more easy and therefore more agreeable to the fallen race than is righteousness.

That God could have given Adam such a vivid impression of the many evil results of sin as would have deterred him from it, we need not question, but we believe that God foresaw that an actual experience of the evil would be the surest and most lasting lesson to serve man eternally; and for that reason God did not prevent but permitted man to take his choice, and to feel the consequences of evil. Had opportunity to sin never been permitted, man could not have resisted it, consequently there would have been neither virtue nor merit in his right-doing. God seeketh such to worship him as worship in spirit and in truth. He desires intelligent and willing obedience, rather than ignorant, mechanical service. He already had in operation inanimate mechanical agencies accomplishing his will, but his design was to make a nobler thing, an intelligent creature in his own likeness, a lord for earth, whose loyalty and righteousness would be based upon an appreciation of right and wrong, of good and evil.

The principles of right and wrong, as *principles,* have always existed, and must always exist; and all perfect, intelligent creatures in God's likeness must be free to choose either, though the right principle *only* will forever continue to be active. The Scriptures inform us that when the activity of the evil principle has been permitted long enough to accomplish God's purpose, it will forever cease to be active, and that all who continue to submit to its control shall forever cease to exist. (1 Cor. 15:25, 26; Heb. 2:14) Right-doing and right-doers, only, shall continue forever.

But the question recurs in another form: Could not man have been made acquainted with evil in some other way than by experience? There are four ways of knowing things, namely, by intuition, by observation, by experience, and by information received through sources accepted as positively truthful. An intuitive knowledge would be a direct apprehension, without the process of reasoning, or the necessity for proof. Such knowledge belongs only to the divine Jehovah, the eternal fountain of all wisdom and truth, who, of necessity and in the very nature of things, is superior to all his creatures. Therefore, man's knowledge of good and evil could not be intuitive. Man's knowledge might have come by observation, but in that event there must needs have been some exhibition of evil and its results for man to observe. This would imply the permission of evil somewhere, among some beings, and why not as well among men, and upon the earth, as among others elsewhere?

Why should not man be the illustration, and get his knowledge by practical experience? It is so: man is gaining a practical experience, and is furnishing an illustration to others as well, being "made a spectacle to angels."

Adam already had a knowledge of evil by information, but that was insufficient to restrain him from trying the experiment. Adam and Eve knew God as their Creator, and hence as the one who had the right to control and direct them; and God had said of the forbidden tree, "In the day thou eatest thereof, dying thou shalt die." They had, therefore, a theoretical knowledge of evil, though they had never observed or experienced its effects. Consequently, they did not appreciate their Creator's loving authority and his beneficent law, nor the dangers from which he thereby proposed to protect them. They therefore yielded to the temptation which God wisely permitted, the ultimate utility of which his wisdom had traced.

Few appreciate the severity of the temptation under

which our first parents fell, nor yet the justice of God in attaching so severe a penalty to what seems to many so slight an offense; but a little reflection will make all plain. The Scriptures tell the simple story of how the woman, the weaker one, was deceived, and thus became a transgressor. Her experience and acquaintance with God were even more limited than Adam's, for he was created first, and God had directly communicated to him before her creation the knowledge of the penalty of sin, while Eve probably received her information from Adam. When she had partaken of the fruit, she, having put confidence in Satan's deceptive misrepresentation, evidently did not realize the extent of the transgression, though probably she had misgivings, and slight apprehensions that all was not well. But, although deceived, Paul says she was a transgressor—though not so culpable as if she had transgressed against greater light.

Adam, we are told, unlike Eve, was not deceived (1 Tim. 2:14), hence he must have transgressed with a fuller realization of the sin, and with the penalty in view, knowing certainly that he must die. We can readily see what was the temptation which impelled him thus recklessly to incur the pronounced penalty. Bearing in mind that they were perfect beings, in the mental and moral likeness of their Maker, the godlike element of love was displayed with marked prominence by the perfect man toward his beloved companion, the perfect woman. Realizing the sin and fearing Eve's death, and thus his loss (and that without hope of recovery, for no such hope had been given), Adam, in despair, recklessly concluded not to live without her. Deeming his own life unhappy and worthless without her companionship, he wilfully shared her act of disobedience in order to share the death-penalty which he probably supposed rested on her. Both were "in the transgression," as the Apostle shows. (Rom. 5:14; 1 Tim. 2:14) But Adam and Eve were one and not "twain"; hence Eve shared the sentence which her conduct helped to bring upon Adam. Rom. 5:12, 17-19

God not only foresaw that, having given man freedom of choice, he would, through lack of *full* appreciation of sin and its results, accept it, but he also saw that, becoming acquainted with it, he would still choose it, because that acquaintance would so impair his moral nature that evil would gradually become more agreeable and more desirable to him than good. Still, God designed to *permit evil*, because, having the remedy provided for man's release from its consequences, he saw that the result would be to lead him, through experience, to a full appreciation of "the exceeding sinfulness of sin" and of the matchless brilliancy of virtue in contrast with it—thus teaching him the more to love and honor his Creator, who is the source and fountain of all goodness, and forever to shun that which brought so much woe and misery. So the final result will be greater love for God, and greater hatred of all that is opposed to his will, and consequently the firm establishment in everlasting righteousness of all such as shall profit by the lessons God is now teaching through the permission of sin and correlative evils. However, a wide distinction should be observed between the indisputable fact that God has permitted sin, and the serious error of some which charges God with being the author and instigator of sin. The latter view is both blasphemous and contradictory to the facts presented in the Scriptures. Those who fall into this error generally do so in an attempt to find another plan of salvation than that which God has provided through the *sacrifice* of Christ as our ransom-price. If they succeed in convincing themselves and others that God is responsible for all sin and wickedness and crime,* and that man as an innocent tool in his hands was forced into sin, then they have cleared the way for the theory that not a sacrifice for our sins, nor mercy in any form, was needed, but simply and only JUSTICE. Thus, too, they lay a foundation for another part of their false theory, viz., universalism, claiming that as God caused all the sin and wickedness and crime in all, he will also cause the deliverance of all mankind from sin and death. And reasoning that God willed and caused the sin, and that none could resist him, so they claim that when he shall will righteousness all will likewise be powerless to resist him. But in all such reasoning, man's noblest quality, liberty of will or *choice*, the most striking feature of his likeness to his Creator, is entirely set aside; and man is theoretically degraded to a

---

*Two texts of Scripture (Isa. 45:7 and Amos 3:6) are used to sustain this theory, but by a misinterpretation of the word *evil* in both texts. Sin is always an evil, but an evil is not always a sin. An earthquake, a conflagration, a flood or a pestilence would be a calamity, an *evil;* but none of these would be sins. The word *evil* in the texts cited signifies *calamities.* The same Hebrew word is translated *affliction* in Psa. 34:19; 107:39; Jer. 48:16; Zech. 1:15. It is translated *trouble* in Psa. 27:5; 41:1; 88:3; 107:26; Jer. 51:2; Lam. 1:21. It is translated *calamities, adversity,* and *distress* in 1 Sam. 10:19; Psa. 10:6; 94:13; 141:5; Eccl. 7:14; Neh. 2:17. And the same word is in very many places rendered *harm, mischief, sore, hurt, misery, grief* and *sorrow.*

In Isa. 45:7 and Amos 3:6 the Lord would remind Israel of his covenant made with them as a nation—that if they would obey his laws he would bless them and protect them from the calamities common to the world in general; but that if they would forsake him he would bring calamities (evils) upon them as chastisements. See Deut. 28:1-14,15-32; Lev. 26:14-16; Josh. 23:6-11,12-16.

When calamities came upon them, however, they were inclined to consider them as accidents and not as chastisements. Hence God sent them word through the prophets, reminding them of their covenant and telling them that their calamities were from him and by his will for their correction. It is absurd to use these texts to prove God the author of sin, for they do not at all refer to sin.

mere machine which acts only as it is acted upon. If this were the case, man, instead of being the lord of earth, would be inferior even to insects; for they undoubtedly have a will or power of choice. Even the little ant has been given a power of will which man, though by his greater power he may oppose and thwart, cannot destroy.

True, God has power to force man into either sin or righteousness, but his Word declares that he has no such purpose. He could not consistently force man into sin for the same reason that "he cannot deny himself." Such a course would be inconsistent with his righteous character, and therefore an impossibility. And he seeks the worship and love of only such as worship him in spirit and in truth. To this end he has given man a liberty of *will* like unto his own, and desires him to *choose* righteousness. *Permitting* man to choose for himself led to his fall from divine fellowship and favor and blessings, into death. By his experience in sin and death, man learns practically what God offered to teach him theoretically, without his experiencing sin and its results. God's foreknowledge of what man would do is not used against him, as an excuse for degrading him to a mere machine-being: on the contrary, it is used in man's favor; for God, foreseeing the course man would take if left free to choose for himself, did not hinder him from tasting sin and its bitter results experimentally, but he began at once to provide a means for his recovery from his first transgression by providing a Redeemer, a great Savior, able to save to the uttermost all who would *return unto God* through him. To this end—that man might have a free *will* and yet be enabled to profit by his first failure in its misuse, in disobedience to the Lord's will—God has provided not only a *ransom* for all, but also that a knowledge of the opportunity thus offered of reconciliation with himself shall be testified to all in due time. 1 Tim. 2:3-6

The severity of the penalty was not a display of hatred and malice on God's part, but the necessary and inevitable, final result of evil, which God thus allowed man to see and feel. God can sustain life as long as he sees fit, even against the destructive power of actual evil; but it would be as impossible for God to sustain such a life everlastingly, as it is for God to lie. That is, it is *morally impossible.* Such a life could only become more and more a source of unhappiness to itself and others; therefore, God is too good to sustain an existence so useless and injurious to itself and others, and, his sustaining power being withdrawn, destruction, the natural result of evil, would ensue. Life is a favor, a gift of God, and it will be continued everlastingly only to the obedient.

No injustice has been done to Adam's posterity in not affording them each an individual trial. Jehovah was in no sense bound to bring us into existence; and, having brought us into being, no law of equity or justice binds him to perpetuate our being everlastingly, nor even to grant us a trial under promise of everlasting life if obedient. Mark this point well. The present life, which from the cradle to the tomb is but a process of dying, is, notwithstanding all its evils and disappointments, a boon, a favor, even if there were no hereafter. The large majority so esteem it, the exceptions (suicides) being comparatively few; and these our courts of justice have repeatedly decided to be mentally unbalanced, as otherwise they would not thus cut themselves off from present blessings. Besides, the conduct of the perfect man, Adam, shows us what the conduct of his children would have been under similar circumstances.

Many have imbibed the erroneous idea that God placed our race on trial for life with the alternative of *eternal torture,* whereas nothing of the kind is even hinted at in the penalty. The favor or blessing of God to his obedient children is life—continuous life—free from pain, sickness and every other element of decay and death. Adam was given this blessing in the full measure, but was warned that he would be deprived of this "gift" if he failed to render obedience to God—"In the day that thou eatest thereof, dying, thou shalt die." He knew nothing of a *life* in torment, as the penalty of sin. Life everlasting is nowhere promised to any but the obedient. Life is God's gift, and death, the opposite of life, is the penalty he prescribes.

Eternal torture is nowhere suggested in the Old Testament Scriptures, and only a few statements in the New Testament can be so misconstrued as to appear to teach it; and these are found either among the symbolisms of Revelation, or among the parables and dark sayings of our Lord, which were *not understood* by the people who heard them (Luke 8:10), and which seem to be but little better comprehended today. "The wages of sin is death." (Rom. 6:23) "The soul that sinneth, it shall die." Ezek. 18:4

Many have supposed God unjust in allowing Adam's condemnation to be shared by his posterity, instead of granting each one a trial and chance for everlasting life similar to that which Adam enjoyed. But what will such say if it now be shown that the world's opportunity and trial for life will be much more favorable than was Adam's; and that, too, *because* God adopted this plan of permitting Adam's race to share his penalty in a natural way? We believe this to be the case, and will endeavor to make it plain.

God assures us that as condemnation *passed upon* all *in* Adam, so he has arranged for a new head, father or life-giver for the race, into whom all may be transferred by faith and obedience and that as all *in* Adam shared the curse of death, so all *in* Christ will share the blessing of restitution; the Church being an exception. (Rom. 5:12, 18, 19) Thus seen, the death of Jesus, the undefiled, the sinless one, was a complete settlement toward God of the sin of Adam. As one man had sinned, and all in him had shared his curse, his penalty, so Jesus, having paid the penalty of that one sinner, bought not only Adam, but all his posterity—all men—who by heredity shared his weaknesses and sins and the penalty of these—death. Our Lord, "the *man* Christ Jesus," himself unblemished, approved, and with a perfect seed or race in him, unborn, likewise untainted with sin, gave his *all* of human life and title as the full *ransom-price* for Adam and the race or seed in him when sentenced.

After fully purchasing the lives of Adam and his race, Christ offers to adopt as his seed, his children, all of Adam's race who will accept the terms of his New Covenant and thus by faith and obedience come into the family of God and receive everlasting life. Thus the Redeemer will "see *his seed* [as many of Adam's seed as will accept *adoption*, upon his conditions] and prolong his days [resurrection to a higher than human plane, being granted him by the Father as a reward for his obedience]," and all in the most unlikely way; by the sacrifice of life and posterity. And thus it is written: "As all in Adam die, *even so* all in Christ shall be made alive." *Corrected translation,* 1 Cor. 15:22

The injury we received through Adam's fall (we suffered no injustice) is, by God's favor, to be more than offset with favor through Christ; and all will sooner or later (in God's "due time") have a full opportunity to be restored to the same standing that Adam enjoyed before he sinned. Those who do not receive a full knowledge and, by faith, an enjoyment of this favor of God in the present time (and such are the great majority, including children and heathen) will assuredly have these privileges in the next age, or "world to come," the dispensation or age to follow the present. To this end, "all that are in their graves . . . shall come forth." As each one (whether in this age or the next) becomes fully aware of the ransom-price given by our Lord Jesus, and of his subsequent privileges, he is considered as on trial, as Adam was; and obedience brings lasting life, and disobedience lasting death—the "second death." Perfect obedience, however, without perfect ability to render it, is not required of any. Under the Covenant of Grace, members of the Church during the Gospel age, have had the righteousness of Christ imputed to them by faith, to make up their unavoidable deficiencies through the weakness of the flesh. Divine Grace will also operate toward "whosoever will" of the world during the Millennial age. Not until physical perfection is reached (which will be the *privilege* of all before the close of the Millennial age) will absolute moral perfection be expected. That new trial, the result of the ransom and the New Covenant, will differ from the trial in Eden, in that in it the acts of each one will affect only his own future.

But would not this be giving some of the race a *second* chance to gain everlasting life? We answer—The *first* chance for everlasting life was lost for himself and all of his race, "yet in his loins," by father Adam's disobedience. Under that original trial "condemnation passed upon all men;" and God's plan was that through Christ's redemption-sacrifice Adam, and *all* who lost life in his failure, should, after having tasted of the exceeding sinfulness of sin and felt the weight of sin's penalty, be given the opportunity to turn unto God through faith in the Redeemer. If any one chooses to call this a "second chance," let him do so: it must certainly be Adam's second chance, and in a sense at least it is the same for all of the redeemed race, but it will be the first *individual* opportunity of his descendants, who, when born, were already under condemnation to death. Call it what we please, the facts are the same; viz., all were sentenced to death because of Adam's disobedience, and all will enjoy (in the Millennial age) a *full opportunity* to gain everlasting life under the favorable terms of the New Covenant.

This, as the angels declared, is "Good tidings of great joy which shall be unto all people." And, as the Apostle declared, this grace of God—that our Lord Jesus "gave himself a *ransom for all*"—must be "testified" to all "in due time." (Rom. 5:17-19; 1 Tim. 2:4-6) Men, not God, have limited to the Gospel age this chance or opportunity of attaining life. God, on the contrary, tells us that the Gospel age is merely for the selection of the Church, the royal priesthood, through whom, during a succeeding age, all others shall be brought to an accurate knowledge of the truth and granted full opportunity to secure everlasting life under the New Covenant.

But what advantage is there in the method pursued? Why not give all men an individual chance for life now, at once, without the long process of Adam's trial and condemnation, the share by his offspring in his condemnation, the redemption of all by Christ's sacrifice, and the new offer to all of everlasting life upon the New Covenant conditions? If evil must be permitted because of man's free moral agency, why is its extermination accomplished by such a peculiar and circuitous method? Why allow so much misery to intervene, and to come upon many who will ultimately receive the gift of life as obedient children of God?

Ah! that is the point on which interest in this subject centers. Had God ordered differently the propagation of our species, so that children would not partake of the results of parental sins—weaknesses, mental, moral and physical—and had the Creator so arranged that all should have a favorable Edenic condition for their testing, and that transgressors only should be condemned and "cut off," how many might we presume would, under all those favorable conditions, be found worthy, and how many unworthy of life?

If the one instance of Adam be taken as a criterion (and

he certainly was in every respect a sample of perfect manhood), the conclusion would be that none would have been found perfectly obedient and worthy; because none would possess that clear knowledge of and experience with God, which would develop in them full confidence in his laws, beyond their personal judgment. We are assured that it was Christ's knowledge of the Father that enabled him to trust and obey implicitly. (Isa. 53:11) But let us suppose that one-fourth would gain life; or even more, suppose that one-half were found worthy, and that the other half would suffer the wages of sin—death. Then what? Let us suppose the other half, the obedient, had neither experienced nor witnessed sin: might they not forever feel a curiosity toward things forbidden, only restrained through fear of God and of the penalty? Their service could not be so hearty as though they knew good and evil; and hence had a full appreciation of the benevolent designs of the Creator in making the laws which govern his own course as well as the course of his creatures.

Then, too, consider the half that would thus go into death as the result of their own wilful sin. They would be lastingly cut off from life, and their only hope would be that God would in love remember them as his creatures, the work of his hands, and provide another trial for them. But why do so? The only reason would be a hope that if they were re-awakened and tried again, some of them, by reason of their larger *experience,* might then choose obedience and live.

But even if such a plan were as good in its results as the one God has adopted, there would be serious objections to it.

How much more like the wisdom of God to confine sin to certain limits, as his plan does. How much better even our finite minds can discern it to be, to have but one perfect and impartial law, which declares the wages of wilful sin to be death—destruction—cutting off from life. God thus limits the evil which he permits, by providing that the Millennial reign of Christ shall accomplish the full extinction of evil and also of wilful evil-doers, and usher in an eternity of righteousness, based upon full knowledge and perfect free-will obedience by perfect beings.

But there are two other objections to the plan suggested, of trying each individual separately at first. One Redeemer was quite sufficient in the plan which God adopted, because only *one* had sinned, and only *one* had been condemned. (Others shared *his* condemnation.) But if the first trial had been an individual trial, and if one-half of the race had sinned and been individually condemned, it would have required the sacrifice of a redeemer for each condemned individual. One unforfeited life could redeem one forfeited life, but no more. The one perfect man, "the man Christ Jesus," who redeems the fallen Adam (and our losses through him), could not have been "a ransom [a corresponding price] for ALL" under any other circumstances than those of the plan which God chose.

If we should suppose the total number of human beings since Adam to be one hundred billions, and that only one-half of these had sinned, it would require all of the fifty billions of obedient, perfect men to die in order to give a *ransom* [a corresponding price] for all the fifty billions of transgressors; and so by this plan also death would pass upon all. And such a plan would involve *no less* suffering than is at present experienced.

The other objection to such a plan is that it would seriously disarrange God's plans relative to the selection and exaltation to the divine nature of a "little flock," the body of Christ, a company of which Jesus is the Head and Lord. God could not justly *command* the fifty billions of obedient sons to give their rights, privileges and lives as ransoms for the sinners; for under his own law their obedience would have won the right to lasting life. Hence, if those perfect men were asked to become ransomers of the fallen ones, it would be God's plan, as with our Lord Jesus, to set some special reward before them, so that they, for the joy set before them, might endure the penalty of their brethren. And if the same reward should be given them that was given to our Lord Jesus, namely, to partake of a new nature, the divine, and to be highly exalted above angels and principalities and powers, and every name that is named—next to Jehovah (Eph. 1:20, 21), then there would be an immense number on the divine plane, which the wisdom of God evidently did not approve. Furthermore, these fifty billions, under such circumstances, would all be on an *equality*, and none among them chief or head, while the plan God *has adopted* calls for but one Redeemer, one highly exalted to the divine nature, and then a "little flock" of those whom he redeemed, and who "walk in his footsteps" of suffering and self-denial, to share his name, his honor, his glory and his nature, even as the wife shares with the husband.

Those who can appreciate this feature of God's plan, which, by condemning all in *one* representative, opened the way for the ransom and restitution of all by *one* Redeemer, will find in it the solution of many perplexities. They will see that the condemnation of *all* in one was the reverse of an injury: it was a great favor to *all* when taken in connection with God's plan for providing justification for *all* through another one's sacrifice. Evil will be forever extinguished when God's purpose in permitting it shall have been accomplished, and when the benefits of the ransom are made co-extensive with the penalty of sin. It is impossible, however, to appreciate rightly this feature of the plan of God without a full recognition of the sinfulness of sin, the nature of its penalty—death, the importance and value of the *ransom* which our Lord Jesus gave, and the positive and complete restoration of the individual to favorable conditions, conditions under which he will have full and ample trial, before being adjudged worthy of the reward (lasting life), or of the penalty (lasting death).

In view of the great plan of redemption, and the consequent "restitution of all things," through Christ, we can see that blessings result through the permission of evil which, probably, could not otherwise have been so fully realized.

Not only are men benefited to all eternity by the experience gained, and angels by their observation of man's experiences, but all are further advantaged by a fuller acquaintance with God's character as manifested in his plan. When his plan is fully accomplished, all will be able to read clearly his wisdom, justice, love and power. They will see the justice which could not violate the divine decree, nor save the justly condemned race without a full cancellation of their penalty by a willing redeemer. They will see the love which provided this noble sacrifice and which highly exalted the Redeemer to God's own right hand, giving him power and authority thereby to restore to life those whom he had purchased with his precious blood. They will also see the power and wisdom which were able to work out a glorious destiny for his creatures, and so to overrule every opposing influence as to make them either the willing or the unwilling agents for the advancement and final accomplishment of his grand designs. Had evil not been permitted and thus overruled by divine providence, we cannot see how these results could have been attained. The permission of evil for a time among men thus displays a far-seeing wisdom, which grasped all the attendant circumstances, devised the remedy, and marked the final outcome through his power and grace.

During the Gospel dispensation sin and its attendant

evils have been further made use of for the discipline and preparation of the Church. Had sin not been permitted, the sacrifice of our Lord Jesus and of his Church, the reward of which is the divine nature, would have been impossible.

It seems clear that substantially the same law of God which is now over mankind, obedience to which has the reward of life, and disobedience the penalty of death, must ultimately govern all of God's intelligent creatures; and that law, as our Lord defined it, is briefly comprehended in the one word, *Love*. "Thou shalt love the Lord thy God with all thy heart, and with all thy soul, and with all thy strength, and with all thy mind; and thy neighbor as thyself." (Luke 10:27) Ultimately, when the purposes of God shall have been accomplished, the glory of the divine character will be manifest to all intelligent creatures, and the temporary permission of evil will be seen by all to have been a wise feature in the divine policy. Now, this can be seen only by the eye of faith, looking onward through God's Word at the things spoken by the mouth of all the holy prophets since the world began—the restitution of all things.

The Day is at Hand

"Poor, fainting pilgrim, still hold on thy way—the dawn is near!
True, thou art weary now; but yon bright ray becomes more clear.
    Bear up a little longer; wait for rest;
    Yield not to slumber, though with toil oppressed.

"The night of life is mournful, but look on—the dawn is near!
Soon will earth's shadowed scenes and forms be gone; yield not to fear!
    The mountain's summit will, ere long, be gained,
    And the bright world of joy and peace attained.

" 'Joyful through hope' thy motto still must be—the dawn is near!
What glories will that dawn unfold to thee! be of good cheer!
    Gird up thy loins; bind sandals on thy feet:
    The way is dark and long; the end is sweet."

STUDY VIII
THE DAY OF JUDGMENT

"GOD hath appointed a day in the which he will judge the
world in righteousness by that man whom he hath
ordained"—"Jesus Christ, the righteous." "For the Father
judgeth no man, but hath committed all judgment unto the
Son." Acts 17:31; 1 John 2:1; John 5:22

A very vague and indefinite idea prevails in regard to the
day of judgment. The view generally entertained is that
Christ will come to earth, seated upon a great white throne,
and that he will summon saint and sinner in rank and file
before him to be judged, amidst great convulsions of
nature—earthquakes, opening graves, rending rocks and
falling mountains; that the trembling sinners will be brought
from the depths of everlasting woe to hear their sins
rehearsed, only to be again returned to an eternal and
merciless doom; and that the saints will be brought from
heaven to witness the misery and despair of the condemned,
to hear again the decision in their own cases, and to return.
According to the prevailing theory, all receive their sentence
and reward at death; and this, which by way of distinction is
commonly called the general judgment, is merely a repetition

of that first judgment, but for no conceivable purpose, since they claim that a decision which is final and unalterable is rendered at death.

The entire time supposed to be assigned to this stupendous work of judging billions is a twenty-four hour day. A discourse recently delivered to a Brooklyn congregation voiced the general view on this subject. It affected to give a detailed account of the work of the Day of Judgment, representing it as completed within the limits of a single literal day.

This is a very crude conception, and is entirely out of harmony with the inspired Word. It is drawn from a too literal interpretation of our Lord's parable of the sheep and the goats. (Matt. 25:31-46) It illustrates the absurdity of attempting to force a literal interpretation upon figurative language. A parable is never an exact statement, but merely an illustration of a truth by something which is in many respects like it. If this parable were a literal statement of the manner in which the judgment will be conducted, it would apply to literal sheep and goats, just as it reads, and not to mankind at all. Let us now look at a more Scriptural as well as a more reasonable view of the work and the result of the great Judgment Day which God hath appointed, with which reasonable and Scriptural conclusions all parables and figures should and do agree.

The term *judgment* signifies more than simply the rendering of a verdict. It includes the idea of a trial, as well as a decision based upon that trial. And this is true not only of the English word judgment, but also of the Greek word which it translates.

The term *day*, both in the Scriptures and in common usage, though most frequently used to represent a period of twelve or twenty-four hours, really signifies any definite or special period of time. Thus, for instance, we speak of

Noah's day, Luther's day, Washington's day; and thus in the Bible the entire time of creation is called a day, where we read of "the day that Jehovah God made the earth and the heavens" (Gen. 2:4)—a long, definite period. Then we read of "the day of temptation in the wilderness"—forty years (Heb. 3:8, 9); "the day of salvation" (2 Cor. 6:2); also the "day of vengeance," "day of wrath" and "day of trouble"— terms applied to a period of forty years in the close of the Jewish age, and to a similar period of trouble in the end of the Gospel age. Then again we read of the "day of Christ," the "day of judgment," and "his day"—terms applicable to the Millennial age, in which Messiah will reign over, rule and judge the world in righteousness, granting trial as well as rendering sentence. And of that period it is written: He shall judge the world in righteousness, and in his day shall show who is that blessed and only potentate, the King of kings and Lord of lords. (Acts 17:31; 1 Tim. 6:15) Why any should suppose this day of judgment to be of but twelve or twenty-four hours, while recognizing the wider meaning of the word *day* in other similar cases, is beyond comprehension, except upon the supposition that they have been influenced by tradition, without proper evidence or investigation.

Those who will carefully consult a complete concordance of the Bible with reference to the Day of Judgment, and note the kind and amount of work to be accomplished within that period, will soon see the absurdity of the common view, and the necessity for giving to the term *day* its wider significance.

While the Scriptures speak of a great judgment or trial day yet future, and show that the masses of mankind are to have their complete trial and final sentence in that day, they also teach that there have been other judgment days, during which certain elect *classes* have been on trial.

The first great judgment [trial and sentence] was at the beginning, in Eden, when the whole human race, as represented in its head, Adam, stood on trial before God. The result of that trial was the verdict—Guilty, disobedient, unworthy of life; and the penalty inflicted was death—"Dying thou shalt die." (Gen. 2:17, margin) And so "In Adam all die." That trial time in Eden was the world's first judgment day, and the decision of the Judge (Jehovah) has ever since been enforced.

"The wrath of God *is revealed* from heaven against all unrighteousness." It may be seen in every funeral procession. Every tomb is a witness to it. It is felt in every ache and pain we experience—all of which are results of the first trial and sentence—the righteous sentence of God, that we are unworthy of life and the blessings originally provided for man when obedient and in God's likeness. But mankind are to be recovered from the sentence of that first trial by the one sacrifice for all, which the great Redeemer provides. All are to be rescued from the grave and from the sentence of death—destruction—which in view of this redemption is no longer to be considered death in the full, everlasting sense of the word, but rather a temporary sleep; because in the Millennial morning all will be awakened by the Life-giver who redeemed all. Only the Church of believers in Christ are yet in any sense released or "escaped" from this original sentence and penalty; and their escape is not yet *actual*, but only so reckoned by faith. "We are saved *by hope*" only. Our actual release from this death penalty (incurred in Adam and escaped from by getting into Christ) will not be fully experienced until the resurrection morning, when we shall be satisfied to awake in our Redeemer's likeness. But the fact that we who have come to a knowledge of God's gracious plan in Christ "have *escaped the corruption* that is [still] on the world," so far from proving that others will have no future hope of escape, proves rather the contrary of this; for we are first-fruits unto God of his creatures. Our escape from death in Adam to life in Christ is but a foretaste of the deliverance of whosoever wills to be delivered from the bondage of corruption [death] to the liberty of life proper to all whom God shall recognize as sons. All who will may be delivered from death to life, regardless of the distinctions of nature God has provided for his sons on different planes of being. The Gospel age is the trial-day for life or death to those called to the divine nature.

But God has appointed a day, in which he will judge the world. How can this be? Has God changed his mind? Has he concluded that his decision in the trial of the first man and the general sentence were unjust, too severe, that he now concludes to judge the world individually? No; were such the case, we should have no better guarantee of a just decision in the future trial than in the past. It is not that God considers his decision in the first judgment unjust, but that he has provided a *redemption* from the penalty of the first judgment, in order that he may grant another judgment (trial) under more favorable conditions to the entire race—all having then had experience with sin and its results. God has not changed one iota from his original purpose, which he formed before the world began. He distinctly informs us that he changes not, and that he will by no means clear the guilty. He will exact the full penalty which he justly pronounced. And that full penalty has been provided by the Redeemer or substitute whom God himself provided—Jesus Christ, who, "by the grace [favor] of God, tasted death for every man." Our Lord having provided a ransom for Adam's race, with his own life, can justly give a new offer of life to them all. This offer to the Church is under

the Covenant of sacrifice (Psa. 50:5; Rom. 12:1): to the world
it will be under the New Covenant. Rom. 14:9; Heb. 10:16;
Jer. 31:31

We are further informed that when God gives the
world this individual trial, it will be under Christ as Judge,
whom Jehovah will thus honor because of his obedience
even unto death for our redemption. God has highly
exalted him, even to the divine nature, that he may be a
Prince and a Savior (Acts 5:31), that he may be able to
recover from death and grant judgment to all whom he
purchased with his own precious blood. God has
committed all judgment unto the Son, and has given him
all power in heaven and in earth. John 5:22

It is, then, the highly exalted, glorified Christ, who so loved
the world as to give his life as its ransom-price, who is to be
the Judge of the world in its promised future trial. And it is
Jehovah himself who has appointed him to that office, for that
very purpose. Since such are the plain declarations of the
Scriptures, there is nothing to dread, but on the contrary there
is great cause for rejoicing on the part of all, in looking
forward to the Judgment Day. The character of the Judge is a
sufficient guarantee that the judgment will be just and
merciful, and with due consideration for the infirmities of all,
until the willing and obedient are brought back to the original
perfection lost in Eden.

A judge, in ancient times, was one who executed justice
and relieved the oppressed. Note, for instance, how, when
under oppression by their enemies because of transgression
against the Lord, Israel was time and again released and
blessed by the raising up of judges. Thus we read, "When
the children of Israel cried unto Jehovah, Jehovah raised
up a *deliverer*, . . . Othniel. And the spirit of Jehovah came
upon him, and he *judged* Israel, and went out to war, and
prevailed, and the land had rest forty years." (Judges 3:9-11)

So, though the world has long been under the power and oppression of the adversary, Satan, yet shortly he who pays for the sins of all with his own precious blood will take his great power and reign. He will *deliver* and *judge* those whom he so loved as to redeem.

With this conclusion *all* the prophetic declarations agree. It is written: "With righteousness shall he judge the world, and the people with equity." Psa. 98:9

This coming judgment will be on exactly the same principles as the first. The same law of obedience will be presented, with the same reward of life, and the same penalty of death. And as the first trial had a beginning, progressed, and culminated with a sentence, so also will the second; and the sentence will be life to the righteous, and death to the unrighteous. The second trial will be more favorable than the first, because of the experience gained under the results of the first trial. Unlike the first trial, the second trial will be one in which every man will stand the test for himself alone, and not for another. None will then die because of Adam's sin, or because of inherited imperfections. It shall no more be said, "The fathers have eaten a sour grape and the children's teeth are set on edge; but *he that eateth the sour grape,* his teeth shall be set on edge." "The soul that sinneth, it shall die." (Ezek. 18:4; Jer. 31:29, 30) And it will be true of the world then, as it is of the Church now, that a man will not be judged according to that which he hath not, but according to that which he hath. (2 Cor. 8:12) Under the reign of Christ, mankind will be gradually educated, trained and disciplined until they reach perfection. And when they have reached perfection, perfect harmony with God will be required, and any who then fall short of perfect obedience will be cut off, being judged unworthy of life. The sin which brought death to the race through Adam was simply one disobedient act; but by that act he fell from his perfection. God had a right to demand perfect obedience of him, since he was created perfect; and he will demand the same of all men when the great work of restoring them is complete. None will be permitted to have everlasting life who then in the slightest degree fall short of perfection. To fall short of perfection, then, will be to sin wilfully against full light and perfect ability.

Any who sin wilfully, against full light and ability, will perish in the second death. And should any one, during that age of trial, under its full blaze of light, spurn the offered favors, and make no progress toward perfection for a hundred years, he will be reckoned unworthy of life and will be "cut off," though at a hundred years he would be in the period of comparative childhood. Thus it is written of that day: "As a lad shall one die a hundred years old; and as a sinner shall be accursed he who dieth at a hundred years old." (Isa. 65:20— *Leeser*) Thus all must have at least one hundred years of trial; and, if not so obstinate as to refuse to make progress, their trial will continue throughout the entire day of Christ, reaching a culmination only at its close.

The conclusion of the world's coming judgment is clearly shown in the parable of the sheep and the goats (Matt. 25:31-46), in Rev. 20:15; 21:8 and in 1 Cor. 15:25. These and other scriptures show that at its close the two classes will have been completely separated—the obedient and the disobedient; those in harmony with the letter and the spirit of God's law, and those out of harmony with it. They enter into everlasting life, and the others are remanded to death, extinction ("second death"), the same sentence as in the first judgment, from which they had been reckonedly released by Christ who secured the right to release them by the giving of their ransom—by his death. This will be their second death. No ransom will be given for them, and there will be no release or resurrection for them, their sin being a wilful, individual sin against full light and opportunity, under a most favorable, individual trial.

We do not wish to be understood as ignoring the present responsibility of the world, which every man has, according to the measure of light enjoyed, whether it be much or little, whether it be the light of nature or of revelation. "The eyes of the Lord are in every place, beholding the evil and the good," and "God shall bring every work into judgment, with every secret thing, whether it be good or whether it be evil." (Prov. 15:3; Eccl. 12:14) The good and the evil deeds of the present time will receive a *just* recompense of reward either now or hereafter. "Some men's sins are open beforehand, going before to judgment, and some they follow after." (1 Tim. 5:24) No others than the Lord's favored "little flock" have as yet sufficient light to incur the final penalty, the second death. We here merely broach the subject of the world's present accountability, leaving the particulars for subsequent consideration.

A period of about six thousand years intervenes between the world's first and second judgment days, and during this long period God has been selecting two special classes from among men, and specially trying, disciplining and training them to be his honored instruments during the period or day of the world's judgment.

These two classes are respectively designated by Paul (Heb. 3:5, 6) as the house of sons and the house of servants, the former being composed of those overcomers tried and found faithful during the Christian dispensation, and the latter being composed of the faithful overcomers who preceded the Christian dispensation. These special selections in no sense interfere with the judgment or trial promised to the world of mankind in the age to follow this Gospel Dispensation. Those who successfully pass the trial for either of these special classes will not come into judgment with the world, but will enter upon their reward when the world is coming into judgment. They will be God's agents in the blessing of the world—in giving to men the instruction and training necessary for their final testing and judgment. "Do ye not know that the saints shall judge the world?" 1 Cor. 6:2

These specially selected classes, like the rest of mankind, were once under the Adamic condemnation, but became sharers by faith in the benefits of Christ's death. After being first justified by faith in God's promises, and having then fulfilled the subsequent conditions of their respective callings, they are accounted worthy of high exaltation to stations of honor and authority.

The trial or judgment of both these classes has been much more severe than the trial of the world will be in its judgment day; because these have had to withstand Satan, the prince of this world, with all his wiles and ensnarements, while in the world's judgment day Christ will be reigning, and Satan will be bound, that he may not deceive the nations. (Rev. 20:3) These have suffered persecution for righteousness' sake, while then men will be rewarded for righteousness, and punished only for unrighteousness. These have had great stumbling blocks and snares in the way, which will be removed when the world is placed on trial. But though the trial of these two special companies has been much more severe than the trial of the world will be, the rewards are correspondingly greater.

Under the sophistries of the great deceiver, Satan, both the world and the Church nominal have been robbed of the blessed assurances of the coming time of righteous judgment. They know that the Bible tells of a coming judgment day, but they regard it with only fear and dread; and because of this fear, there is to them no more unwelcome tidings than that the day of the Lord is at hand. They put it far away from them, and do not wish to hear it even mentioned.

They have no idea of the blessings in store for the world under that glorious reign of him whom God hath appointed to judge the world in righteousness. Among the greatest of the blinding influences which Satan has devised to keep men in ignorance of the truth regarding the judgment day have been the errors which have crept into the creeds and hymn books of the various religious sects. Many have come to esteem these errors as of paramount importance to the Word of God.

How differently did the prophets and apostles regard that promised day of judgment! Note the exultant prophetic utterance of David (1 Chron. 16:31-34). He says:

"Let the heavens be glad,
And let the earth rejoice;
And let men say among the nations, Jehovah reigneth.
Let the sea roar, and the fulness thereof;
Let the fields rejoice, and all that are therein.
Then shall the trees of the wood sing aloud
At the presence of Jehovah,
BECAUSE HE COMETH
TO JUDGE THE EARTH.
O give thanks unto Jehovah, for he is good;
For his mercy endureth forever."

To the same day the Apostle also points, assuring us that it will be a glorious and desirable day, and that for it the whole creation is groaning and travailing in pain together—waiting for the great Judge to deliver and to bless the world, as well as to exalt and glorify the Church. Rom. 8:21, 22

In John 5:28, 29 a precious promise for the world of a coming *judgment-trial* for life everlasting is, by a mistranslation, turned into a fearful imprecation. According to the Greek, they that have done evil—that have failed of divine approval—will come forth unto resurrection [raising up to perfection] by judgments, "stripes," disciplines. See the Revised Version.

Afterward

"God's ways are equal: storm or calm,
      Seasons of peril and of rest,
The hurting dart, the healing balm,
      Are all apportioned as is best.
In judgments oft misunderstood,
      In ways mysterious and obscure,
He brings from evil lasting good,
      And makes the final gladness sure.
While Justice takes its course with strength,
      Love bids our faith and hope increase:
He'll give the chastened world at length
      His afterward of peace.

"When the dread forces of the gale
      His sterner purposes perform,
And human skill can naught avail
      Against the fury of the storm,
Let loving hearts trust in him still,
      Through all the dark and devious way;
For who would thwart his blessed will,
      Which leads through night to joyous day?
Be still beneath his tender care;
      For he will make the tempest cease,
And bring from out the anguish here
      An afterward of peace.

"Look up, O Earth; no storm can last
      Beyond the limits God hath set.
When its appointed work is past,
      In joy thou shalt thy grief forget.
Where sorrow's plowshare hath swept through,
      Thy fairest flowers of life shall spring,
For God shall grant thee life anew,
      And all thy wastes shall laugh and sing.
Hope thou in him; his plan for thee
      Shall end in triumph and release.
Fear not, for thou shalt surely see
      His afterward of peace."

STUDY IX
RANSOM AND RESTITUTION

THE RESTITUTION GUARANTEED BY THE RANSOM—NOT EVERLASTING LIFE, BUT A TRIAL FOR IT, SECURED BY THE RANSOM—THE CONDITIONS AND ADVANTAGES OF THE TRIAL—CHRIST'S SACRIFICE NECESSARY—HOW THE RACE COULD BE AND WAS REDEEMED BY THE DEATH OF ONE—FAITH AND WORKS STILL NECESSARY—THE WAGES OF WILFUL SIN CERTAIN—WILL THERE BE ROOM ON THE EARTH FOR THE RESURRECTED MILLIONS?—RESTITUTION VERSUS EVOLUTION.

FROM the outline of God's revealed plan, as thus far sketched, it is evident that his design for mankind is a restitution or restoration to the perfection and glory lost in Eden. The strongest, and the conclusive, evidence on this subject is most clearly seen when the extent and nature of the ransom are fully appreciated. The restitution foretold by the apostles and prophets must follow the ransom as the just and logical sequence. According to God's arrangement in providing a ransom, all mankind, unless they wilfully resist the saving power of the Great Deliverer, must be delivered from the original penalty, "the bondage of corruption," death, else the ransom does not avail for all.

Paul's reasoning on the subject is most clear and emphatic. He says (Rom. 14:9), "For to this end Christ died and lived again, that he might be Lord [ruler, controller] of both the dead and the living." That is to say, the object of our Lord's death and resurrection was not merely to bless and rule over and restore the living of mankind, but to give him authority over, or full control of, the dead as well as the living, insuring the benefits of his ransom as much to the one as to the other.* He "gave himself a ransom [a corresponding price] for all," in order that he might bless all, and give to every man an individual trial for life. To claim that he gave "ransom for *all*," and yet to claim that only a mere handful of the ransomed ones will ever receive any benefit from it, is absurd; for it would imply either that God accepted the ransom-price and then unjustly refused to grant the release of the redeemed, or else that the Lord, after redeeming all, was either unable or unwilling to carry out the original benevolent design. The unchangeableness of the divine plans, no less than the perfection of the divine justice and love, repels and contradicts such a thought, and gives us assurance that the original and benevolent plan, of which the "ransom for all" was the basis, will be fully carried out in God's "due time," and will bring to faithful believers the blessing of release from the Adamic condemnation and an opportunity to return to the rights and liberties of sons of God, as enjoyed before sin and the curse.

Let the actual benefits and results of the ransom be clearly seen, and all objections to its being of universal application must vanish. The "ransom for all" given by "the man Christ Jesus" does not give or guarantee everlasting life or blessing to any man; but it does guarantee to every man *another opportunity or trial for life everlasting.* The first trial of man, which resulted in the loss of the blessings at first conferred, is really turned into a blessing of experience to the loyal-hearted, by reason of the *ransom* which God has provided. But the fact that men are ransomed from the first

---

*We may properly recognize an additional and a still broader meaning in the Apostle's words; namely, that the entire human family was included in the expression "the dead." From God's standpoint the entire race, under sentence of death, is treated as though already dead (Matt. 8:22); hence the expression "the living" would apply beyond the human family to some whose lives had not been forfeited—the angels.

penalty does not guarantee that they may not, when individually tried for everlasting life, fail to render the obedience without which none will be permitted to live everlastingly. Man, by reason of present experience with sin and its bitter penalty, will be fully forewarned; and when, as a result of the ransom, he is granted another, an individual trial, under the eye and control of him who so loved him as to give his life for him, and who would not that any should perish, but that all should turn to God and live, we may be sure that only the wilfully disobedient will receive the penalty of the second trial. That penalty will be the second death, from which there will be no ransom, no release, because there would be no object for another ransom or a further trial. All will have fully seen and tasted both good and evil; all will have witnessed and experienced the goodness and love of God; all will have had a full, fair, individual trial for life, under most favorable conditions. More could not be asked, and more will not be given. That trial will decide forever who would be righteous and holy under a thousand trials; and it will determine also who would be unjust, and unholy and filthy still, under a thousand trials.

It would be useless to grant another trial for life under exactly the same circumstances; but though the circumstances of the tried ones will be different, more favorable, the terms or conditions of their individual trial for life will be the same as in the Adamic trial. The law of God will remain the same—it changes not. It will still say, "The soul that sinneth, it shall die"; and the condition of man will be no more favorable, so far as surroundings are concerned, than the conditions and surroundings in Eden; but the great difference will be the increased *knowledge*. The *experience* with evil, contrasted with the experience with good, which will accrue to each during the trial of the coming age, will constitute the advantage by reason of which the results of the second trial will differ so widely from the results of the first, and on account of which divine Wisdom and Love provided the "ransom for all," and thus guaranteed to all the blessing of a new trial. No more favorable trial, no more favorable law, no more favorable conditions or circumstances, can in any way be conceived of as reasons for another ransom or a further trial for any beyond the Millennial age.

The ransom given does not excuse sin in any; it does not propose to *count* sinners as saints, and usher them thus into everlasting bliss. It merely releases the accepting sinner from the first condemnation and its results, both direct and indirect, and places him again on trial for life, in which trial his own wilful obedience or wilful disobedience will decide whether he may or may not have life everlasting.

Nor should it be assumed, as so many seem disposed to assume, that all those who live in a state of civilization, and see or possess a Bible, have thus a full opportunity or trial for life. It must be remembered that the fall has not injured all of Adam's children alike. Some have come into the world so weak and depraved as to be easily blinded by the god of this world, Satan, and led captive by besetting and surrounding sin; and all are more or less under this influence, so that, even when they would do good, evil is present and more powerful through surroundings, etc., and the good which they would do is almost impossible, while the evil which they would not do is almost unavoidable.

Small indeed is the number of those who in the present time truly and experimentally learn of the liberty wherewith Christ makes free those who accept of his ransom, and put themselves under his control for future guidance. Yet only these few, the Church, called out and tried beforehand for the special purpose of being co-workers with God in blessing the world—witnessing now, and ruling, blessing and judging the world in its age of trial—yet enjoy to any extent the benefits of the ransom, or are *now* on trial for life.

These few have *reckoned* to them (and they receive *by faith*) all the blessings of restitution which will be provided for the world during the coming age. These, though not perfect, not restored to Adam's condition actually, are treated in such a manner as to compensate for the difference. Through faith in Christ they are *reckoned* perfect, and hence are restored to perfection and to divine favor, as though no longer sinners. Their imperfections and unavoidable weaknesses, being offset by the ransom, are not imputed to them, but are covered by the Redeemer's perfection. Hence the Church's trial, because of her reckoned standing in Christ, is as fair as that which the world will have in its time of trial. The world will all be brought to a full knowledge of the truth, and each one, as he accepts of its provisions and conditions, will be treated no longer as a sinner, but as a son, for whom all the blessings of restitution are intended.

One difference between the experiences of the world under trial and the experiences of the Church during her trial will be that the obedient of the world will begin at once to receive the blessings of restitution by a gradual removal of their weaknesses—mental and physical; whereas the Gospel Church, consecrated to the Lord's service even unto death, goes down into death and gets her perfection instantaneously in the first resurrection. Another difference between the two trials is in the more favorable surroundings of the next age as compared with this, in that then society, government, etc., will be favorable to righteousness, rewarding faith and obedience, and punishing sin; whereas now, under the prince of this world, the Church's trial is under circumstances unfavorable to righteousness, faith, etc. But this, we have seen, is to be compensated for in the prize of the glory and honor of the divine nature offered to the Church, in addition to the gift of everlasting life.

Adam's death was sure, though it was reached by nine hundred and thirty years of dying. Since he was himself dying, all his children were born in the same dying condition and without right to life; and, like their parents, they all die after a more or less lingering process. It should be remembered, however, that it is not the pain and suffering in dying, but death—the extinction of life—in which the dying culminates, that is the penalty of sin. The suffering is only incidental to it, and the penalty falls on many with but little or no suffering. It should further be remembered that when Adam forfeited life, he forfeited it forever; and not one of his posterity has ever been able to expiate his guilt or to regain the lost inheritance. All the race are either dead or dying. And if they could not expiate their guilt before death, they certainly could not do it when dead—when not in existence. The penalty of sin was not simply to die, with the privilege and right thereafter of returning to life. In the penalty pronounced there was no intimation of release. (Gen. 2:17) The restitution, therefore, is an act of free grace or favor on God's part. And as soon as the penalty had been incurred, even while it was being pronounced, the free favor of God was intimated, which, when realized, will so fully declare his love.

Had it not been for the gleam of hope, afforded by the statement that the seed of the woman should bruise the serpent's head, the race would have been in utter despair; but this promise indicated that God had some plan for their benefit. When to Abraham God swore that in his seed all the families of the earth should be blessed, it implied a resurrection or restitution of all; for many were then dead, and others have since died, unblessed. Nevertheless, the promise is still sure: all shall be blessed when the times of restitution or refreshing shall come. (Acts 3:19) Moreover, since blessing indicates favor, and since God's favor was withdrawn and his curse came instead because of sin, this promise of a future blessing implied the removal of the curse, and consequently a return of his favor. It also implied either that God would relent, change his decree and clear the guilty race, or else that he had some plan by which it could be *redeemed*, by having man's penalty paid by another.

God did not leave Abraham in doubt as to which was his plan, but showed, by various typical sacrifices which all who approached him had to bring, that he could not and did not relent, nor excuse the sin; and that the only way to blot it out and abolish its penalty would be by a sufficiency of sacrifice to meet that penalty. This was shown to Abraham in a very significant type: Abraham's son, in whom the promised blessing centered, had first to be a sacrifice before he could bless, and Abraham received him from the dead in a figure. (Heb. 11:19) In that figure Isaac typified the true seed, Christ Jesus, who died to redeem men, in order that the redeemed might all receive the promised blessing. Had Abraham thought that the Lord would excuse and clear the guilty, he would have felt that God was changeable, and therefore could not have had full confidence in the promise made to him. He might have reasoned, If God has changed his mind once, why may he not change it again? If he relents concerning the curse of death, may he not again relent concerning the promised favor and blessing? But God leaves us in no such uncertainty. He gives us ample assurance of both his justice and his unchangeableness. He could not clear the guilty, even though he loved them so much that "he spared not his own Son, but delivered him up [to death] for us all."

As the entire race was in Adam when he was condemned, and lost life through him, so when Jesus "gave himself a ransom for all" his death involved the possibility of an unborn race in his loins. A full satisfaction, or corresponding price, for all men was thus put into the hands of Justice—to be applied "in due time," and he who thus *bought all* has full authority to restore all who come unto God by him.

"As by the offence of one, judgment came upon all men to condemnation, even so by the righteousness of one, the free gift came upon all men unto justification of life. For as by one man's disobedience many were made sinners, so by the obedience of one shall many be made righteous." (Rom. 5:18,19) The proposition is a plain one: As many as have shared death on account of Adam's sin will have life-privileges offered to them by our Lord Jesus, who died for them and sacrificially became *Adam's substitute* before the broken law, and thus "gave himself a ransom for all." He died, "the just for the unjust, that he might bring us to God." (1 Peter 3:18) It should never be overlooked, however, that all of God's provisions for our race recognize the human will as a factor in the securing of the divine favors so abundantly provided. Some have overlooked this feature in examining the text just quoted—Rom. 5:18, 19. The Apostle's statement, however, is that, as the sentence of condemnation extended to all the seed of Adam, even so, through the obedience of our Lord Jesus Christ to the Father's plan, by the sacrifice of himself on our behalf, a free gift is extended to all—a gift of forgiveness, which, if accepted, will constitute a justification or basis for life everlasting. And "as by one man's disobedience many *were* made sinners, so by the obedience of one many *shall be* [not *were*] made righteous." If the ransom alone, without our acceptance of it, made us righteous, then it would have read, by the obedience of one many *were* made righteous.

But though the ransom-price has been given by the Redeemer only a few during the Gospel age have been made righteous—justified—"through faith in his blood." But since Christ is the propitiation (satisfaction) for the sins of the whole world, all men may on this account be absolved and released from the penalty of Adam's sin by him—under the New Covenant.

There is no unrighteousness with God; hence "If we confess our sins, he is faithful and *just* to forgive us our sins and to cleanse us from all unrighteousness." (1 John 1:9) As he would have been unjust to have allowed us to escape the pronounced penalty before satisfaction was rendered, so also he here gives us to understand that it would be unjust were he to forbid our restitution, since by his own arrangement our penalty has been paid for us. The same unswerving justice that once condemned man to death now stands pledged for the release of all who, confessing their sins, apply for life through Christ. "It is God that justifieth—who is he that condemneth? It is Christ that died; yea, rather, that is risen again, who is even at the right hand of God, who also maketh intercession for us." Rom. 8:33, 34

The completeness of the ransom is the very strongest possible argument for the restitution of all mankind who will accept it on the proffered terms. (Rev. 22:17) The very character of God for justice and honor stands pledged to it; every promise which he has made implies it; and every typical sacrifice pointed to the great and sufficient sacrifice—"the Lamb of God, which taketh away the SIN OF THE WORLD"—who is "the propitiation [satisfaction] for our sins [the Church's], and not for ours only, but also for the sins of the whole world." (John 1:29; 1 John 2:2) Since death is the penalty or wages of sin, when the sin is canceled the wages must in due time cease. Any other view would be both unreasonable and unjust. The fact that no recovery from the Adamic loss is yet accomplished, though nearly two thousand years have elapsed since our Lord died, is no more an argument against restitution than is the fact that four thousand years elapsed before his death a proof that

God had not planned the redemption before the foundation of the world. Both the two thousand years since and the four thousand years before the death of Christ were appointed times for other parts of the work, preparatory to "the times of restitution of all things."

Let no one hastily suppose that there is in this view anything in conflict with the teaching of the Scriptures that faith toward God, repentance for sin and reformation of character are indispensable to salvation. This feature will be treated more at length hereafter, but we now suggest that only the few have ever had a sufficiency of light to produce full faith, repentance and reformation. Some have been blinded in part, and some completely, by the god of this world, and they must be recovered from blindness as well as from death, that they, *each for himself*, may have a *full* chance to prove, by obedience or disobedience, their worthiness or unworthiness of life everlasting. Then those who prove themselves unworthy of life will die again—the second death—from which there will be no redemption, and consequently no resurrection. The death which comes on account of Adam's sin, and all the imperfections which follow in its wake, will be removed because of the redemption which is in Christ Jesus; but the death which comes as a result of individual, wilful apostasy is final. This sin hath never forgiveness, and its penalty, the second death, will be *everlasting*—not everlasting dying, but everlasting death—a death unbroken by a resurrection.

The philosophy of the plan of redemption will be treated in a succeeding volume. Here we merely establish the fact that the redemption through Christ Jesus is to be as far-reaching in its blessed results and opportunities as was the sin of Adam in its blight and ruin—that all who were condemned and who suffered on account of the one may as surely, "in due time," be set free from all those ills on account of the other. However, none can appreciate this

Scriptural argument who do not admit the Scriptural statement that death—extinction of being—is the wages of sin. Those who think of death as life in torment not only disregard the meaning of the words *death* and *life*, which are opposites, but involve themselves in two absurdities. It is absurd to suppose that God would perpetuate Adam's existence forever in torment for any kind of a sin which he could commit, but especially for the comparatively small offence of eating forbidden fruit. Then, again, if our Lord Jesus redeems mankind, died in our stead, became our ransom, went into death that we might be set free from it, is it not evident that the death which he suffered for the unjust was of exactly the same kind as that to which all mankind were condemned? Is he, then, suffering eternal torture for our sins? If not, then so surely as he *died* for our sins, the punishment for our sins was death, and not life in any sense or condition.

But, strange to say, finding that the theory of eternal torture is inconsistent with the statements that "the Lord hath laid upon him the iniquity of us all," and that Christ "died for our sins," and seeing that one or the other must be dropped as inconsistent, some are so wedded to the idea of eternal torture, and so prize it as a sweet morsel, that they hold to it regardless of the Scriptures, and deliberately deny that Jesus paid the world's ransom-price, though this truth is taught on every leaf of the Bible.

Is Restitution Practicable?

Some have supposed that if the billions of the dead were resurrected, there would not be room for them on the earth; and that if there should be room for them, the earth would not be capable of sustaining so large a population. It is even claimed by some that the earth is one vast graveyard, and that if all the dead were awakened they would trample one upon another for want of room.

This is an important point. How strange it would be if we should find that while the Bible declares a resurrection for all men, yet, by actual measurement, they could not find a footing on the earth! Now let us see: figure it out and you will find this an unfounded fear. You will find that there is an abundance of room for the "restitution of all," as "God hath spoken by the mouth of all his holy prophets."

Let us assume that it is six thousand years since the creation of man, and that there are fourteen hundred millions of people now living on the earth. Our race began with one pair, but let us make a very liberal estimate and suppose that there were as many at the beginning as there are now; and, further, that there never were fewer than that number at any time, though actually the flood reduced the population to eight persons. Again, let us be liberal, and estimate three generations to a century, or thirty-three years to a generation, though, according to Gen. 5, there were but eleven generations from Adam to the flood, a period of one thousand six hundred and fifty-six years, or about one hundred and fifty years to each generation. Now let us see: six thousand years are sixty centuries; three generations to each century would give us one hundred and eighty generations since Adam; and fourteen hundred millions to a generation would give two hundred and fifty-two billions (252,000,000,000) as the total number of our race from creation to the present time, according to this liberal estimate, which is probably more than twice the actual number.

Where shall we find room enough for this great multitude? Let us measure the land, and see. The State of Texas, United States, contains two hundred and thirty-seven thousand square miles. There are twenty-seven million eight hundred and seventy-eight thousand four hundred square feet in a square mile, and, therefore, six trillion six hundred and seven billion one hundred and eighty million eight hundred thousand (6,607,180,800,000) square feet in Texas. Allowing ten square feet as the surface covered by each dead body, we find that Texas, as a cemetery, would at this rate hold six hundred and sixty billion seven hundred and eighteen million and eighty thousand (660,718,080,000) bodies, or nearly three times as many as our exaggerated estimate of the numbers of our race who have lived on the earth.

A person standing occupies about one and two-thirds square feet of space. At this rate the present population of the earth (one billion four hundred million persons) could stand on an area of eighty-six square miles—an area much less than that of the city of London or of Philadelphia. And the island of Ireland (area, thirty-two thousand square miles) would furnish standing room for more than twice the number of people who have ever lived on the earth, even at our exaggerated estimate.

There is not much difficulty, then, in settling this objection. And when we call to mind the prophecy of Isaiah (35:1-6), that the earth shall yield her increase; that the desert shall rejoice and blossom as the rose; that in the wilderness shall waters break out, and streams in the desert, we see that God indicates that he has foreseen all the necessities of his plan, and will make ample provision for the needs of his creatures in what will seem a very natural way.

Restitution Versus Evolution

It may be objected by some that the testimony of the Scriptures concerning human restitution to a former estate is out of harmony with the teachings of science and philosophy, which, with *apparent* reason, point us to the superior intelligence of this twentieth century, and claim this as conclusive evidence that primeval man must have been, in comparison, very lacking in intelligence, which they claim is the result of development. From this standpoint, a restitution to a former estate would be far from desirable, and certainly the reverse of a blessing.

At first sight such reasoning appears plausible, and many seem inclined to accept it as truth without careful examination, saying, with a celebrated Brooklyn preacher, If Adam fell at all his fall was upward, and the more and faster we fall from his original state the better for us and for all concerned.

Thus philosophy, even in the pulpit, would make the Word of God of no effect, and if possible convince us that the apostles were fools when they declared that death and every trouble came by the first man's disobedience, and that these could be removed and man restored to divine favor and life only by means of a ransom. (Rom. 5:10, 12, 17-19, 21; 8:19-22; Acts 3:19-21; Rev. 21:3-5) But let us not hastily conclude that this philosophy is impregnable; for should we be obliged to discard the doctrines of the apostles relative to the origin of sin and death, and of restitution to an original perfection, we should, in honesty, be obliged to reject their testimony entirely and on every subject, as uninspired and consequently without special weight or authority. Let us, then, in the light of facts, briefly examine this growingly popular view and see how deep is its philosophy.

Says an advocate and representative of this theory:

"Man was first in a stage of existence in which his animal nature predominated, and the almost purely physical ruled him; then he slowly grew from one state to another until now, when the average man has attained to a condition in which, it might be said, he is coming under the rule of the brain. Hence this age may be regarded and designated as the Brain Age. Brain pushes the great enterprises of the day. Brain takes the reins of government; and the elements of the earth, air and water are being brought under subjection.

Man is putting his hand on all physical forces, and slowly but surely attaining such power over the domain of nature as gives evidence that ultimately he may exclaim, in the language of Alexander Selkirk, 'I am monarch of all I survey.' "

The fact that at first glance a theory appears reasonable should not lead us hastily to accept it, and to attempt to twist the Bible into harmony with it. In a thousand ways we have proved the Bible, and know beyond peradventure that it contains a superhuman wisdom which makes its statements unerring. We should remember, too, that while scientific research is to be commended, and its suggestions considered, yet its conclusions are by no means infallible. And what wonder that it has proven its own theories false a thousand times, when we remember that the true scientist is merely a student attempting, under many unfavorable circumstances, and struggling against almost insurmountable difficulties, to learn from the great Book of Nature the history and destiny of man and his home.

We would not, then, either oppose or hinder scientific investigation; but in hearing suggestions from students of the Book of Nature, let us carefully compare their deductions, which have so often proved in part or wholly erroneous, with the Book of Divine Revelation, and prove or disprove the teachings of scientists by "the law and the testimony. If they speak not according to this word, it is because there is no light in them." (Isa. 8:20) An accurate knowledge of both books will prove them to be harmonious; but until we have such knowledge, God's Revelation must take precedence, and must be the standard among the children of God, by which the supposed findings of fallible fellowmen shall be judged.

But while holding to this principle, let us see whether there is not some other reasonable solution of the increased knowledge and skill and power of man than the theory of Evolution—that though originally developed from a very low order of being, man has now reached the superior or "Brain Age." Perhaps after all we shall find that the inventions and conveniences, the general education and wider diffusion and increase of knowledge, are not attributable to a greater brain capacity, but to more favorable circumstances for the use of brains. That the brain capacity today is greater than in by-gone ages, we deny; while we freely admit that, owing to advantageous circumstances, the use of what brain capacity men have today is more general than at any former period, and hence makes a much larger showing. In the study of painting and sculpture, do not the students of this "Brain Age" go back to the great masters of the past? Do they not by so doing acknowledge a brain power and originality of design as well as a skill of workmanship worthy of imitation? Does not the present "Brain Age" draw largely upon the original designs of the past ages for its architecture? Do not the orators and logicians of this "Brain Age" study and copy the methods and syllogisms of Plato, Aristotle, Demosthenes and others of the past? Might not many of the public speakers of today well covet the tongue of a Demosthenes or an Apollos, and much more the clear reasoning power of the Apostle Paul?

To go still further back: while we might well refer to the rhetorical powers of several of the prophets, and to the sublime poetic paintings interspersed throughout the Psalms, we refer these "Brain Age" philosophers to the wisdom and logic, no less than to the fine moral sensibilities, of Job and his comforters. And what shall we say of Moses, "learned in all the wisdom of the Egyptians"? The laws given through him have been the foundation for the laws of all civilized nations, and are still recognized as the embodiment of marvelous wisdom.

The exhuming of ancient buried cities reveals a knowledge of the arts and sciences in ages past which is surprising some of the philosophers of this so-called "Brain Age." The ancient methods of embalming the dead, of tempering copper, of making elastic glass and Damascus steel, are among the achievements of the remote past which the brain of the present age, with all its advantages, is unable either to comprehend or to duplicate.

Going back four thousand years to about Abraham's time, we find the Great Pyramid of Egypt—an object of wonder and amazement to the most learned scientists of today. Its construction is in exact accord with the most advanced attainments of this "Brain Age" in the sciences of Mathematics and Astronomy. It teaches, positively, truths which can today be only approximated by the use of modern instruments. So striking and clear are its teachings that some of the foremost astronomers of the world have unhesitatingly pronounced it to be of divine origin. And even if our "Brain Age" evolutionists should admit that it is of divine arrangement, and that its wisdom is superhuman, they must still admit that it is of human construction. And the fact that in that remote day any set of men had the mental capacity to work out such a divine arrangement as very few men today would be capable of doing with a model before them, and with all modern scientific appliances at hand, proves that our "Brain Age" develops more self-conceit than circumstances and facts warrant.

If, then, we have proven that the mental capacity of today is not greater than that of past ages, but probably less, how shall we account for the increase of general knowledge, modern inventions, etc.? We trust we shall be able to show this reasonably and in harmony with Scripture. The inventions and discoveries which are now proving so valuable, and which are considered proof that this is the "Brain

Age," are really very modern—nearly all having come within the past century, and among the most important are those of the last threescore years; for instance, the application of steam and electricity—in telegraphy, railroading and steamboating, and to the machinery of the various mechanical industries. If, then, these be evidences of increased brain power, the "Brain Age" must be only beginning, and the logical deduction is that another century will witness every form of miracle as an everyday occurrence; and at the same ratio of increase, where would it eventuate?

But let us look again: Are all men inventors? How very few there are whose inventions are really useful and practical, compared with the number who appreciate and use an invention when put into their hand! Nor do we speak disparagingly of that very useful and highly-esteemed class of public servants when we say that the smaller number of them are men of great brain-power. Some of the most brainy men in the world, and the deepest reasoners, are not mechanical inventors. And some inventors are intellectually so sluggish that all wonder how they ever stumbled into the discoveries they made. The great principles (electricity, steam power, etc.), which many men in many years work out, apply and improve upon, time and again, were generally discovered apparently by the merest accident, without the exercise of great brain power, and comparatively unsought.

From a human standpoint we can account for modern inventions thus: The invention of printing, in A.D. 1440, may be considered the starting point. With the printing of books came records of the thoughts and discoveries of thinkers and observers, which, without this invention, would never have been known to their successors. With books came a more general education and, finally, common schools. Schools and colleges do not increase human capacity, but they do make mental exercise more general, and hence help to develop the capacity already possessed. As knowledge becomes more general and books more common, the generations possessing these have a decided advantage over previous generations; not only in that there are now a thousand thinkers to one formerly, to sharpen and stimulate each other with suggestions, but also in that each of the later generations has, through books, the combined experience of the past in addition to its own. Education and the laudable ambition which accompanies it, enterprise, and a desire to achieve distinction and a competency, aided by the record and descriptions of inventions in the daily press, have stimulated and brightened man's perceptive powers, and put each upon the alert to discover or to invent, if possible, something for the good and convenience of society. Hence we suggest that modern invention, looked at from a purely human standpoint, teaches, not an increase of brain capacity, but a sharpened perception from natural causes.

And now we come to the Scriptures to see what they teach on the subject; for while we believe, as suggested above, that invention and the increase of knowledge, etc., among men are the results of *natural* causes, yet we believe that these natural causes were all planned and ordered by Jehovah God long ago, and that in due time they have come to pass—by his overruling providence, whereby he "worketh all things after the counsel of his own will." (Eph. 1:11) According to the plan revealed in his Word, God purposed to permit sin and misery to misrule and oppress the world for six thousand years, and then in the seventh millennium to restore all things, and to extirpate evil—destroying it and its consequences by Jesus Christ, whom he hath afore ordained to do this work. Hence, as the six thousand years of the reign of evil began to draw to a close, God permitted circumstances to favor discoveries, in the study of both his Book of Revelation and his Book of Nature, as well as in the preparation of mechanical and chemical appliances useful in the blessing and uplifting of mankind during the Millennial age, now about to be introduced. That this was God's plan is clearly indicated by the prophetic statement: "O Daniel, shut up the words, and seal the book, even to *the time of the end*; [then] many shall run to and fro, and KNOWLEDGE [not capacity] shall be increased," "and none of the wicked shall understand [God's plan and way], but the wise shall understand;" "and there shall be a time of trouble such as never was since there was a nation, even to that same time." Dan. 12:1, 4, 10

To some it may appear strange that God did not so arrange that the present inventions and blessings should sooner have come to man to alleviate the curse. It should be remembered, however, that God's plan has been to give mankind a full appreciation of the curse, in order that when the blessing comes upon all they may forever have decided upon the unprofitableness of sin. Furthermore, God foresaw and has foretold what the world does not yet realize, namely, that his choicest blessings would lead to and be productive of greater evils if bestowed upon those whose hearts are not in accord with the righteous laws of the universe. Ultimately it will be seen that God's present permission of increased blessings is a practical lesson on this subject, which may serve as an example of this principle to all eternity—to angels as well as to restored men. How this can be, we merely suggest:

First: So long as mankind is in the present fallen or depraved condition, without stringent laws and penalties and a government strong enough to enforce them, the selfish propensities will hold more or less sway over all. And with the unequal individual capacities of men considered, it cannot possibly happen otherwise than that the result of the invention of labor-saving machinery must, after the flurry and stimulus occasioned by the manufacture of machinery, tend to make the rich richer, and the poor poorer. The manifest tendency is toward monopoly and self-aggrandizement, which places the advantage directly in the hands of those whose capacity and natural advantages are already the most favorable.

Secondly: If it were possible to legislate so as to divide the present wealth and its daily increase evenly among all classes, which is not possible, still, without human perfection or a supernatural government to regulate human affairs, the results would be even more injurious than the present condition. If the advantages of labor-saving machinery and all modern appliances were evenly divided, the result would, ere long, be a great decrease of hours of labor and a great increase of leisure. Idleness is a most injurious thing to fallen beings. Had it not been for the necessity of labor and sweat of face, the deterioration of our race would have been much more rapid than it has been. Idleness is the mother of vice; and mental, moral and physical degradation are sure to follow. Hence the wisdom and goodness of God in withholding these blessings until it was *due time* for their introduction as a preparation for the Millennial reign of blessing. Under the control of the supernatural government of the Kingdom of God, not only will all blessings be equitably divided among men, but the leisure will be so ordered and directed by the same supernatural government that its results will produce virtue and tend upward toward perfection, mental, moral and physical. The present multiplication of inventions and other blessings of increasing knowledge is permitted in this "day of preparation" to come about in so natural a way that men flatter themselves that it is because this is the "Brain Age"; but it will be permitted in great measure to work out in a manner very much to the disappointment, no doubt, of these wise philosophers. It is the very increase of these blessings that is already beginning to bring upon the world the time of trouble, which will be such as never has been since there was a nation.

The prophet Daniel, as quoted above, links together the increase of knowledge and the time of trouble. The knowledge causes the trouble, because of the depravity of the race. The increase of knowledge has not only given the world wonderful labor-saving machinery and conveniences, but it has also led to an increase of medical skill whereby thousands of lives are prolonged, and it has so enlightened mankind that human butchery, war, is becoming less popular, and thus, too, other thousands are spared to multiply still further the race, which is increasing more rapidly today, perhaps, than at any other period of history. Thus, while mankind is multiplying rapidly, the necessity for his labor is decreasing correspondingly; and the "Brain Age" philosophers have a problem before them to provide for the employment and sustenance of this large and rapidly increasing class whose services, for the most part supplanted by machinery, can be dispensed with, but whose necessities and wants know no bounds. The solution of this problem, these philosophers must ultimately admit, is beyond their brain capacity.

Selfishness will continue to control the wealthy, who hold the power and advantage, and will blind them to common sense as well as to justice; while a similar selfishness, combined with the instinct of *self-preservation* and an increased knowledge of their rights, will nerve some and inflame others of the poorer classes, and the result of these *blessings* will, for a time, prove terrible—a time of trouble, truly, such as was not since there was a nation—and this, because man in a depraved condition cannot properly use these blessings unguided and uncontrolled. Not until the Millennial reign shall have rewritten the law of God in the restored human heart will men be capable of using full liberty without injury or danger.

The day of trouble will end in due time, when he who spake to the raging Sea of Galilee will likewise, with authority, command the raging sea of human passion, saying, "Peace! Be still!" When the Prince of Peace shall "stand up" in authority, a great calm will be the result. Then the raging and clashing elements shall recognize the authority of "Jehovah's Anointed," "the glory of the Lord shall be revealed, and all flesh shall see it together"; and in the reign of the Christ thus begun "shall all the families of the earth be blessed."

Then men will see that what they attributed to evolution or natural development and the smartness of the "Brain Age" was, instead, the flashings of Jehovah's lightnings (Psa. 77:18) in "the day of his preparation" for the blessing of mankind. But as yet only the saints can see, and only the wise in heavenly wisdom can understand this; for "The secret of the Lord is with them that fear him; and he will show them his covenant." (Psa. 25:14) Thanks be to God, that while general knowledge has been increased, he has also arranged that his children need "not be unfruitful in the knowledge of the Lord" and in the appreciation of his plans. And by this appreciation of his Word and plans we are enabled to discern and to withstand the vain philosophies and foolish traditions of men which contradict the Word of God.

The Bible account of man's creation is that God created him perfect and upright, an earthly image of himself; that man sought out various inventions and defiled himself (Gen. 1:27; Rom. 5:12; Eccl. 7:29); that, all being sinners, the race was unable to help itself, and none could by any means redeem his brother or give to God a ransom for him (Psa. 49:7, 15); that God in compassion and love had made provision for this; that, accordingly, the Son of God became a man, and gave man's ransom-price; that, as a reward for this sacrifice, and in order to the completion of the great work of atonement, he was highly exalted, even to the divine nature; and that in due time he will bring to pass a restitution of the race to the original perfection and to every blessing then possessed. These things are clearly taught in the Scriptures, from beginning to end, and are in direct opposition to the Evolution theory; or, rather, such "babblings of science, falsely so called," are in violent and irreconcilable conflict with the Word of God.

* * *

"Still o'er earth's sky the clouds of anger roll,
And God's revenge hangs heavy on her soul;
Yet shall she rise—though first by God chastised—
In glory and in beauty then baptized.

"Yes, Earth, thou shalt arise; thy Father's aid
Shall heal the wound his chastening hand hath made;
Shall judge the proud oppressor's ruthless sway,
And burst his bonds, and cast his cords away.

"Then on your soil shall deathless verdure spring;
Break forth, ye mountains, and ye valleys, sing!
No more your thirsty rocks shall frown forlorn,
The unbeliever's jest, the heathen's scorn.

"The sultry sands shall tenfold harvests yield,
And a new Eden deck the thorny field.
E'en now we see, wide-waving o'er the land,
The mighty angel lifts his golden wand,

"Courts the bright vision of descending power,
Tells every gate and measures every tower;
And chides the tardy seals that yet detain
Thy Lion, Judah, from his destined reign."

—*Heber*

STUDY X
SPIRITUAL AND HUMAN NATURES
SEPARATE AND DISTINCT

COMMON MISAPPREHENSIONS—EARTHLY OR HUMAN AND HEAVENLY OR SPIRITUAL NATURES—EARTHLY GLORY AND HEAVENLY GLORY—BIBLE TESTIMONY REGARDING SPIRIT BEINGS—MORTALITY AND IMMORTALITY—CAN MORTAL BEINGS HAVE EVERLASTING LIFE?—JUSTICE IN THE BESTOWMENT OF FAVORS—A SUPPOSED PRINCIPLE EXAMINED—VARIETY IN PERFECTION—GOD'S SOVEREIGN RIGHTS—GOD'S PROVISIONS FOR MAN A SATISFYING PORTION—THE ELECTION OF THE BODY OF CHRIST—HOW THEIR CHANGE OF NATURE IS EFFECTED.

FAILING to see that the plan of God for mankind in general contemplates a restitution to their former estate—the human perfection lost in Eden—and that the Christian Church, as an exception to this general plan, is to have a change of nature from human to spiritual, Christian people generally have supposed that none will be saved except those who reach the spiritual nature. The Scriptures, however, while holding out promises of life and blessing and restitution to all the families of the earth, offer and promise the change to spiritual nature only to the Church selected during the Gospel age; and not a single passage can be found which sustains such hopes for any others.

If the masses of mankind are saved from all the degradation, weakness, pain, misery and death which result from sin, and are restored to the condition of human perfection enjoyed before the fall, they are as really and completely saved from that fall as those who, under the special "high-calling" of the Gospel age, become "partakers of the divine nature."

173

The failure to understand rightly what constitutes a perfect man, the misapprehension of the terms mortal and immortal, and wrong ideas of justice, have together tended to this error, and mystified many scriptures otherwise easily understood. It is a common view, though unsupported by a single text of Scripture, that a perfect man has never been on earth; that all that is seen of man on earth is only the partially developed man, and that to reach perfection he must become spiritual. This view makes confusion of the Scriptures instead of developing that harmony and beauty which result from "rightly dividing the word of truth."

The Scriptures teach that there have been two, and only two, perfect men—Adam and Jesus. Adam was created in the image of God: that is, with the similar mental powers of reason, memory, judgment and will, and the moral qualities of justice, benevolence, love, etc. "Of the earth, earthy," he was an earthly image of a spiritual being, possessing qualities of the same kind, though differing widely in degree, range and scope. To such an extent is man an image of God that God can say even to the fallen man, "Come, let us reason together."

As Jehovah is ruler over all things, so man was made a ruler over all earthly things—After our likeness, let him have dominion over the beasts, fowl, fish, etc. (Gen. 1:26) Moses tells us (Gen. 1:31) that God recognized the man whom he *had made*—not merely commenced to make, but completed— and God considered his creature *"very good,"* that is, perfect; for in God's sight nothing short of perfection is *very good*, in his intelligent creatures.

The perfection of man, as created, is expressed in Psa. 8:5-8: "Thou hast made him a little lower than the angels, and hast crowned him with glory and honor. Thou madest him to have dominion over the works of thy hands; thou hast put all things under his feet: all sheep and oxen, yea, the beasts of the field, the fowl of the air and the fish of the sea." It has been suggested by some who would make the Bible conform to a theory of evolution, that the statement, "a little," in Heb. 2:7, might be understood to mean a little *while* lower, and not a little *degree* lower than the angels. There is, however, neither authority nor reason for such an interpretation. This is a quotation from Psa. 8:5, and a critical comparison of the Hebrew and Greek texts can leave no doubt as to the import. The idea, clearly expressed, is a little lower in degree than angels.

David, in the psalm, refers to man in his original estate, and prophetically intimates that God has not abandoned his original plan to have man in his own image and the king of earth, and that he will *remember* him, redeem him and restore him to the same again. The Apostle (Heb. 2:7) calls attention to the same fact—that God's original purpose has not been abandoned; that man, originally grand and perfect, the king of earth, is to be remembered, and visited, and restored. He then adds, We see not this promised restitution yet, but we do see the first step God is taking toward its accomplishment. We see Jesus crowned with this glory and honor of perfect manhood, that he, as a fitting ransom or substitute might by God's favor taste death for every man, and thus prepare the way for the restitution of man to all that was lost. Rotherham, one of the most scrupulous translators, renders this passage as follows:

> "What is man, that thou rememberest him;
> Or man's son, that thou visitest him?
> Thou madest him *less some little* than messengers:
> With glory and honor thou crownedst him,
> And didst appoint him over the works of thy hands."

Nor should it be inferred that a little lower in degree means a little less perfect. A creature may be perfect, yet on a lower plane of being than another; thus, a perfect horse would be lower than a perfect man, etc. There are various natures, animate and inanimate. To illustrate, we arrange the following table:

Grades of Heavenly or Spiritual Being	Grades of Earthly or Animal Being	Grades in the Vegetable Domain	Grades in the Mineral Domain
Divine	Human	Trees	Gold
———	Brute	Shrubs	Silver
———	Fowl	Grasses	Copper
Angelic	Fish	Mosses	Iron

Each of the minerals mentioned may be pure, yet gold ranks the highest. Though each of the orders of plants should be brought to perfection, they would still differ in nature and rank. Likewise with animals: if each species should be brought to perfection, there would still be variety; for perfecting a nature does not change a nature.* The grades of spiritual being, also, though perfect, stand related to each other as higher and lower in nature or kind. The divine nature is the highest and the superior of all spiritual natures. Christ at his resurrection was made *"so much better"* than perfect angels as the divine is superior to the angelic nature. Heb. 1:3-5

Note carefully that while the classes named in the above table are distinct and separate, yet a comparison between them may be instituted, thus: The highest grade of mineral is inferior to, or *a little lower* than, the lowest grade of vegetable,

---

*The word *nature* is sometimes used in an accommodated sense, as, for instance, when it is said that a dog has a *savage nature*, or that a horse has a *gentle nature*, or is *bad natured*. But in using the word thus it signifies merely the *disposition* of the one described as compared with others, and does not, strictly speaking, relate to nature.

because in vegetation there is life. So the highest grade of vegetable is *a little lower* than the lowest grade of animal life, because animal life, even in its lowest forms, has intelligence enough to be conscious of existence. Likewise man, though the highest of animal or earthly beings, is "a little lower than the angels," because angels are spiritual or heavenly beings.

There is a wonderful contrast between man as we now see him, degraded by sin, and the perfect man that God made in his image. Sin has gradually changed his features, as well as his character. Multiplied generations, by ignorance, licentiousness and general depravity, have so blurred and marred humanity that in the large majority of the race the likeness of God is almost obliterated. The moral and intellectual qualities are dwarfed; and the animal instincts, unduly developed, are no longer balanced by the higher. Man has lost physical strength to such an extent that, with all the aid of medical science, his average length of life is now about thirty years, whereas at first he survived nine hundred and thirty years under the same penalty. But though thus defiled and degraded by sin and its penalty, death, working in him, man is to be restored to his original perfection of mind and body, and to glory, honor and dominion, during and by the Millennial reign of Christ. The things to be restored by and through Christ are those things which were lost through Adam's transgression. (Rom. 5:18, 19) Man did not lose a heavenly but an earthly paradise. Under the death penalty, he did not lose a spiritual but a human existence; and all that was lost was purchased back by his Redeemer, who declared that he came to seek and to save that which was lost. Luke 19:10

In addition to the above, we have proof that the perfect man is not a spiritual being. We are told that our Lord, before he left his glory to become a man, was "in a form of

God"—a spiritual form, a spirit being; but since to be a ransom for mankind he had to be a man, of the same nature as the sinner whose substitute in death he was to become, it was necessary that his nature be changed. And Paul tells us that he took not the nature of angels, one step lower than his own, but that he came down two steps and took the nature of men—he became a man; he was "made flesh." Heb. 2:16; Phil. 2:7, 8; John 1:14

Notice that this teaches not only that angelic nature is not the only order of spirit being, but that it is a lower nature than that of our Lord before he became a man; and he was not then so high as he is now, for "God hath highly exalted him," because of his obedience in becoming man's willing ransom. (Phil. 2:8, 9) He is now of the highest order of spirit being, a partaker of the divine (Jehovah's) nature.

But not only do we thus find proof that the divine, angelic and human natures are separate and distinct, but this proves that to be a perfect man is not to be an angel, any more than the perfection of angelic nature implies that angels are divine and equal with Jehovah; for Jesus took *not* the *nature of angels*, but a different nature—the *nature of men*; not the imperfect human nature as we now possess it, but the *perfect* human nature. He became *a man*; not a depraved and nearly dead being such as men are now, but a man in the full vigor of perfection.

Again, Jesus must have been a perfect man else he could not have kept a perfect law, which is the full measure of a *perfect man's ability*. And he must have been a perfect man else he could not have given a ransom (a corresponding price—1 Tim. 2:6) for the forfeited life of the perfect man Adam; "For since by *man* came death, by *man* came also the resurrection of the dead." (1 Cor. 15:21) Had he been in the least degree imperfect, it would have proved that he was under condemnation, and therefore he could not have been an acceptable sacrifice; neither could he have kept perfectly the law of God. A perfect man was tried, and failed, and was condemned; and only a perfect man could give the *corresponding price* as the Redeemer.

Now we have the question fairly before us in another form, viz.: If Jesus in the flesh was a perfect man, as the Scriptures thus show, does it not prove that a perfect man is a human, fleshly being—not an angel, but a little lower than the angels? The logical conclusion is unmistakable; and in addition we have the inspired statement of the Psalmist (Psa. 8:5-8) and Paul's reference to it in Heb. 2:7-9.

Neither was Jesus a combination of the two natures, human and spiritual. The blending of two natures produces neither the one nor the other, but an imperfect, hybrid thing, which is obnoxious to the divine arrangement. When Jesus was in the flesh he was a perfect human being; previous to that time he was a perfect spiritual being; and since his resurrection he is a perfect spiritual being of the highest or divine order. It was not until the time of his consecration even unto death, as typified in his baptism— at thirty years of age (manhood, according to the Law, and therefore the right time to consecrate himself as *a man*)— that he received the earnest of his inheritance of the divine nature. (Matt. 3:16,17) The human nature had to be *consecrated to death* before he could receive even the *pledge* of the divine nature. And not until that consecration was actually carried out and he had actually sacrificed the human nature, even unto death, did our Lord Jesus become a full partaker of the divine nature. After becoming a man he became obedient unto death; *wherefore*, God hath highly exalted him to the divine nature. (Phil. 2:8, 9) If this scripture is true, it follows that he was not exalted to the divine nature until the human nature was actually sacrificed—dead.

Thus we see that in Jesus there was no mixture of natures, but that twice he experienced a change of nature; first, from spiritual to human; afterward, from human to the highest order of spiritual nature, the divine; and in each case the one was given up for the other.

In this grand example of perfect humanity, which stood unblemished before the world until sacrificed for the world's redemption, we see the perfection from which our race fell in Adam, and to which it is to be restored. In becoming man's ransom, our Lord Jesus gave the *equivalent* for that which man lost; and therefore all mankind may receive again, through faith in Christ, and obedience to his requirements, not a spiritual, but a glorious, perfect *human* nature—"that which was lost."

The perfect faculties and powers of the perfect human being may be exercised indefinitely, and upon new and varied objects of interest, and knowledge and skill may be vastly increased; but no such increase of knowledge or power will effect a change of nature, or make it more than perfect. It will be only the expanding and developing of the perfect human powers. Increase of knowledge and skill will doubtless be man's blessed privilege to all eternity; yet he will still be man, and will be merely learning to use more fully the powers of human nature already possessed. Beyond its wide limits he cannot hope, nor will he desire, to advance, his desires being limited to the scope of his powers.

While Jesus as a man was an illustration of perfect human nature, to which the mass of mankind will be restored, yet since his resurrection he is the illustration of the glorious divine nature which the overcoming Church will, at resurrection, share with him.

Because the present age is devoted mainly to the development of this class which is offered a *change* of nature, and because the apostolic epistles are devoted to the instruction of this "little flock," it should not be inferred that God's plans end with the completion of this chosen company. Nor, on the other hand, should we go to the opposite extreme, and suppose that the special promises of the divine nature, spiritual bodies, etc., made to these, are God's design for all mankind. To these are the "exceeding great and precious promises," over and above the other precious promises made to all mankind. To rightly divide the Word of truth, we should observe that the Scriptures recognize the perfection of the divine nature in the "little flock," and the perfection of the human nature in the restored world, as two separate things.

Let us now inquire more particularly, What are spirit beings? what powers are theirs? and by what laws are they governed? Many seem to think, because they do not understand the nature of a spirit being, that it must be a mere myth, and on this subject much superstition prevails. But Paul does not appear to have such an idea. Though he intimates that a human being is incapable of understanding the higher, spiritual nature (1 Cor. 2:14), yet he plainly states, as if to guard against any mythical or superstitious notions, that there is a spiritual body, as well as a natural (human) body, a celestial as well as a terrestrial, and a glory of the earthly as well as of the heavenly. The glory of the earthly, as we have seen, was lost by the first Adam's sin, and is to be restored to the race by the Lord Jesus and his Bride (the Christ, Head and body) during the Millennial reign. The glory of the heavenly is as yet unseen except as revealed to the eye of faith by the Spirit through the Word. These glories are distinct and separate. (1 Cor. 15:38-49) We know to some extent what the natural, earthly, terrestrial body is, for we now have such, though we can only approximately estimate the glory of its perfection. It is flesh, blood and bones; for "that which is born of the flesh is flesh." And since they are two distinct kinds of bodies, we know that the spiritual, whatever it may be, is not composed of flesh, blood and bones: it is heavenly, celestial, spiritual—"That which is born of the Spirit is spirit." But what a spirit body is, we know not, for "It doth not yet appear what we shall be; but . . . we shall be like him"—like our Lord Jesus. John 3:6; 1 John 3:2

We have no record of any being, either spiritual or human, ever having been changed from one nature to another, except the Son of God; and this was an exceptional case, for an exceptional purpose. When God made angels he doubtless intended them to remain angels forever, and so with men, each being perfect on his own plane. At least the Scriptures give no intimation of any different purpose. As in the inanimate creation there is a pleasing and almost endless variety, so in the living and intelligent creation the same variety in perfection is possible. Every creature in its perfection is glorious; but, as Paul says, the glory of the celestial (heavenly) is one kind of glory, and the glory of the terrestrial (earthly) is another and a different glory.

By examining the facts recorded of our Lord Jesus after his resurrection, and of angels, who are also spirit beings, thus "comparing spiritual things with spiritual" (1 Cor. 2:13), we may gain some general information with regard to spirit beings. First, then, angels can be and frequently are present, yet invisible. "The angel of the Lord encampeth round about them that fear him"; and "Are they not all ministering spirits, sent forth to minister for them who shall be heirs of salvation?" (Psa. 34:7; Heb. 1:14) Have they ministered visibly or invisibly? Undoubtedly the latter. Elisha was surrounded by a host of Assyrians; his servant was fearful; Elisha prayed to the Lord, and the young man's eyes were opened, and he saw the mountains round about them full of chariots of fire and horsemen of fire (or like fire). Again, while to Balaam the angel was invisible, the ass, his eyes being opened, saw him.

Secondly, angels can assume human bodies and appear *as* men. The Lord and two angels so appeared to Abraham, who had a supper prepared for them, of which they ate. At first Abraham supposed them to be three men, and it was not until they were about to go that he discovered one of them to be the Lord, and the other two, angels, who afterward went down to Sodom and delivered Lot. (Gen. 18:1, 2) An angel appeared to Gideon as a man, but afterward made himself known. An angel appeared to the father and mother of Samson, and they thought him a man until he ascended up to heaven in the flame of the altar. Judges 6:11-22; 13:20

Thirdly, spirit beings are glorious in their normal condition, and are frequently referred to as glorious and bright. The countenance of the angel who rolled away the stone from the door of the sepulchre was "as the lightning." Daniel caught a glimpse of a spiritual body, which he described, saying, His eyes were as lamps of fire, his countenance as the lightning, his arms and feet like in color to polished brass, and his voice as the voice of a multitude. Before him Daniel fell as a dead man. (Dan. 10:6, 10, 15, 17) Saul of Tarsus caught a similar glimpse of Christ's glorious body shining above the brightness of the sun at noonday. Saul lost his sight and fell to the ground.

Thus far we have found spirit beings truly glorious; yet, except by the opening of men's eyes to see them, or by their appearing *in flesh* as men, they are invisible to men. This conclusion is further confirmed when we examine the particular details of these manifestations. The Lord was seen of Saul alone, the men traveling with him hearing the voice, but seeing no one. (Acts 9:7) The men that were with Daniel did not see the glorious being he describes, but a great fear fell on them, and they ran and hid themselves. Again, this glorious being declared, "The prince of the kingdom of Persia withstood me one and twenty days." (Dan. 10:13) Did Daniel, the man greatly beloved of the Lord, fall as dead before this one whom Persia's prince withstood one and twenty days? How is this? Surely he did not appear in glory to the prince! No; either he was *invisibly* present with him, or else he appeared *as* a man.

Our Lord, since his resurrection, is a spirit being; consequently the same powers which we find illustrated in angels (spiritual beings) should also be possessed by him. And such is the case, as we shall see more fully in a succeeding chapter.

Thus we find that the Scriptures regard the spiritual and the human natures as separate and distinct, and furnish no evidence that the one will evolve or develop into the other; but, on the contrary, they do show that only a few will ever be changed from the human to the divine nature, to which Jesus, their head, has already been exalted. And this remarkable and special feature in Jehovah's plan is for the remarkable and special purpose of preparing these as God's agents for the great future work of restoring all things.

Let us now examine the terms

Mortality and Immortality.

We shall find their true significance in exact harmony with what we have learned from our comparison of Bible statements concerning human and spiritual beings, and earthly and heavenly promises. These words are usually given very uncertain meanings, and wrong ideas of their meanings produce erroneous views of subjects with which they stand connected, in general and in Scripture usage.

"*Mortality*" signifies a state or condition of *liability to death*; not a condition of death, but a condition in which death is a *possibility*.

"*Immortality*" signifies a state or condition *not liable to death*; not merely a condition of freedom from death, but a condition in which death is an *impossibility*.

The common but erroneous idea of *mortality* is, a state or condition in which death is unavoidable, while the common idea of the significance of *immortality* is more nearly correct.

The word *immortal* signifies *not mortal*; hence the very construction of the words indicates their true definitions. It is because of the prevalence of a wrong idea of the word *mortal* that so many are confused when trying to determine whether Adam was mortal or immortal before his transgression. They reason that if he had been *immortal* God would not have said, "In the day that thou eatest thereof thou shalt surely die"; because it is impossible for an immortal being to die. This is a logical conclusion. On the other hand, say they, Had he been *mortal*, wherein could have consisted the threat or penalty of the statement, "Thou shalt surely die"; since if mortal (according to their erroneous definition) he could not have avoided death anyhow?

The difficulty, it will be perceived, is in the false meaning given to the word *mortality*. Apply the correct definition, and all is clear. Adam was mortal—that is, in a condition in which death was a possibility. He had life in full and perfect measure, yet *not inherent life*. His was a life *sustained* by "every tree of the garden" save the one tree forbidden; and so long as he continued in obedience to and in harmony with his Maker, his life was secure—the sustaining elements would not be denied. Thus seen, Adam had life; and death was entirely avoidable, yet he was in such a condition that death was possible—he was *mortal*.

The question arises, then, If Adam was mortal and on trial, was he on trial for immortality? The general answer would be, Yes. We answer, No. His trial was to see whether he was worthy or unworthy of a continuance of the life and blessings already possessed. Since it was nowhere promised that if obedient he would become immortal, we are bound to leave all such speculations out of the question. He was promised a *continuance of the blessings then enjoyed* so long as obedient, and threatened with the loss of all—death—if disobedient. It is the false idea of the meaning of the word *mortal* that leads people in general to conclude that all beings who do not die are immortal. In this class they therefore include our heavenly Father, our Lord Jesus, the angels, and all mankind. This, however, is an error: the great mass of mankind saved from the fall, as well as the angels of heaven, will always be mortal; though in a condition of perfection and bliss, they will always be of that mortal nature which could suffer death, the wages of sin, if they would commit sin. The security of their existence will be conditioned, as it was with Adam, upon obedience to the all-wise God, whose justice, love and wisdom, and whose power to cause all things to work together for good to those who love and serve him, will have been fully demonstrated by his dealings with sin in the present time.

Nowhere in the Scriptures is it stated that angels are immortal, nor that mankind restored will be immortal. On the contrary, immortality is ascribed only to the divine nature—originally to Jehovah only; subsequently to our Lord Jesus in his present highly exalted condition; and finally by promise to the Church, the body of Christ, when glorified with him. 1 Tim. 6:16; John 5:26; 2 Pet. 1:4; 1 Cor. 15:53, 54

Not only have we evidence that immortality pertains only to the divine nature, but we have proof that angels are mortal, in the fact that Satan, who was once a chief of their number, is to be destroyed. (Heb. 2:14) The fact that he can be destroyed proves that angels as a class are mortal.

Thus considered, we see that when incorrigible sinners are blotted out, both immortal and mortal beings will live forever in joy and happiness and love—the first class possessing a nature incapable of death, having inherent life—life in themselves (John 5:26); and the latter having a nature susceptible to death, yet, because of perfection of being and knowledge of the evil and sinfulness of sin, giving no cause for death. They, being approved of God's law, shall be everlastingly supplied with those elements necessary to sustain them in perfection, and shall never die.

The proper recognition of the meaning of the terms *mortal* and *immortal*, and of their use in the Scriptures, destroys the very foundation of the doctrine of eternal torment. It is based upon the unscriptural theory that God created man immortal, that he cannot cease to exist, and that God cannot destroy him; hence the argument is that the incorrigible must *live on* somewhere and somehow, and the conclusion is that since they are out of harmony with God their eternity must be one of misery. But God's Word assures us that he has provided against such a perpetuation of sin and sinners: that man is mortal, and that the full penalty of wilful sin against full light and knowledge will not be a life in torment, but a second death. "The soul that sinneth, it shall die."

"Who Art Thou that Repliest Against God?"
Romans 9:20

It is the mistaken idea of some that justice requires that God should make no difference in the bestowment of his favors among his creatures; that if he exalts one to a high position, *in justice* he must do the same for all, unless it can be shown that some have forfeited their *rights*, in which case such might justly be assigned to a lower position.

If this principle be a correct one, it would show that God had no right to create Jesus higher than the angels, and then further to exalt him to the divine nature, unless he intended to do the same for all the angels and for all men. And to carry the principle still further, if some men are to be highly exalted and made partakers of the divine nature, all men must eventually be elevated to the same position. And why not carry the principle to its extreme limit, and apply the same law of progression to the brute and insect creation, and say that since they are all God's creatures they must all eventually attain to the very highest plane of existence—the divine nature? This is a manifest absurdity, but as reasonable as any other deduction from this assumed principle.

Perhaps none would be inclined to carry the erroneous assumption so far. Yet if it were a principle founded in simple justice, where could it stop short and still be just? And if such were indeed the plan of God, where would be the pleasing variety in all his works? But such is not God's plan. All nature, both animate and inanimate, exhibits the glory and diversity of divine power and wisdom. And as "the heavens declare the glory of God, and the firmament showeth his handiwork" in wonderful variety and beauty, much more shall his intelligent creation exhibit in variety the superior glory of his power. We so conclude—from the express teaching of the Word of God, from reason and from the analogies of nature.

It is very important that we have right ideas of justice. A *favor* should never be esteemed as a justly merited recompense. An act of simple justice is no occasion for special gratitude, nor is it any proof of love; but God commendeth his great love to his creatures, in an endless train of unmerited favors, which should call forth their love and praise in return.

God had a right, if he chose, to make us merely the creatures of a brief space of time, even if we had never sinned. Thus he has made some of his lower creatures. He might have permitted us to enjoy his blessings for a season, and then, without injustice, might have blotted us all out of existence. In fact, even so brief an existence would be a favor. It is only of his favor that we have an existence at all. How much greater favor is the redemption of the existence once forfeited by sin! And further, it is of God's favor that we are men and not beasts; it is purely of God's favor that angels are by nature a little higher than men; and it is also of God's favor that the Lord Jesus and his bride become partakers of the divine nature. It becomes all his intelligent creatures, therefore, to receive with gratitude whatever God bestows. Any other spirit justly merits condemnation, and, if indulged, will end in abasement and destruction. A man has no right to aspire to be an angel, never having been invited to that position; nor has an angel any right to aspire to the divine nature, that never having been offered to him.

It was the aspiration of Satan's pride which brought his abasement, and will end in his destruction. (Isa. 14:14) "Whosoever exalteth himself shall be abased; and he that humbleth himself shall be exalted" (Luke 14:11), but not necessarily to the highest position.

Partly from false ideas of justice, and partly from other causes, the subject of election as taught in the Scriptures has been the occasion of much dispute and misunderstanding. That the Scriptures teach election few would deny, but on just what principle the election or selection is based is a matter of considerable difference of opinion, some claiming that it is an arbitrary, unconditional election, and others that it is conditional. There is a measure of truth, we believe, in both of these views. An election on God's part is the expression of his choice for a certain purpose, office or condition. God has elected or chosen that some of his creatures should be angels, that some should be men, that some should be beasts, birds, insects, etc., and that some should be of his own divine nature. And though God selects according to certain *conditions* all who will be admitted to the divine nature, yet it cannot be said that these more than others *merit* it; for it is purely of favor that any creature has existence on any plane.

"So then it is not of him that willeth, nor of him that runneth, but of God that showeth mercy"—kindness or favor. (Rom. 9:16) It is not because the chosen ones were better than others, that God gave them the invitation to the divine nature, for he passed by the angels who had not sinned and called some of the redeemed sinners to divine honors. God has a right to do as he pleases with his own; and he chooses to exercise this right for the accomplishment of his plans. Since, then, all we have is of divine favor, "Who art thou, O man, that repliest against God? Shall the thing formed say unto him who formed it, Why hast thou made me thus? Hath not the potter power over the clay, to make one vessel unto honor and another unto dishonor"—or less honor? (Rom. 9:20, 21) All were created by the same divine power—some to have higher nature and greater honor, and some to have lower nature and less honor.

"Thus saith the Lord, the Holy One of Israel, his [man's] maker: *Ask* me of things to come. Concerning my children, and concerning the work of my hands, *command* ye me? I have made the earth, and created man upon it: I, even my hands, have stretched out the heavens, and all their hosts have I commanded." "Thus saith the Lord that created the heavens, God himself that formed the earth and made it; he hath established it, he created it not in vain, he formed it to be inhabited: I am the Lord, and there is none else." (Isa. 45:11, 12, 18) None have a right to dictate to God. If he established the earth, and if he formed it not in vain, but made it to be inhabited by restored, perfect men, who are we that we should reply against God, and say that it is unjust not to change their nature and make them all partakers of a spiritual nature either like unto the angels, or like unto his own divine nature? How much more becoming to come humbly to God's Word and to *"Ask"* concerning things to come, than to *"command"* or to assert that he must carry out our ideas? Lord, keep back thy servants from presumptuous sins: let them not have dominion over us. None of God's children, we believe, would knowingly dictate to the Lord; yet how easily and almost unconsciously many fall into this error.

The human race are God's children by creation—the work of his hands—and his plan with reference to them is clearly revealed in his Word. Paul says that the first man (who was a sample of what the race will be when perfect) was of the earth, earthy; and his posterity, with the exception of the Gospel Church, will in the resurrection still be earthy, human, adapted to the earth. (1 Cor. 15:38, 44) David declares that man was made only a little lower than the angels, and crowned with glory, honor, dominion, etc. (Psa. 8:4-8) And Peter, our Lord, and all the prophets since the world began, declare that the human race is to be restored to that glorious perfection, and is again to have dominion over earth, as its representative, Adam, had. Acts 3:19-21

It is this portion that God has elected to give to the human race. And what a glorious portion! Close your eyes for a moment to the scenes of misery and woe, degradation and sorrow that yet prevail on account of sin, and picture before your mental vision the glory of the perfect earth. Not a stain of sin mars the harmony and peace of a perfect society; not a bitter thought, not an unkind look or word; love, welling up from every heart, meets a kindred response in every other heart, and benevolence marks every act. There sickness shall be no more; not an ache nor a pain, nor any evidence of decay—not even the fear of such things. Think of all the pictures of comparative health and beauty of human form and feature that you have ever seen, and know that perfect humanity will be of still surpassing loveliness. The inward purity and mental and moral perfection will stamp and glorify every radiant countenance. Such will earth's society be; and weeping bereaved ones will have their tears all wiped away, when thus they realize the resurrection work complete. Rev. 21:4

And this is the change in human society only. We call to mind also that the earth, which was "made to be inhabited" by such a race of beings, is to be a fit and pleasing abode for them, as represented in the Edenic paradise, in which the representative man was at first placed. Paradise shall be restored. The earth shall no more bring forth thorns and briers, and require the sweat of man's face to yield his bread, but "the earth shall [easily and naturally] yield her increase." "The desert shall blossom as the rose"; the lower animal creation will be perfect, willing and obedient servants; nature with all its pleasing variety, will call to man from every direction to seek and know the glory and power and love of God; and mind and heart will rejoice in him. The restless desire for something new, that now prevails, is not a natural but an abnormal condition, due to our imperfection, and to our present unsatisfactory surroundings. It is not God-like restlessly to crave something new. Most things are old to God; and he rejoices most in those things which are old and perfect. So will it be with man when restored to the image of God. The perfect man will not know or appreciate fully, and hence will not prefer, the glory of spiritual being, because of a different nature, just as fishes and birds, for the same reason, prefer and enjoy each their own nature and element most. Man will be so absorbed and enraptured with the glory that surrounds him on the human plane that he will have no aspiration to, nor preference for, another nature or other conditions than those possessed. A glance at the present experience of the Church will illustrate this. "How hardly," with what difficulty, shall those who are rich in this world's goods enter into the kingdom of God. The few good things possessed, even under the present reign of evil and death, so captivate the human nature that we need special help from God to keep our eye and purpose fixed on the spiritual promises.

That the Christian Church, the body of Christ, is an exception to God's general plan for mankind, is evident from the statement that its selection was determined in the divine plan before the foundation of the world (Eph. 1:4, 5), at which time God not only foresaw the fall of the race into sin, but also predetermined the justification, the sanctification and the glorification of this class, which, during the Gospel age, he has been calling out of the world to be conformed to the image of his Son, to be partakers of the divine nature and to be fellow-heirs with Christ Jesus of the Millennial Kingdom for the establishment of universal righteousness and peace. Rom. 8:28-31

This shows that the election or choice of the Church was a predetermined thing on God's part; but mark, it is not an unconditional election of the *individual members* of the Church. Before the foundation of the world God determined that such a company should be selected for such a purpose within a specific time—the Gospel age. While we cannot doubt that God could have foreseen the action of each individual member of the Church, and could have foreknown just who would be worthy and therefore constitute the members of that "little flock," yet this is not the way in which God's Word presents the doctrine of election. It was not the thought of an individual predestination which the apostles sought to inculcate, but that *a class* was predetermined in God's purpose to fill the honorable position, the selection of which would be upon conditions of severe trials of faith and obedience and the sacrifice of earthly privileges, etc., even unto death. Thus by an individual trial, and by individually "overcoming," the individual members of the *predetermined class* are being chosen or accepted into all the blessings and benefits predetermined of God for this class.

The word "glorified" in Rom. 8:30, from the Greek *doxazo*, signifies *honored*. The position to which the Church is elected is one of great honor. No man could think of aspiring to so great an honor. Even our Lord Jesus was first invited before he aspired to it, as we read: "So also Christ glorified [*doxazo*—honored] not himself to be made an High Priest, but he that said unto him, 'Thou art my Son, today have I begotten thee.'" The heavenly Father thus honored our Lord Jesus; and all of the elect body who are to be joint-heirs with him will be thus honored by Jehovah's favor. The Church, like its Head, experiences a beginning of the "honor" when *begotten* of God to spiritual nature through the word of truth (James 1:18), and will be fully ushered into the honor when *born* of the Spirit, spiritual beings—in the image of the glorified Head. Those whom God would thus honor must be perfect and pure; and since we were by inheritance sinners, he not only called or invited us to the honor, but also provided *justification* from sin through the death of his Son, to enable us to receive the honor to which he calls us.

In selecting the little flock, God makes a very general call—"many are called." All are not called. The call was confined at first, during our Lord's ministry, to Israel after the flesh; but now, as many as the servants of God meet (Luke 14:23) are to be urged or constrained (not compelled) to come to this special feast of favor. But even of those who hear and come, all are not worthy. Wedding garments (the imputed righteousness of Christ) are provided, but some will not wear them, and must be rejected; and of those who do put on the robes of justification, and who receive the honor of being begotten to a new nature, some fail to make their calling and election sure by faithfulness to their covenant. Of those worthy to appear with the Lamb in glory, it is declared, "They are *called* and *chosen* and *faithful*." Rev. 14:1; 17:14

The call is true; the determination of God to select and exalt a Church is unchangeable; but who will be of this chosen class is conditional. All who would share the predestined honors must fulfil the conditions of the call. "Let us therefore fear, lest, a promise being left us of entering into his rest, any of you should seem to come short of it." (Heb. 4:1) While the great favor is not *of* him that willeth, nor *of* him that runneth, it is *to* him that willeth and *to* him that runneth, when called.

Having thus, we trust, clearly vindicated God's *absolute right and purpose* to do what he will with his own, we call attention to the fact that the principle which characterizes the bestowment of all God's favors is the general good of all.

While, then, on the authority of the Scriptures, we reckon it an established fact that the human and spiritual natures are separate and distinct—that the blending of the two natures is no part of God's design, but would be an imperfection, and that the change from one nature to another is not the rule, but the exception, in the single instance of the Christ—it becomes a matter of deep interest to learn how the change is to be accomplished, upon what conditions it may be attained and in what manner it will be effected.

The conditions on which the Church may be exalted with her Lord to the divine nature (2 Pet. 1:4) are precisely the same as the conditions on which he received it; even by following in his footprints (1 Pet. 2:21), presenting herself a living sacrifice, as he did, and then faithfully carrying out that consecration vow until the sacrifice terminates in death. This change of nature from human to divine is given as a reward to those who, within the Gospel age, sacrifice the *human nature*, as did our Lord, with all *its* interests, hopes and aims, present and future—even unto death. In the resurrection such will awake, not to share with the rest of mankind in the blessed restitution to human perfection and all its accompanying blessings, but to share the likeness and glory and joy of the Lord, as partakers with him of the divine nature. Rom. 8:17; 2 Tim. 2:12

The beginning and development of the new nature is likened to the beginning and development of human life. As in the one case there is a begetting and then a birth, so also in the other. The saints are said to be begotten of God through the Word of truth. (1 Pet. 1:3; 1 John 5:18; James 1:18) That is, they receive the first impulse in the divine life from God through his Word. When, having been justified freely by faith in the ransom, they hear the call, "Present your bodies a living sacrifice, holy, [ransomed, justified— and therefore] acceptable unto God, which is your reasonable service" (Rom. 12:1); and when, in obedience to that call, they fully consecrate their justified humanity to God, a living sacrifice, side by side with that of Jesus, it is accepted of God; and in that very act the spiritual life is begun. Such find themselves at once thinking and acting as the new [transformed] mind prompts, even to the crucifixion of the human desires. From the moment of consecration these are reckoned of God as "new creatures."

Thus to these *embryo* "new creatures" old things [human desires, hopes, plans, etc.] pass away, and all things become new. The embryo "new creature" continues to grow and develop, as the old human nature, with its hopes, aims, desires, etc., is crucified. These two processes progress simultaneously, from the time consecration begins until the death of the human and the birth of the spiritual result. As the Spirit of God continues to unfold, through his Word, more and more of his plans, he thus quickens even our mortal bodies (Rom. 8:11), enabling these mortal bodies to render him service; but in due time we will have new bodies—spiritual, heavenly, adapted in all respects to the new, divine mind.

The *birth* of the "new creature" is in the resurrection (Col. 1:18); and the resurrection of this class is designated the *first* (or choice) resurrection. (Rev. 20:6) It should be remembered that we are not actually spirit beings until the resurrection, though from the time we receive the spirit of adoption we are reckoned as such. (Rom. 8:23-25; Eph. 1:13, 14; Rom. 6:10, 11) When we become spirit beings actually, that is, when we are born of the Spirit, we will no longer be fleshly beings; for "that which is born of the Spirit *is spirit.*"

This birth to the spiritual nature in the resurrection must be preceded by a begetting of the Spirit at consecration, just as surely as the birth of the flesh is preceded by a begetting of the flesh. All that are born of the flesh in the likeness of the first Adam, the earthly, were first begotten of the flesh; and some have been begotten *again*, by the Spirit of God through the word of truth, that in due time they may be born of the Spirit into the heavenly likeness, in the first resurrection: "As we have borne the image of the earthly, *we* [the Church] shall also bear the image of the heavenly"—unless there be a falling away. 1 Cor. 15:49; Heb. 6:6

Though the acceptance of the heavenly call and our consecration in obedience to it be decided at one particular moment, the bringing of every thought into harmony with the mind of God is a gradual work; it is a gradual bending heavenward of that which naturally bends earthward. The Apostle terms this process a transforming work, saying, "Be not conformed to this world; but be ye transformed [to the heavenly nature] by the *renewing of your minds*, that ye may prove what is that good and acceptable and perfect will of God." Rom. 12:2

It should be noticed that these words of the Apostle are not addressed to the unbelieving world, but to those whom he recognizes as brethren, as shown by the preceding verse—"I beseech you, therefore, *brethren*, . . . that ye present your bodies living sacrifices, holy and acceptable unto God."

It is commonly believed that when a man is converted or turned from sin to righteousness, and from unbelief and opposition to God to reliance upon him, that is the transforming which Paul meant. Truly that is a great change—*a* transformation, but not *the* transformation that Paul here refers to. That is a transformation of character; but Paul refers to a transformation of nature promised to believers during the Gospel age, on certain conditions, and he was urging *believers* to fulfil those conditions. Had not such a transformation of *character* already taken place in those whom he addressed, he could not have termed them brethren—brethren, too, who had something "holy and acceptable unto God" to offer in sacrifice; for only those who are justified by faith in the ransom are reckoned of God as holy and acceptable. Transformation of *nature* results to those who, during the Gospel age, present their justified humanity a living sacrifice, as Jesus presented his perfect humanity a sacrifice, laying down all right and claim to future *human* existence, as well as ignoring present human gratification, privileges, rights, etc. The first thing sacrificed is the human will; and thenceforth we may not be guided either by our own or by any other human will, but only by the divine will. The divine will becomes our will, and we reckon the human will as not ours, but as the will of another, to be ignored and sacrificed. The divine will having become our will, we begin to think, to reason and to judge from the divine standpoint: God's plan becomes our plan, and God's ways become our ways. None can fully understand this transformation who have not in good faith presented themselves as sacrifices, and in consequence come to experience it. Previously we might enjoy anything that was not actually sinful; for the world and all its good things were made for man's enjoyment, the only difficulty being to subdue the sinful propensities. But the consecrated, the transformed, in addition to the effort to subdue sin, must sacrifice the present good things and devote all their energies to the service of God. And those faithful in service and sacrifice will indeed realize daily that this world is not their resting place, and that here they have no continuing city. But their hearts and hopes will be turned to that "rest that remaineth for the people of God." And that blessed hope in turn will quicken and inspire to continued sacrifice.

Thus, through consecration, the mind is renewed or transformed, and the desires, hopes and aims begin to rise toward the spiritual and unseen things promised, while the human hopes, etc., die. Those thus transformed, or in process of change, are reckoned "new creatures," begotten of God, and partakers to that extent of the divine nature. Mark well the difference between these "new creatures" and those believers and "brethren" who are only justified. Those of the latter class are still of the earth, earthy, and, aside from sinful desires, their hopes, ambitions, and aims are such as will be fully gratified in the promised restitution of all things. But those of the former class are not of this world, even as Christ is not of this world, and their hopes center in the things unseen, where Christ sitteth at the right hand of God. The prospect of earthly glory, so enchanting to the natural man, would no longer be a satisfying portion to those begotten of this heavenly hope, to those who see the glories of the heavenly promises, and who appreciate the part assigned them in the divine plan. This new, divine mind is the earnest of our inheritance of the complete divine nature—mind and body. Some may be a little startled by this expression, a divine body; but we are told that Jesus is now the express image of his Father's person, and that the overcomers will "be *like* him and see him as he *is*." (1 John 3:2) "There is a natural [human] body, and there is a spiritual body." (1 Cor. 15:44) We could not imagine either our divine Father or our Lord Jesus as merely great minds without bodies. Theirs are glorious spiritual bodies, though it doth not yet appear how great is the glory, and it shall not, until we also shall share the divine nature.

While this transforming of the *mind* from human to spiritual is a gradual work, the change from a human to a spiritual *body* will not be gradual, but instantaneous. (1 Cor. 15:52) Now, as Paul says, we have this treasure (the divine mind) in earthen vessels, but in due time the treasure will be in a glorious vessel appropriate to it—the spiritual body.

We have seen that the human nature is a likeness of the spiritual. (Gen. 5:1) For instance, God has a will, so have men and angels; God has reason and memory, so have his intelligent creatures—angels and men. The character of the mental operations of each is the same. With the same data for reasoning, and under similar conditions, these different natures are able to arrive at the same conclusions. Though the mental faculties of the divine, the angelic and the human natures are similar, yet we know that the spiritual natures have powers beyond and above the human—powers which result, we think, not from different faculties, but from the wider range of the same faculties and the different circumstances under which they operate. The human nature is a perfect earthly image of the spiritual nature, having the same faculties, but confined to the earthly sphere, and with ability and disposition to discern only so much beyond it as God sees fit to reveal for man's benefit and happiness.

The divine is the highest order of the spiritual nature; and how immeasurable is the distance between God and his creatures! We are able to catch only glimpses of the glory of the divine wisdom, power and goodness as in panoramic view he causes some of his mighty works to pass before us. But we may measure and comprehend the glory of perfect humanity.

With these thoughts clearly in mind, we are able to appreciate how the change from the human to the spiritual nature is effected, viz., by carrying the same mental powers over to higher conditions. When clothed with the heavenly body, we shall have the heavenly powers which belong to that glorious body; and we shall have the range of thought and scope of power which belong to it.

The change or transformation of mind, from earthly to heavenly, which the consecrated experience here, is the beginning of that change of nature. It is not a change of brain, nor a miracle in its changed operation, but it is the will and the bent of mind that are changed. Our will and sentiments represent our individuality; hence we are transformed, and reckoned as actually belonging to the heavenly nature, when our wills and sentiments are thus changed. True, this is but a very small beginning; but a begetting, as this is termed, is always but a small beginning; yet it is the earnest or assurance of the finished work. Eph. 1:13, 14

Some have asked, How shall we know ourselves when changed? How shall we then know that we are the same beings that lived and suffered and sacrificed that we might be partakers of this glory? Will *we* be the same conscious beings? Most assuredly, yes. If *we* be dead with Christ, *we* shall also live with him. (Rom. 6:8) Changes which daily occur to our human bodies do not cause us to forget the past, or to lose our identity.*

These thoughts may help us to understand also how the Son, when changed from spiritual to human conditions—to human nature and earthly limitations—was a man; and though it was the same being in both cases, under the first conditions he was spiritual and under the second conditions he was human. Because the two natures are separate and

---

*Our human bodies are constantly changing. Science declares that each seven years witnesses a complete change in our component atoms. So the promised change from human to spiritual bodies will not destroy either memory or identity, but will increase their power and range. The same divine mind that now is ours, with the same memory, the same reasoning powers, etc., will then find its powers expanded to immeasurable heights and depths, in harmony with its new spiritual body; and memory will trace all our career from earliest human infancy, and we will be able, by contrast, fully to realize the glorious reward of our sacrifice. But this could not be the case if the human were not an *image* of the spiritual.

distinct, and yet the one a likeness of the other, therefore, the same mental faculties (memory, etc.) being common to both, Jesus could realize his former glory which he had before becoming a man, but which he had not when he had become a man, as his words prove—"Father, glorify thou me with thine own self, with the glory which I *had* with thee before the world was" (John 17:5)—the glory of the spiritual nature. And that prayer is more than answered in his present exaltation to the highest form of spirit being, the divine nature.

Referring again to Paul's words, we notice that he does not say, Do not conform yourselves to this world, but transform yourselves into the divine likeness; but he says, "*Be* not conformed, . . . but *be* ye transformed." This is well expressed; for we do not either conform or transform ourselves; but we do either submit ourselves to be conformed to the world by the worldly influences, the spirit of the world around us, or submit ourselves to the will of God, the holy will or Spirit, to be transformed by heavenly influences exercised through the Word of God. You that are consecrated, to which influences are you submitting? The transforming influences lead to present sacrifice and suffering, but the end is glorious. If you are developing under these transforming influences, you are proving daily what is that good and acceptable and perfect will of God.

Let such as have laid their all upon the altar of sacrifice continually bear in mind that, while the Word of God contains both earthly and heavenly promises, only the latter belong to us. Our treasure is in heaven: let our hearts continually be there. Our calling is not only to the spiritual nature, but to the highest order of the spiritual, the divine nature—"so much better than the angels." (2 Pet. 1:4; Heb. 1:4) This heavenly calling is confined to the Gospel age: it was never made before it, and it will cease with its close. An earthly calling was made, though imperfectly understood, before the heavenly calling, and we are told that it will be continued after the Gospel age. Life [for those restored as human beings] and immortality [the prize for which the body of Christ is running] have both been brought to light during this age. (2 Tim. 1:10) Both the human and spiritual natures will be glorious in their perfection, yet distinct and separate. No insignificant feature of the glory of God's finished work will be the beautiful variety, yet wonderful harmony, of all things, animate and inanimate—harmony with each other and harmony with God.

The Church of God

"Zion, arise, break forth in songs
　　Of everlasting joy;
To God eternal praise belongs,
　　Who doth thy foes destroy.
Thou Church of God, awake! awake!
　　For light beams from on high;
From earth and dust thy garments shake,
　　Thy glory's drawing nigh.

"To raise thee high above the earth,
　　God will his power employ;
He'll turn thy mourning into mirth,
　　Thy sorrow into joy.
In shining robes thyself array,
　　Put on thy garments pure;
Thy King shall lead thee in the way
　　That's holy, safe and sure."

STUDY XI
THE THREE WAYS—THE BROAD WAY, THE NARROW WAY, THE HIGHWAY

"WIDE is the gate of destruction, and broad that way leading thither; and many are they who enter through it. How narrow is the gate of life! how difficult that way leading thither! and how few are they who find it!" Matt. 7:13, 14, *Diaglott translation*

"And a highway shall be there, and a way, and it shall be called the way of holiness; the unclean shall not pass over it; but it shall be for those: the wayfaring men, though fools, shall not err therein. No lion shall be there, nor any ravenous beast shall go up thereon, nor be found there; but they that walk there shall be delivered." Isa. 35:8, 9

Three ways, the "broad road," the "narrow way" and the "highway," are thus brought to our attention in the Scriptures.

The Broad Road to Destruction

This road is thus named because it is most easy to the degenerate human race. Six thousand years ago, as a sinner condemned to destruction, Adam (and the race represented in him) started upon this road, and after nine hundred and thirty years he reached its end—destruction. As years and centuries have rolled on, the downward path has become more and more smoothly worn, and the race has sped more and more rapidly to destruction, the way becoming daily more glazed and slimed and slippery with sin. And not only

205

does the way grow more slippery, but mankind daily loses the power of resistance, so that now the average length of human life is about thirty-five years. Men now reach the end of the road—destruction—nine hundred years quicker than did the first man.

For six thousand years the race has steadily pursued the broad, downward way. Only a few, comparatively, have tried to change their course and retrace their steps. In fact, to retrace all the steps, and reach the original perfection, has been impossible, though the effort of some to do so has been commendable, and not without beneficial results. For six thousand years sin and death have reigned relentlessly over mankind, and driven them upon this broad road to destruction. And not until the Gospel age was a *way* of escape brought to light. Though in previous ages rays of hope were dimly seen in types and shadows, which were joyfully hailed and acted upon by a few, yet life and immortality were not brought to light until the appearing of our Lord and Savior, Jesus Christ, and the proclamation by the apostles of the good tidings of redemption and remission of sins and a consequent *resurrection from the destruction*. (2 Tim. 1:10) The teachings of Jesus and the apostles bring to light *life*—a restitution or restoration to life for all mankind, as based upon the merit and sacrifice of the Redeemer; and they show this to be the significance of many Old Testament types. They also bring to light *immortality*, the prize of the high calling of the Gospel Church.

Although a way of escape from the broad road to destruction has been brought to light through the gospel, the great mass of mankind heeds not the good tidings, because depraved by sin and blinded by the Adversary. Those who now gratefully accept the promise of life, restoration to human existence, through Christ, have pointed out to them a new way which has been opened up, by which consecrated believers may go beyond the human nature and be changed to a higher nature—the spiritual. This new way "consecrated for *us*"—the royal priesthood (Heb. 10:20)—our Lord called

"The Narrow Way to Life."

Our Master tells us that it is because of the narrowness of this way that the many prefer to remain on the broad road to destruction. "Strait [difficult] is the gate and narrow is the way that leadeth unto life, and few there be that find it."

Before considering this way and its dangers and difficulties, let us notice the end to which it leads—life. As already seen, life may be enjoyed on various planes of being, higher as well as lower than human. Life is a broad and comprehensive term, but here our Lord uses it in reference to that highest form of life, pertaining to the divine nature—immortality—the prize for which he invited us to run. What is life? We not only realize it in ourselves, but we see its operation in lower animals, and even in vegetation, and we are told of its existence in higher forms, angelic and divine. How shall we define a term so comprehensive?

While we may not be able to discover the secret springs of life in all, we may safely assume that the Divine Being, Jehovah, is the great fountain of all life, from which all these springs are supplied. All living things result from and depend on him for life. All life, whether in God or in his creatures, is the same: it is an energizing principle, not a substance. It is a principle which *inheres* in God, but which in his creatures *results* from certain causes which God has ordained, and of it he is therefore the cause, the author or fountain. Hence the creature is in no sense a part or an offspring of the Creator's essence or nature, as some imagine, but he is God's handiwork infused with life.

Recognizing the fact that only in the divine nature is life independent, unlimited, exhaustless, ever continuous and neither produced nor controlled by circumstances, we see that of necessity Jehovah is superior to those physical laws and supplies which he ordained for the sustenance of his creatures. It is this quality, which pertains only to the divine nature, that is described by the term *immortality*. As shown in the preceding chapter, *immortal* signifies death-proof, consequently disease and pain-proof. In fact, *immortality* may be used as a synonym for *divinity*. From the divine, immortal fountain proceed all life and blessing, every good and perfect gift, as from the sun the earth receives her light and vigor.

The sun is the great fountain of light to the earth, illuminating all things, producing many varieties of color and shades of light, according to the nature of the object upon which it shines. The same sunlight shining upon a diamond, upon a brick, and upon various kinds of glass, produces strikingly different effects. The light is the same, but the objects upon which it shines differ in their capacity to receive and to transmit it. So with life: it all flows from the one exhaustless fountain. The oyster has life, but its organism is such that it cannot make use of much life, just as the brick cannot reflect much of the light of the sun. So with each of the higher manifestations of life, in beast, fish and fowl. Like the various kinds of glass under sunlight, so these various creatures show forth differently the various organic powers they possess, when life animates their organisms.

The polished diamond is so adapted to the light that it appears as though it possessed it within itself, and were itself a miniature sun. So with man, one of the masterpieces of God's creation, made only "a little lower than the angels." He was so grandly formed as to be able to receive and retain life by the use of the means which God supplied, and never grow dim. Thus was Adam before he fell grander than any other earthly creature, not by reason of any difference in the *life principle* implanted, but because of a grander *organism*. Yet, let us remember that as the diamond can reflect no light except when shone upon by the sun, so man can possess and enjoy life only as the supply of life is continued. Man has not inherent life: he is no more a fountain of life than a diamond is a fountain of light. And one of the very strongest evidences that we have not an exhaustless supply of life in ourselves, or, in other words, that we are not immortal, is that since sin entered, death has passed upon all our race.

God had arranged that man in Eden should have access to life-sustaining trees, and the paradise in which he was placed was abundantly supplied with numbers of "every [kind of] tree" good for food or for adornment. (Gen. 2:9, 16, 17) Among the trees of life good for food was one forbidden. While for a time forbidden to eat of the tree of knowledge, he was permitted to eat freely of trees which sustained life perfectly; and he was separated from them only after transgression, that thereby the death-penalty might go into effect. Gen. 3:22

Thus the glory and beauty of humanity are seen to be dependent on the continued supply of life, just as the beauty of the diamond is dependent on the continued supply of sunlight. When sin deprived humanity of the right to life, and the supply was withheld, immediately the jewel began to lose its brilliancy and beauty, and finally it is deprived of its last vestige in the tomb. His beauty consumes away like a moth. (Psa. 39:11) As the diamond loses its beauty and brilliancy when the light is withdrawn, so man loses life when God withholds the supplies from him. "Yea, man giveth up the ghost [life] and where is he?" (Job 14:10) "His sons come to honor, and he knoweth it not; and they are brought low, but he perceiveth it not of them." (Verse 21) "For there is no work, nor device, nor knowledge, nor wisdom, in the grave whither thou goest." (Eccl. 9:10) But since a ransom has been found, since the death penalty has been provided by the Redeemer, the jewel is to have its beauty restored, and is again to reflect perfectly the Creator's image when the Sun of Righteousness shall arise with healing in his wings. (Mal. 4:2) It is because of the sin-offering, the sacrifice of Christ, that "All that are in their graves shall come forth." There shall be a restitution of all things; first an opportunity or offer of restitution to all, and ultimately the attainment of human perfection by all who will obey the Redeemer.

This, however, is not the reward to which Jesus refers as the end of the narrow way. From other scriptures we learn that the reward promised to those who walk the narrow way is the "divine nature"—life inherent, life in that superlative degree which only the divine nature can possess—immortality. What a hope! Dare we aspire to such a height of glory? Surely not without positive and explicit invitation could any rightfully thus aspire.

From 1 Tim. 6:14-16 we learn that the immortal or divine nature was originally the possession of divinity only. We read: "He [Jesus] in his time [the Millennial age] will show who is the blessed and only potentate—the King of kings and Lord of lords, who only hath immortality, dwelling in the light which no man can approach unto, whom no man hath seen nor can see." All other beings, angels, men, beasts, birds, fish, etc., are but vessels holding each its measure of life, and all differing in character, capacity, and quality according to the organism which it has pleased the Creator to provide for each.

Further, we learn that Jehovah, who alone possessed immortality originally, has highly exalted his Son, our Lord Jesus, to the same divine, immortal nature; hence he is now the express image of the Father's person. (Heb. 1:3) So we read, "As the Father hath LIFE IN HIMSELF [God's definition of "immortality"—*life in himself*—not drawn from other sources, nor dependent on circumstances, but independent, inherent life], *so* hath he given to the Son to have LIFE IN HIMSELF." (John 5:26) Since the resurrection of the Lord Jesus, then, two beings are immortal; and, amazing grace! the same offer is made to the Bride of the Lamb, being selected during the Gospel age. Yet not all of the great company who are nominally of the Church will receive this great prize, but only that "little flock" of overcomers who so run as to obtain it; who follow closely in the Master's footsteps; who, like him, walk the narrow way of sacrifice, even unto death. These, when born from the dead in the resurrection, will have the divine nature and form. This immortality, the independent, self-existent, divine nature, is the life to which the narrow way leads.

This class is not to be raised from the tomb human beings; for we are assured by the Apostle that, though sown in the tomb natural bodies, they will be raised spiritual bodies. These all shall be "changed," and even as they once bore the image of the earthly, human nature, they shall bear the image of the heavenly. But "it doth not yet appear what we shall be"—what a spiritual body is; but "we know that when he shall appear, we shall be *like him*," and share in "the glory to be revealed." 1 John 3:2; Col. 1:27; 2 Cor. 4:17; John 17:22; 1 Pet. 5:10; 2 Thess. 2:14

Not only is this high calling to a *change of nature* confined exclusively to the Gospel age, but it is the only offer of this age. Hence our Lord's words quoted at the beginning of this chapter include on the broad road to destruction all who are not on the way to the only prize *now offered*. All others are still on the broad road—these only have as yet escaped the condemnation that is on the world. This, the only way of life now open, because of its difficulty, finds few who care to walk in it. The masses of mankind in their weakness prefer the broad, easy way of self-gratification.

The narrow way, while it ends in life, in immortality, might be called a way of death, since its prize is gained through the sacrifice of the human nature even unto death. It is the narrow way *of* death *to* life. Being reckoned free from the Adamic guilt and the death penalty, the consecrated voluntarily surrender or *sacrifice* those human rights, reckoned theirs, which in due time they, with the world in general, would have actually received. As "the man Christ Jesus" laid down or sacrificed his life for the world, so these become joint-sacrificers with him. Not that his sacrifice was insufficient and that others were *needed*; but while his is all-sufficient, these are permitted to serve and to suffer with him in order to become his bride and joint-heir. So, then, while the world is under condemnation to death, and is dying *with* Adam, this "little flock," through the process of faith reckonings and sacrifice, already described, are said to die *with* Christ. They sacrifice and die *with* him as human beings, in order to become partakers of the divine nature and glories *with* him; for we believe that if we be dead *with* him, we shall also live *with* him. If we suffer *with* him, we shall also be glorified *together*. Rom. 8:17 and 2 Tim. 2:11, 12

In the beginning of the Millennial age, those who now walk the narrow way will have gained the great prize for which they ran, immortality; and being thus clothed with the divine nature and power, they will be prepared for the great work of restoring and blessing the world during that age. With the end of the Gospel age, the narrow way to immortality will close, because the select "little flock" that it was designed to test and prove will have been completed. "Now is the accepted [Greek, *dektos*, acceptable or receivable] time"—the time in which sacrificers, coming in the merit of Jesus and becoming dead with him, are *acceptable* to God—a sacrifice of sweet odor. Death, as the Adamic penalty, will not be permitted forever; it will be abolished during the Millennial age; as a *sacrifice* it will be acceptable and rewarded only during the Gospel age.

It is only as *"new creatures"* that the saints of this age are on the way to life; and only as human beings are we consecrated to destruction, as sacrifices. If, as human creatures, we be dead with Christ, as new, spiritual beings, we shall live with him. (Rom. 6:8) The mind of God in us, the transformed mind, is the germ of the new nature.

The new life would be easily choked; and Paul assures us that when begotten of the spirit through the truth, if we live after the flesh, we shall die (lose our life), but if we, through the spirit, do mortify (put to death) the deeds of the body (the disposition of the human nature), we (as new creatures) shall live; for the sons of God are those led by the spirit of God. (Rom. 8:13, 14) This is a thought of utmost importance to all the consecrated; for if we have covenanted with God to sacrifice the human nature, and if that sacrifice was accepted by him, it is useless to attempt to take it back. The human is reckoned of God as dead now, and must actually die, never again to be restored. All that can be gained, then, by turning back to live after the flesh, is a little human gratification at the expense of the new spiritual nature.

There are, however, many consecrated ones desirous of

the *prize*, and who have been begotten of the spirit, who are partially overcome by the allurements of the world, the desires of the flesh, or the arts of the devil. They partially lose sight of the prize set before us, and try to walk upon a middle road—to keep the favor of God and the favor of the world, forgetting that "the friendship of the world is enmity with God" (James 4:4), and that the instructions to those running the race for the prize are, Love not the world, and, Seek not honor one of another, but that honor which cometh from God only. 1 John 2:15; John 5:44

These, who love the present world, but who have not wholly forsaken the Lord and despised their covenant, receive a scourging and purifying by the fire of affliction. As the Apostle expresses it, they are delivered over to Satan for the destruction of the flesh, that the spirit (the newly begotten nature) may be saved in the day of the Lord Jesus. (1 Cor. 5:5) And if rightly exercised by the discipline, they will finally be received into the spiritual condition. They will have everlasting, spirit life as angels have it, but will lose the prize of immortality. They will serve God in his temple, and stand *before* the throne, having palms in their hands (Rev. 7:9-17); but though that will be glorious, it will not be so glorious as the position of the "little flock" of overcomers, who will be kings and priests unto God, seated with Jesus *in the throne* as his bride and joint-heir, and with him crowned with immortality.

Ours is a rugged, steep, narrow way, and were it not that strength is furnished for each successive step of the journey, we could never reach the goal. But our Captain's word is encouraging: Be of good cheer; I have overcome; my grace is sufficient for thee, for my strength is made perfect in weakness. (John 16:33; 2 Cor. 12:9) The difficulties of this way are to act as a separating principle to sanctify and refine a "peculiar people" to be "heirs of God and joint-heirs with Jesus Christ." In view of these things, let us come boldly to the throne of grace, that we may obtain mercy and find grace to help in time of need, while we fight the good fight of faith and lay hold on "the crown of glory"— immortality, the divine nature. 2 Tim. 4:8; 1 Peter 5:4

The Highway of Holiness

While the special hope of the Gospel age is so surpassingly glorious, and the way to it is correspondingly difficult—narrow, hedged in by hardships and dangers at every step—so that few find it, and obtain the great prize at its end, the new order of things in the age to come is to be entirely different. As a different hope is held out, so also a different *way* leads to it. The way to immortality has been a way which required the sacrifice of the otherwise lawful and proper hopes, ambitions and desires—the sacrifice forever of the human nature. But the way to human perfection, to restitution, the hope of the world, requires only the putting away of sin: not the sacrifice of human rights and privileges, but their proper enjoyment. It will lead to personal purification and restoration to the image of God as enjoyed by Adam before sin entered the world.

The way back to actual human perfection is to be made very plain and easy; so plain that none may mistake the way; so plain that "the wayfaring man, and those unacquainted therewith, shall not go astray" (Isa. 35:8—*Leeser*); so plain that none will need to teach his neighbor, saying, Know the Lord, for all shall know the Lord from the least unto the greatest. (Jer. 31:34) Instead of being a narrow way that few can find, it is termed "a highway," a public roadway—not a narrow, steep, rugged, difficult, hedged byway, but a way specially prepared for *easy* travel—specially arranged for the convenience and comfort of the travelers. Verses 8 and 9 show that it is a public road, open to all the redeemed—every man. Every man for whom Christ died, who will recognize and avail himself of the opportunities and blessings purchased by the precious blood, may go up on this Highway of Holiness to the grand goal of perfect restitution to human perfection and everlasting life.

Nor will these be *reckoned* justified and granted a reckoned standing of holiness and perfection in the sight of God; when started upon this highway of holiness they may go up thereon to *actual* perfection, as a result of endeavor and obedience, to which all things will be made favorable by their Redeemer, then reigning in power. Each individual will, according to his necessities, be aided by the wise and perfect administration of the new kingdom. This, as will occur to some, is the legitimate result of the ransom. Since our Lord, the man Christ Jesus, gave himself a ransom for all, and desires all to come to a knowledge of the truth, and thereby to actual perfection, why does he not at once make a good and broad highway for all? Why does he not remove the obstructions, the stumbling-stones, the pitfalls and snares? Why not help the sinner back to full harmony with God, instead of making the way narrow, rugged, thorny, hard to find, and still harder to walk in? A failure rightly to divide the Word of truth, and to see that the present narrow way leads to the special prize, and is for the trial and selection of a little flock of joint-heirs, the body of Christ, which, when selected and exalted with their Head, shall bless all nations, has led some to very confused ideas on the subject. Failing to see God's plan, many try to preach a highway of holiness, an easy way to life, in the present age, when no such way exists, and they confuse and compromise the matter to fit the facts and the Scriptures with their mistaken theories. On the highway soon to be opened, only sinful things will be prohibited, while those who travel the narrow way must deny themselves and sacrifice many things not sinful, as well as war continually against besetting sins. This is a pathway of sacrifice, as that of the coming age is to be a highway of righteousness.

Of that highway it is significantly stated in symbolic language that "No lion shall be there, nor any ravenous beast shall go up thereon; it shall not be found there." (Isa. 35:9) How many frightful lions are now in the way of those who would be glad to forsake sinful ways, and to pursue righteousness! There is the lion of a degenerate public sentiment, which deters many from venturing to obey the dictates of conscience in matters of everyday life—dress, home, and business arrangements, etc. The lion of temptation to strong drink hinders thousands who would be glad to see it removed. Prohibitionists and temperance workers now find a herculean task on their hands, which only the authority and power of the next age can remove; and the same may be said of other worthy efforts at moral reform. "Nor shall any ravenous beast go up thereon." No giant corporations, organized to advance selfish, individual interests at the expense of the general good, will be tolerated. "They shall not hurt nor destroy in all my holy mountain" (kingdom) saith the Lord. (Isa. 11:9) Though there will be difficulties to labor against in overcoming propensities to evil, etc., yet, in comparison with the narrow way of this age, that will be an easy way. The stones (stumbling-stones) shall all be gathered out, and the standard of truth shall be lifted up for the people. (Isa. 62:10) Ignorance and superstition will be things of the past, and righteousness will receive its due reward, while to evil will be meted out its just deserts. (Mal. 3:15, 18) By wholesome chastisements, fitting encouragements and plain instructions, as returned prodigals, mankind will be trained and disciplined up to the grand perfection from which father Adam fell. Thus "the ransomed of the Lord *shall return* [from destruction, by the grand highway of holiness] . . . with songs and everlasting joy upon their heads; they shall obtain joy and gladness, and sorrow and sighing shall flee away." (Isa. 35:10) Our Lord referred to but two of these ways, because the third was not yet due to be opened up—just as when announcing the good tidings, he said, "This scripture is fulfilled in your ears," but omitted mentioning the "day of vengeance," because it was not then due. (Compare Luke 4:19 and Isa. 61:2.) Now, however, as the narrow way draws to a close, the grand highway of righteousness begins to be seen more and more distinctly, in the light of the dawning day.

Thus we have found a "Broad Road," on which at present the masses of mankind travel, deluded by the "prince of this world," and led by perverted tastes. We have found that it was opened up and that our race was started in its headlong course upon it by "*one man's* disobedience." We have found that the "Highway of Holiness" is to be opened up by our Lord, who gave himself a ransom for all and redeems *all* from the destruction to which the "Broad Road" leads, and that it will, in due time, be accessible and easy for all the redeemed ones whom he bought with his own precious blood. We have found, furthermore, that the present "Narrow Way," opened up by the merit of the same precious blood, is a special way leading to a special prize, and is made specially narrow and difficult as a *test* and discipline for those now being selected to be made partakers of the *divine* nature and joint-heirs with our Lord Jesus in the Kingdom of glory soon to be revealed for the blessing of all. Such as have *this hope*—who see this prize— may count all other hopes as but loss and dross in comparison. Phil. 3:8-15

STUDY XII
EXPLANATION OF CHART
REPRESENTING THE PLAN OF THE AGES

THE AGES—THE HARVESTS—PLANES OF ACTUAL AND RECKONED STANDING—
THE COURSE OF OUR LORD JESUS—THE COURSE OF HIS FOLLOWERS—
THREE CLASSES IN THE NOMINAL CHURCH—SEPARATION IN THE HARVEST—
THE ANOINTED CLASS GLORIFIED—THE GREAT TRIBULATION CLASS—THE
TARES BURNED—THE WORLD BLESSED—THE OUTCOME GLORIOUS.

IN THE back of this volume is attached a chart representing the plan of God for the world's salvation. By it we have sought to aid the mind, through the eye, in understanding something of the progressive character of God's plan, and the progressive steps which must be taken by all who ever attain the complete "change" from the human to the divine nature.

First, we have an outline of the three great dispensations, *A, B, C*—the first of these, *A*, lasting from man's creation to the flood; the second, *B*, from the flood to the commencement of the Millennial reign of Christ, at his second advent; and the third, or "Dispensation of the Fulness of Times," *C*, lasting from the beginning of Christ's reign for "ages to come." (Eph. 1:10; 2:7) These three great dispensations are frequently referred to in the Scriptures: *A* is called "the world that was"; *B* by our Lord Jesus is called "this world," by Paul "the present evil world," by Peter "the world that now is." *C* is called "the world to come, wherein dwelleth righteousness," in contrast with the present evil world. Now evil rules and the righteous suffer, while in the world to come this order is to be reversed: righteousness will rule and evil-doers will suffer, and finally all evil will be destroyed.

In each of these three great dispensations, epochs or "worlds" God's plan with reference to men has a distinct and separate outline; yet each is but a part of the one great plan which, when complete, will exhibit the divine wisdom—though these parts considered separately fail to show their deep design. Since the first "world" ("heavens and earth," or that order of things) passed away at the time of the flood, it follows that it must have been a different order from "this present evil world," of which our Lord said Satan is the prince; hence the prince of this present evil world was not the prince of the world that was before the flood, although he was not without influence then. Several scriptures throw light on God's dealings during that time, and thus give a clear insight into his plan as a whole. The thought suggested by these is that the first "world," or the dispensation before the flood, was under the supervision and special ministration of angels, who were permitted to try what they could do to recover the fallen and degenerate race. Doubtless, with God's permission, they were anxious to try it; for their interest was manifested in the singing and shouting for joy over the works of creation. (Job 38:7) That angels were the permitted, though unsuccessful rulers of that first epoch is not only indicated by all references to that period, but it may reasonably be inferred from the Apostle's remark when, contrasting the present dispensation with the past and the future, he says (Heb. 2:5), "Unto the angels hath he not put in subjection the world to come." No; that world is to be under the control of the Lord Jesus and his joint-heirs; and hence it will not only be a more righteous administration than that of "the present evil world," but it will also be more successful than that of the first world or dispensation under the "ministration of angels," whose inability to reclaim the race is manifest from the fact that man's wickedness became so great that God in his wrath and righteous indignation destroyed with a flood the whole of the race then living with the exception of eight persons. Gen. 7:13

During the "present evil world," man is permitted to try governing himself; but by reason of the fall he is under the control of Satan, the "prince of this world," against whose secret machinations and intrigues he has vainly striven in his efforts at self-government during the long period from the flood to the present time. This attempted reign of man under Satan is to end in the greatest time of trouble the world has ever known. And thus will have been proven the futility, not only of angelic power to save the race, but also of man's own efforts to reach satisfactory conditions.

The second of these great dispensations, *B*, is composed of three distinct ages, each of which, as a progressive step, leads upward and onward in God's plan.

Age *D* was the one during which God's special dealings were with such patriarchs as Abraham, Isaac and Jacob.

Age *E* is the Jewish Age, or the period following the death of Jacob, during which all of his posterity were treated by God as his special charge—"his people." To these he showed special favors, and declared, "*You only* have I known (recognized with favor) of all the families of the earth." (Amos 3:2) These, as a nation, were typical of the Christian Church, the "holy nation, the peculiar people." The promises made to them were typical of the "better promises" made to us. Their journey through the wilderness to the land of promise was typical of our journey through the wilderness of sin to the heavenly Canaan. Their sacrifices justified them typically, not really; for the blood of bulls and goats can never take away sin. (Heb. 10:4) But in the Gospel Age, *F*, we have the "better sacrifices," which do make atonement for the sins of the whole world. We have the "royal priesthood," composed of all those who offer themselves to God "living sacrifices," holy and acceptable, through Jesus Christ, who is the Chief or "High Priest of our profession." (Heb. 3:1) In the Gospel age we find the realities of which the Jewish age and its services and ordinances were shadows. Heb. 10:1

The Gospel age, *F*, is the period during which the body of Christ is called out of the world, and shown by faith the crown of life, and the exceeding great and precious promises whereby (by obedience to the call and its requirements) they may become partakers of the divine nature. (2 Pet. 1:4) Evil is still permitted to reign over or rule the world, in order that by contact with it these may be tried to see whether they are willing to give up the human nature with its privileges and blessings, a living sacrifice, being made conformable to Jesus' death, that they may be accounted worthy to be in his likeness in the resurrection. Psa. 17:15

The third great dispensation, *C*, is to be composed of many ages—"The Ages to Come." The first of these, the Millennial age, *G*, is the only one concerning which we have any definite information. It is the thousand years during which Christ will reign over and thereby bless all the families of the earth, accomplishing the "restitution of all things spoken by the mouth of all the holy prophets." (Acts 3:19-21) During that age, sin and death shall be forever blotted out; for "Christ must reign till he hath put all enemies under his feet. . . . The last enemy that shall be destroyed is death"—Adamic death. (1 Cor. 15:25, 26) That will be the great reconstruction period. Associated with Christ Jesus in that reign will be the Church, his bride, his body, even as he promised, saying, "To him that overcometh will I grant to sit with me in my throne, even as I also overcame, and am set down with my Father in his throne." Rev. 3:21

The "Ages to Come," *H*, following the great reconstruction period, are to be ages of perfection, blessedness and happiness, regarding the work of which, the Scriptures are silent. It is enough to know, at this distance, that they will be ages of glory and blessing under divine favor.

Each of these dispensations has its distinct seasons for the beginning and development of its work, and each ends with a harvest manifesting its fruits. The harvest at the close of the Jewish age was a period of forty years, lasting from the beginning of Jesus' ministry, when he was *anointed* of God by the Spirit (Acts 10:37, 38), A.D. 29, until the destruction of Jerusalem, A.D. 70. In this harvest the Jewish age ended and the Gospel age began. There was a lapping of these dispensations, as represented in the diagram.

The Jewish age ended in a measure when, at the end of his three and one-half years' ministry, the Lord rejected that nation, saying, "Your house is left unto you desolate." (Matt. 23:38) Yet there was favor shown them for three and one-half years after this, by the confining to them of the Gospel call, in harmony with the prophet's declaration (Dan. 9:24-27) regarding seventy weeks (of years) of favor toward them, in the midst of the last of which, Messiah should be cut off (die), but not for himself. "Christ died [not for himself, but] for our sins," and thus caused the sacrifice and the oblation to cease, in the midst of the week—three and one-half years before the expiration of the seventy covenant weeks of Jewish favor. When the true sacrifice had been made, of course the typical ones could no longer be recognized by Jehovah.

There was, then, a fuller sense in which that Jewish age closed with the end of the seventieth week, or three and one-half years after the cross—after which the Gospel was preached to the Gentiles also, beginning with Cornelius. (Acts 10:45) This ended their age so far as God's favor toward and recognition of the Jewish church was concerned; their national existence terminated in the great time of trouble which followed.

In that period of the Jewish harvest the Gospel age had its beginning. The design of this age is the call, development and trial of "the Christ of God"—Head and body. This is the Spirit dispensation; hence, it is proper to say that the Gospel age began with the anointing of Jesus "with the Holy Spirit and with power" (Acts 10:38; Luke 3:22; 4:1, 18) at the time of his baptism. In relation to the Church, his body, it commenced three and a half years later.

A "harvest" constitutes the closing period of the Gospel age also, during which there is again a lapping of two ages—the Gospel age ending, and the Restitution or Millennial age beginning. The Gospel age closes by stages, as did its pattern or "shadow," the Jewish age. As there the first seven years of the harvest were devoted in a special sense to a work in and for Israel after the flesh, and were years of favor, so here we find a similar seven years indicated as having the same bearing upon the Gospel Church, to be followed by a period of trouble ("fire") upon the world, as a punishment for wickedness, and as a preparation for the reign of righteousness—of which more again.

The Path to Glory

K, L, M, N, P, R, each represents a different plane. *N* is the plane of *perfect human* nature. Adam was on this plane before he sinned; but from the moment of disobedience he fell to the depraved or sinful plane, *R*, on which all his posterity are born. This corresponds to the "Broad Way" which leads to destruction. *P* represents the plane of typical justification, reckoned as effected by the sacrifices of the Law. It was not actual perfection, for "the Law made nothing perfect."— Heb. 7:19

N represents not only the plane of human perfection, as once occupied by the perfect man, Adam, but also the standing of all justified persons. "Christ died for our sins, according to the Scriptures," and in consequence all believers in Christ—all who accept of his perfect and finished work as their justifier—are, through faith, reckoned of God as justified, as though perfect men, as though they had never been sinners. In God's sight, then, all who accept of Christ as their Redeemer are reckonedly on the plane of human perfection, *N*. This is the only standpoint from which man may approach God, or have any communion with him. All on this plane God calls sons—human sons. Adam was thus a son (Luke 3:38), and had communion before he became disobedient. All who accept of our Lord Jesus' finished ransom work are counted or *reckoned* as restored to primitive purity; and in consequence they have fellowship or communion with God.

During the Gospel age God has made a special offer to justified human beings, telling them that on certain conditions they may experience a change of nature, that they may cease to be earthly, human beings, and become heavenly, spiritual beings, like Christ, their Redeemer. Some believers—justified persons—are satisfied with what joy and peace they have through believing in the forgiveness of their sins, and so do not heed the voice which calls them to come up higher. Others, moved by the love of God as shown in their ransom from sin, and feeling that they are not their own, having been bought with a price, say, "Lord, what wilt thou have me to do?" Such have the Lord's answer through Paul, who says, "I beseech you, *brethren*, by the mercies of God, that ye present your bodies a living *sacrifice*, holy, acceptable to God, your reasonable service." (Rom. 12:1) What does the Apostle mean by thus urging the presentation of ourselves as living sacrifices? He means that we should consecrate to God's service every power and talent we possess, that henceforth we may live not for self, nor for friends, nor for family, nor for the world, nor for anything else but for, and in the obedient service of, him who bought us with his own precious blood.

But since God would not accept of blemished or imperfect typical sacrifices, and since we all became sinners through Adam, can we be acceptable sacrifices? Paul shows that it is only because we are holy that we are acceptable sacrifices. We are not holy like Jesus, who knew no sin, for we are of the condemned race; nor yet because we have entirely succeeded in reaching perfection of conduct, for we reckon not to have attained that perfection to which we are called; but we have this treasure in (fragile and leaky) earthen vessels, that the glory of our ultimate perfection may be seen to be of God's favor, and not of our own ability. But our holiness, and our acceptableness to God as sacrifices, come from the fact that God has justified us freely from all sin, through our faith in Christ's sacrifice on our behalf.

As many as appreciate and obey this call rejoice to be accounted worthy to suffer reproach for the name of Christ, and look not at the things that are seen, but at the things that are not seen—at the "crown of life"—"the prize of our high-calling in Christ Jesus" and "the glory that shall be revealed in us." These, from the moment of consecration to God, are no longer reckoned as men, but as having been begotten of God through the word of truth—no longer human, but thenceforth spiritual children. They are now one step nearer the prize than when they first believed. But their spiritual being is yet imperfect: they are only *begotten*, not yet *born* of the Spirit. They are embryo spiritual children, on plane *M*—the plane of spirit begetting. Because begotten of the Spirit, they are no longer reckoned as human, but as spiritual; for the human nature, once theirs, once justified, they have now given up or reckoned dead—a living sacrifice, holy, acceptable to and accepted of God. They are now new creatures in Christ Jesus: old things (human hopes, will and ambitions) have passed away, and all things have become new; for "ye are not in the flesh, but in the spirit, if so be that the Spirit of God dwell in you." (2 Cor. 5:17; Rom. 8:9) If you have been begotten of the Spirit, "ye (as human beings) are dead, and your life is hid with Christ in God."

Plane *L* represents the condition of *perfect spiritual* being; but before plane *L* can be reached, the conditions of our covenant must be carried out. It is one thing to covenant with God that we will be dead to all human things, and a further thing to perform that covenant throughout our earthly career—keeping the "body under" (dead), keeping our own will out of sight, and performing only the Lord's will. The entrance upon plane *L* is called birth, or the full entrance into life as a spirit being. The entire Church will enter on this plane when gathered out (selected) from the world in the "harvest" or end of the Gospel age. The "dead in Christ shall rise first." Then we, who are alive and remain, shall be changed in a moment—made perfect spiritual beings with bodies like unto Christ's glorious body (for "this mortal must put on immortality"). Then, that which is perfect having come, that which is in part (the begotten condition with the various hindrances of the flesh to which we are now subject) shall be done away.

But there is a still further step to be taken beyond a perfection of spiritual being, viz., to "the glory that shall follow"—plane *K*. We do not here refer to a glory of person, but to a glory of power or office. The reaching of plane *L* brings full personal glory; i.e., glorious being, like unto Christ. But after we are thus perfected, and made entirely like our Lord and Head, we are to be associated with him in the "glory" of power and office—to sit with him in his throne, even as he, after being perfected at his resurrection, was exalted to the right hand of the Majesty on high. Thus shall we enter everlasting glory, plane *K*.

Let us now carefully study the chart and note its illustrations of the various features of the plan of God. In these illustrations we use the pyramid figure to represent perfection, because of its fitness and because of evident reference to it in the Scriptures.

Adam was a perfect being, pyramid *a*. Notice its position—on plane *N*, which represents human perfection. On plane *R*, the plane of sin and imperfection or the depraved plane, the topless pyramid, *b*, an imperfect figure, represents fallen Adam and his posterity—depraved, sinful and condemned.

Abraham and others of that day, justified to fellowship with God on account of faith, are represented by a pyramid (*c*) on plane *N*. Abraham was a member of the depraved human family and by nature belonged with the rest on plane *R*; but Paul tells us that Abraham was justified by faith; that is, he was reckoned of God a sinless and perfect man because of his faith. This, in God's estimation, lifted him up above the world of depraved sinful men to plane *N*; and though actually still imperfect, he was received into the favor that Adam had lost, viz., communion with God as a "friend." (James 2:23) All on the perfect (sinless) plane *N* are friends of God, and he is a friend of theirs; but sinners (on plane *R*) are at enmity against God—"enemies through wicked works."

The world of mankind after the flood, represented by figure *d*, was still on plane *R*—still at enmity, where it continues until the Gospel Church is selected and the Millennial age begins.

"Israel after the flesh," during the Jewish age, when the typical sacrifices of bulls and goats cleansed them (not really, but typically, "for the Law made nothing perfect"—Heb. 7:19), were typically justified, hence they are (*e*) on plane *P*, the plane of typical justification, which lasted from the giving of the Law at Mount Sinai until Jesus made an end of the Law, nailing it to his cross. There the typical justification ended by the institution of the "better sacrifices" than the Jewish types, those which actually "take away the sin of the world" and "make the comers thereunto [actually] perfect." Heb. 10:1

The fire of trial and trouble through which fleshly Israel passed, when Jesus was present, sifting them and taking out of their nominal church the wheat, the "Israelites indeed," and especially when, after the separation of the wheat, he "burned up the chaff [the refuse part of that *system*] with unquenchable fire," is illustrated by figure *f*. It was a time of trouble which they were powerless to avert. See Luke 3:17, 21, 22; 1 Thess. 2:16.

Jesus, at the age of thirty years, was a perfect, mature man (*g*), having left the glory of the spiritual condition and become a *man* in order that he (by the grace of God) should taste death for every man. The justice of God's law is absolute: an eye for an eye, a tooth for a tooth and a life for a life. It was necessary that a perfect *man* should die for mankind, because the claims of justice could be met in no other way. The death of an angel could no more pay the penalty and release man than could the death of "bulls and of goats, which can never take away sin." Therefore, he who is termed "the Beginning of the creation of God" became a *man*, was "made flesh," that he might give that ransom (corresponding price) which would redeem mankind. He must have been a perfect man else he could have done no more than any member of the fallen race to pay the price. He was "holy, harmless, undefiled, and separate from sinners." He took the same form or likeness which sinners have—"the likeness of sinful flesh"—the human likeness. But he took that likeness in its perfection: he did not partake of its sin nor did he share its imperfection, except as he voluntarily shared the sorrows and pains of some during his ministry, taking their pains and infirmities as he imparted to them his vitality and health and strength. It is written that "Himself *took* our infirmities and bare our sicknesses" (Isa. 53:4), and "virtue [life, vitality, vigor] went out of him and healed them all." Mark 5:30; Luke 6:19; Matt. 8:16, 17

Being found in fashion as a (perfect) man, he humbled himself and became obedient unto death. He presented himself to God, saying, "Lo, I come (in the volume of the book it is written of me) to do thy will, O God"—and symbolized this consecration by a baptism in water. When he thus presented himself, consecrated his being, his offering was holy (pure) and acceptable to God, who showed his acceptance by filling him with his Spirit and power—when the holy Spirit came upon him, thus anointing him.

This filling with the Spirit was the begetting to a new nature—the divine—which should be fully developed or born when he had fully accomplished the offering—the sacrifice of the human nature. This begetting was a step up from human conditions, and is shown by pyramid *h*, on plane *M*, the plane of spirit begetting. On this plane Jesus spent three and one-half years of his life—until his human existence ended on the cross. Then, after being dead three days, he was raised to life—to the perfection of spirit being (*i*, plane *L*), born of the Spirit—"the first born from the dead." "That which is *born* of the Spirit is *spirit*." Jesus, therefore, at and after his resurrection, was a spirit—a spirit being, and no longer a human being in any sense.

True, after his resurrection he had power to appear, and did appear, as a man, in order that he might teach his disciples and prove to them that he was no longer dead; but he was not a man, and was no longer controlled by human conditions, but could go and come as the wind (even when the doors were shut), and none could tell whence he came or whither he went. "*So* is every one that is *born* of the Spirit." (John 3:8) Compare 20:19, 26.

From the moment of his consecration to sacrifice, at the time of his baptism, the human had been reckoned dead— and there the new nature was reckoned begun, which was completed at the resurrection, when he reached the perfect spirit plane, *L*—was raised a spiritual body.

Forty days after his resurrection, Jesus ascended to the majesty on high—the plane of divine glory, *K* (pyramid *k*). During the Gospel age he has been in glory (*l*), "set down with the Father on his throne," and Head over his Church on earth—her director and guide. During this entire Gospel age the Church has been in process of development, discipline and trial, to the intent that in the end or harvest of the age she may become his bride and joint-heir. Hence she has fellowship in his sufferings, that she may be also glorified together with him (plane *K*), when the proper time comes.

The steps of the Church to glory are the same as those of her Leader and Lord, who "hath set us an example that we should walk in his footsteps"—except that the Church starts from a lower plane. Our Lord, as we have seen, came into the world on the plane of human *perfection, N*, while all we of the Adamic race are on a lower plane, *R*—the plane of sin, imperfection and enmity against God. The first thing necessary for us, then, is to be *justified*, and thus to reach plane

N. How is this accomplished? Is it by good works? No; sinners can do no good works. We could not commend ourselves to God, so "God commended his love toward us, in that, while we were yet sinners, Christ died for us." (Rom. 5:8) Then the condition upon which we come to the justified or perfect human plane is that Christ died for our sins, redeemed us and lifted us up, "through faith in his blood," to the perfect plane, from which, in Adam, we fell. "We are justified [lifted to plane *N*] by faith." And "*being* justified *by faith*, we have peace with God" (Rom. 5:1), and are no longer esteemed by God as enemies, but as justified human sons, on the same plane as Adam and our Lord Jesus, except that they were actually perfect, while we are merely reckoned so by God. This reckoned justification we realize through faith in God's Word, which says, Ye are "bought," "redeemed," "justified freely from all things." We stand in God's sight blameless, spotless and holy in the robes of Christ's righteousness imputed to us by faith. Our sins he consented to have *imputed* to him, that he might bear our penalty for us; and he died on our behalf, as though he were the sinner. His righteousness is consequently *imputed* to all who accept of his redemption, and brings with it all the rights and blessings originally possessed before sin entered.[1] It restores us to life and to fellowship with God. This fellowship we may have at once by the exercise of faith, and the life and fuller fellowship and joy are assured—in God's "due time."

But remember that while justification is a blessed thing, it does not change our nature:* we are still human beings.

---

[1]See Author's Foreword, *The New Creation*, Vol. VI, pp. iii, iv, of this series for added clarification on justification.

*The word *nature* is used in an accommodated sense when it is said of a man that he is *ill-natured*. Strictly speaking, no man is evil by nature. Human nature is "very good," an *earthly image* of the divine nature. So every

We are saved from the wretched state of sin and alienation from God, and instead of being human sinners we are human sons; and now, because we are sons, God speaks to us as such. During the Gospel age he has been calling for the "little flock" of "joint-heirs," saying, "My son, give me thine heart"—that is, give yourself, all your earthly powers, your will, your talents, your all, to me, even as Jesus hath set you an example; and I will make you a son on a higher plane than the human. I will make you a spiritual son, with a spirit body like the risen Jesus—"the express image of the Father's person." If you will give up all of the earthly hopes, ambitions, aims, etc., consecrate the human nature entirely, and use it up in my service, I will give you a higher nature than the rest of your race; I will make you a "partaker of the divine nature"—an "heir of God and a joint-heir with Jesus Christ, *if so be that you suffer with him*, that you may be also *glorified* together."

Those who rightly value this prize set before them in the gospel gladly lay aside every weight and run with patience the appointed race, that they may win it. Our works were not called for to secure our justification: our Lord Jesus did all the work that could be done to that end, and when, by faith, we accepted of his finished work, we were justified, lifted to plane *N*. But now, if we would go further, we cannot go without works. True, we must not lose our faith, else we will thereby lose our justification; but being justified, and continuing in faith, we are able (through the grace given unto us by our begetting of the Spirit) to do works, to bring forth fruit acceptable to God. And God requires this;

---

man is of a good nature, the difficulty being that this good nature has become depraved. It is then unnatural for a man to be evil, brutal, etc., and natural for him to be God-like. It is in this, its primary sense, that we use the word *nature*, above. We are justified by Christ to a full return to all the privileges and blessings of our human nature—the *earthly* image of God.

for it is the sacrifice we covenanted to make. God requires that we show our appreciation of the great prize by giving all that we have and are for it; not to men, but to God—a sacrifice holy and, through Christ, acceptable to him—our reasonable service.

When we present all these things, we say: Lord, how wouldst thou have me deliver this, my sacrifice, my time, talent, influence, etc., to thee? Then, examining God's Word for an answer, we hear his voice instructing us to deliver our *all* to him as our Lord Jesus did, by doing good unto all men as we have opportunity, especially to the household of faith— serving them with spiritual or with natural food, clothing them in Christ's righteousness or with the earthly raiment, as we may have ability, or as they may need. Having consecrated *all*, we are begotten of the Spirit, we have reached plane *M*; and now, through the power given unto us, if we use it, we will be able to perform all of our covenant, and to come off conquerors, and more than conquerors, through (the power or Spirit of) him who loved us and bought us with his own precious blood. But, thus walking in the footsteps of Jesus,

> "Ne'er think the victory won,
> Nor once at ease sit down.
> Thine arduous work will not be done
> Till thou hast gained thy crown."

The crown will be won when we, like our faithful Brother Paul, have fought a good fight and finished the course, but not sooner. Until then, the flame and incense of our sacrifice of labor and service must ascend daily—a sacrifice of sweet odor unto God, acceptable through Jesus Christ, our Lord.

Those of this overcoming class who "sleep" will be raised spirit beings, plane *L,* and those of the same class who are alive and remain unto the coming of the Lord will be "changed" to the same plane of spirit being, and will not "sleep" for a moment, though the "change" will necessitate the dissolution of the earthen vessel. No longer weak, earthly, mortal, corruptible beings, these will then be fully born of the Spirit—heavenly, spiritual, incorruptible, immortal beings. 1 Cor. 15:44, 52

We know not how long it will be after their "change," or perfecting as spirit beings (plane *L*), before they, as a full and complete company, will be glorified (plane *K*) with the Lord, united with him in power and great glory. This unifying and full glorification of the entire body of Christ with the Head we understand to be the "marriage of the Lamb" to his Bride, when she shall fully enter into the joys of her Lord.

Look again at the chart—*n*, *m*, *p*, *q* are four distinct classes which unitedly represent the nominal Gospel Church as a whole, claiming to be the body of Christ. Both the *n* and *m* classes are on the spirit-begotten plane, *M*. These two classes have existed together throughout the Gospel age; both covenanted with God to become living sacrifices; both were "accepted in the beloved" and begotten by the Spirit as "*new creatures.*" The difference between them is this: *n* represents those who are fulfilling their covenant and are dead with Christ to earthly will, aims and ambitions, while *m* represents the larger company of the spirit-begotten children who have covenanted, but who, alas! shrink back from the performance of their covenant. The *n* class consists of the overcomers who will be the Bride of Christ, who will sit with the Lord in his throne in glory—plane *K*. This is the "little flock" to whom it is the Father's good pleasure to give the Kingdom. (Luke 12:32) Those of the *m* class shrink from the death of the human will, but God still loves them, and therefore will bring them by the way of adversity and trouble to plane *L*, the perfect spiritual plane. But they will have lost the right to plane *K*, the throne of glory, because they were not overcomers. If we prize our Father's love, if we desire our Lord's approval, if we aspire to be members of his body, his Bride, and to sit in his throne, we must fulfil our covenant of sacrifice faithfully and willingly.

The majority of the *nominal* Church is represented by section *p*. Notice that they are not on plane *M*, but on plane *N*. They are justified but not sanctified. They are not fully consecrated to God, and not begotten, therefore, as spirit beings. They are higher than the world, however, because they accept of Jesus as their ransom from sin; but they have not accepted the high-calling of this age to become part of the spiritual family of God. If they continue in faith and fully submit to the righteous laws of Christ's Kingdom, in the Times of Restitution, they will finally attain the likeness of the perfect earthly man, Adam. They will completely recover all that was lost through him. They will attain the same human perfection, mental, moral and physical, and will again be in the image of God, as Adam was; for to all this they were redeemed. And their position of justification, plane *N*, as those who have heard and believed in the salvation through Christ, is a special blessing which they by faith enjoy sooner than the general world (for all shall be brought to an accurate knowledge of the Truth, in the Millennial age). These, however, will have had the advantage of an earlier start and some progress in the right direction. But class *p* fails to improve the real benefit of this faith justification in the present time. It is granted now for the special purpose of enabling some to make the acceptable sacrifice, and to become the *n* class as members of "the body of Christ." Those of class *p* receive the favor of God [justification] *"in vain"* (2 Cor. 6:1): they fail to use it to go on and present themselves acceptable sacrifices, during this time in which sacrifices are acceptable to God. Those of this class, though not "saints," not members of the consecrated "body," are called "brethren" by the Apostle. (Rom. 12:1) In the same sense the entire race, when restored, will forever be brethren of the Christ, and the children of God, though of a different nature. God is the Father of *all* in harmony with him, on every plane and of every nature.

Another class connected with the nominal Church, which never did believe in Jesus as the sacrifice for its sins, and which consequently is not justified—not on plane *N*— is represented below plane *N*, by section *q*. These are "wolves in sheep's clothing;" yet they call themselves Christians, and are recognized as members of the nominal Church. They are not truly believers in Christ as their Redeemer; they belong to plane *R*; they are part of the world, and are out of place in the Church and a great injury to it. In this mixed condition, with these various classes, *n*, *m*, *p*, and *q*, mingling together and all calling themselves Christians, the Church has existed throughout the Gospel age. As our Lord foretold, the nominal kingdom of heaven (the nominal Church) is like a field sown with wheat and tares. And he said he would "let both grow together until the harvest" in the end of the age. In the time of harvest he will say unto the reapers ("the angels"—messengers), Gather together the tares and bind them in bundles to burn them, but gather the wheat into my barn. Matt. 13:38, 41, 49

These words of our Lord show us that while he purposed that both should grow together during the age, and be recognized as members of the nominal Church, he also purposed that there should come a time of separation between these different elements, when those who are truly the Church, his saints (*n*) approved and owned of God, should be made manifest. Matt. 13:39

During the Gospel age the good seed has been growing, and tares or counterfeits also. "The good seed are the children of the kingdom," the spiritual children, classes *n* and *m*, while "the tares are the children of the wicked one." All of class *q*, and many of class *p*, are therefore "tares"; for "no man can serve two masters," and "his servants you are to whom you render service." As those in class *p* do not consecrate their service and talents to the Lord that bought them—a reasonable service—doubtless they give much of their time and talent really in opposition to God, and hence in the service of the enemy.

Now notice on the chart the harvest or end of the Gospel age; notice the two parts into which it is divided— seven years and thirty-three years, the exact parallel of the harvest of the Jewish age.[2] This harvest, like the Jewish one, is to be first a time of trial and sifting upon the Church, and afterward a time of wrath or pouring out of the "seven last plagues" upon the world, including the nominal Church. The Jewish Church was the "shadow" or pattern on the fleshly plane of all that the Gospel Church enjoys on the spiritual plane. That which tried fleshly Israel in the harvest of their age was THE TRUTH then presented to them. The truth then due was the sickle, and it separated the "Israelites indeed" from the nominal Jewish Church; and of the true wheat there was but a fragment compared to the professors. So also is the harvest of this age. The harvest of the Gospel age, like that of the Jewish age, is under the supervision of the chief reaper, our Lord Jesus, who must then be present. (Rev. 14:14) The first work of our Lord in the harvest of this age will be to separate the true from the false. The nominal Church, because of her mixed condition, the

---

[2]See Author's Foreword, *Thy Kingdom Come*, Vol. III, p. i, par. 3 of this series. In the foregoing the author shows the harvest of the Gospel age is of longer duration.

Lord calls "Babylon"—confusion; and the harvest is the time for separating the different classes in the nominal Church, and for ripening and perfecting the *n* class. Wheat will be separated from tares, ripe wheat from unripe, etc. Those in class *n* are a "first fruits" of the wheat, and after being separated they will, in due time, become Christ's Bride, and be forever with and like her Lord.

The separation of this little flock from Babylon is shown by figure *s*. She is on the way to become *one* with the Lord, and to bear his name and share his glory. The glorified Christ, Head and body, is shown by figure *w*. Figures *t, u,* and *v* represent Babylon—the nominal Church—falling, going to pieces during "the time of trouble" in the "day of our Lord." Though this may seem to be a dreadful thing, yet it will actually be of great advantage to all the true wheat. Babylon falls because she is not what she claims to be. The Church nominal contains many hypocrites, who have associated themselves with her because of her honorable standing in the eyes of the world, and who, by their conduct are making Babylon a stench in the nostrils of the world. The Lord always knew their real character, but, according to his purpose he lets them alone until the harvest, when he will "gather out of [or from] his kingdom [true Church, and bind in bundles] all things that offend, and them which do iniquity, and cast them into a furnace of fire [trouble, *destructive* to their nominal system and false profession]. . . . Then shall the righteous [the *n* class] shine forth as the sun in the kingdom of their Father." (Matt. 13:41-43) The trouble coming upon the Church will be occasioned in great measure by the growth of Infidelity and Spiritism, of various kinds, which will be severe trials because Babylon holds so many doctrines contrary to God's Word. As in the harvest of the Jewish age the *cross* of Christ was to the Jew, expecting glory and power, a stumbling block, and to the worldly-wise Greek, foolishness, so in the harvest of the Gospel age it will again be the stone of stumbling and rock of offense.

Every one who has built upon Christ anything else than the gold, silver and precious stones of truth, and a character consistent therewith, will find himself sorely beset during the time of wrath ("fire"); for all the wood, hay and stubble of doctrine and practice will be consumed. Those who have built properly, and who consequently possess the approved character, are represented by figure *s*, while *t* represents the "great company," begotten of the Spirit, but who have built with wood, hay and stubble—wheat, but not fully ripened at the time of the gathering of the first fruits (*s*). They (*t*) lose the prize of the throne and the divine nature, but will finally reach birth as spirit beings of an order lower than the divine nature. Though these are truly consecrated, they are overcome by the worldly spirit to such an extent that they fail to render their lives in sacrifice. Even in "the harvest," while the living members of the Bride are being separated from others by the *truth*, the ears of others, including class *t*, will be dull of hearing. They will be slow to believe and slow to act in that time of separation. They will, no doubt, be greatly dismayed when they afterward realize that the Bride has been completed and united to the Lord, and that they, because so listless and overcharged, have lost that great prize; but the beauty of God's plan, which they will then begin to discern as one of love, both for them and for all the world of mankind, will quite overcome their grief, and they will shout "Alleluia! for the Lord God omnipotent reigneth. Let us be glad, and rejoice, and give honor to him, for the marriage of the Lamb is come, and his wife hath made herself ready." (Rev. 19:6, 7) Notice, too, the abundant provision of the Lord: the message is sent to them— Though you are not the Bride of the Lamb, you may be present at the marriage supper—"Blessed are they which are called unto the marriage supper of the Lamb." (Verse 9) This company will, in due time, through the Lord's chastisements, come fully into harmony with him and his plan, and will wash their robes, that they may ultimately reach a position next to the Bride—*y*, on the spiritual plane, *L.* Rev. 7:14, 15

The time of trouble, as it will affect the world, will be after Babylon has begun to fall and disintegrate. It will be an overturning of all human society and governments, preparing the world for the reign of righteousness. During the time of trouble, fleshly Israel (*e*), which was cast off until the fulness of the Gentiles be come in, will be restored to God's favor, and the Gospel Church, or spiritual Israel, will be completed and glorified. During the Millennial age Israel will be the chief nation of earth, at the head of all on the earthly plane of being, into oneness and harmony with which all the obedient will be gradually drawn.

Their restoration to perfect human nature, as well as that of the world in general, will be a gradual work, requiring all of the Millennial age for its full accomplishment. During that thousand years' reign of Christ, the results of Adamic death will be gradually swallowed up or destroyed. Its various stages— sickness, pain and weakness, as well as the tomb—will yield obedience to the Great Restorer's power, until at the end of that age the great pyramid of our chart will be complete. The Christ (*x*) will be the head of all things—of the great company, of angels, and of men—next to the Father; next in order or rank will be the great company, spirit beings (*y*), and next, angels; then Israel after the flesh (*z*), including only Israelites indeed, at the head of earthly nations; then the world of men (*w*), restored to perfection of being, like the head of the human race, Adam, before he sinned. This restoration will be accomplished gradually during the Millennial age—the "times of restitution." (Acts 3:21) Some, however, will be destroyed from among the people: first, all who, under full light and opportunity, for one hundred years refuse to make progress toward righteousness and perfection (Isa. 65:20); and second, those who, having progressed to perfection, in a final testing at the close of the Millennium prove unfaithful. (Rev. 20:9) Such die the second death, from which there is no resurrection or restitution promised. But one full individual trial is provided. But one ransom will ever be given. Christ dieth no more.

When we look at our Father's great plan for the exaltation of the Church and the blessing through it of Israel and all the families of the earth by a restitution of all things, it reminds us of the song of the angels: "Glory to God in the highest; on earth, peace, good will toward men!" That will be the consummation of God's plan—"the gathering together of all things in Christ." Who will then say that God's plan has been a failure? Who will then say that he has not overruled evil for good, and made the wrath of both men and devils to praise him?

The figure of a pyramid not only serves well the purpose of illustrating perfect beings, but it continues to answer the purpose of illustration in representing the oneness of the whole creation, as in the fulfilment of God's plan it will be *one* when the harmony and perfection of all things will be attained under the headship of Christ, the Head, not only of the Church which is his body, but also of all things in heaven and in earth. Eph. 1:10

Christ Jesus was the "beginning," "the head," "the topstone," the "chief (upper) corner-stone" of this grand structure, which as yet is only commenced; and into harmony with the lines and angles of the top-stone must every understone be built. No matter how many kinds of stones may be in this structure, no matter how many distinct natures there may be among God's sons, earthly and heavenly, they all, to be everlastingly acceptable to him, must be conformed to the image of his Son. All who will be of this building must partake of the spirit of obedience to God, and of love toward him and all his creatures (so amply illustrated in Jesus), the fulfilment of the law—Thou shalt love the Lord with all thy heart, mind, soul and strength, and thy neighbor as thyself.

In the process (as God's Word outlines this gathering together in one of all things, both heavenly and earthly, under one head), Christ Jesus, the Head, was first selected; secondly, the Church, which is his body. Angels and other spirit classes will rank next; then the worthies of Israel and the world. Beginning with the highest, the ordering shall proceed until all who *will* shall have been brought into harmony and oneness.

One peculiarity is that this tried, chief, corner top-stone is laid first and called a *foundation* stone. Thus is illustrated the fact that the foundation of all hope toward God and righteousness is laid, not on the earth, but in the heavens. And those built under it and united to this heavenly foundation are held to it by heavenly attractions and laws. And though this order is the very opposite of an earthly building, how appropriate that the stone in whose likeness the entire structure is to be found should be laid first. And how appropriate also to find that our foundation is laid *upward*, not *downward*; and that we, as living stones, are *"built up* into him in all things." Thus the work will progress during the Millennial age, until every creature, of every nature, in heaven and in earth, will be praising and serving God in conformity with the lines of perfect obedience. The universe will then be clean; for in that day "It shall come to pass that the soul that will not hear that Prophet shall be cut off from among the people"—in the second death. Acts 3:22, 23

The Tabernacle of the Wilderness

The same lesson shown in the Chart of the Ages is here taught in this divinely arranged type, the lessons of which will be more fully examined subsequently. We place it alongside, that the different planes or steps to the Holy of Holies may be duly noted or appreciated, as teaching the same steps already examined in detail.[3] Outside the court of the tabernacle lies the whole world in sin, on the depraved plane, *R*. Entering through the "gate" into the "court," we become believers or *justified* persons, on plane *N*. Those who go forward in consecration press to the door of the Tabernacle, and, entering in (plane *M*), become priests. They are strengthened by the "shew bread," enlightened by the "candlestick" and enabled to offer acceptable incense to God by Jesus Christ at the "Golden Altar." Finally, in the first resurrection, they enter the perfect spiritual condition, or "Most Holy" (plane *L*), and are then associated with Jesus in the glory of the Kingdom, plane *K*.

The Blessed Hope

"A little while, earth's fightings will be over;
    A little while, her tears, be wiped away;
A little while, the power of Jehovah
    Shall turn this darkness to Millennial Day.

"A little while, the ills that now o'erwhelm men
    Shall to the memories of the past belong;
A little while, the love that once redeemed them
    Shall change their weeping into grateful song.

"A little while! 'Tis ever drawing nearer—
    The brighter dawning of that glorious day.
Praise God, the light is hourly growing clearer,
    Shining more and more unto the perfect day."

---

[3] See *Tabernacle Shadows of Better Sacrifices* for a more comprehensive explanation of the Tabernacle types. This publication is available from the Publishers.

STUDY XIII
THE KINGDOMS OF THIS WORLD

The First Dominion—Its Forfeiture—Its Redemption and Restoration—
The Typical Kingdom of God—The Usurper—Two Phases of the Present
Dominion—The Powers that be, Ordained of God—Nebuchadnezzar's View
of Them—Daniel's View and Interpretation—The Kingdoms of this World
Viewed from another Standpoint—The Proper Relationship of the Church
to Present Governments—The Divine Right of Kings Briefly Examined—
Claims of Christendom False—A Better Hope in the Fifth Universal
Empire.

IN THE first chapter of the Divine Revelation, God
declares his purpose concerning his earthly creation and its
government: "And God said, Let us make man in our
image, after our likeness, and let them have dominion over
the fish of the sea, and over the fowl of the air, and over
the cattle, and over all the earth, and over every creeping
thing that creepeth upon the earth. So God created man in
his own image; in the image of God created he him: male
and female created he them. And God blessed them. And
God said to them, Be fruitful and multiply, and fill the
earth, and subdue it; and have dominion over the fish of
the sea, and over the fowl of the air, and over every living
thing that moveth upon the earth."

Thus the dominion of earth was placed in the hands
of the human race as represented in the first man Adam,
who was perfect, and therefore fully qualified to be the lord,
ruler or king of earth. This commission to multiply, and fill,
and subdue, and have dominion over the earth was not to
Adam alone, but to all mankind: "Let *them* have dominion,"

245

etc. Had the human race remained perfect and sinless, this dominion would never have passed out of its hands.

It will be noticed that in this commission no man is given dominion or authority over fellowmen, but the whole race is given dominion over the earth, to cultivate and to make use of its products for the common good. Not only its vegetable and mineral wealth is thus placed at man's command, but also all its varieties of animal life are at his disposal and for his service. Had the race remained perfect and carried out this original design of the Creator, as it grew in numbers it would have been necessary for men to consult together, and to systematize their efforts, and to devise ways and means for the just and wise distribution of the common blessings. And as, in the course of time, it would have been impossible, because of their vast numbers, to meet and consult together, it would have been necessary for various classes of men to elect certain of their number to represent them, to voice their common sentiments, and to act for them. And if all men were perfect, mentally, physically and morally; if every man loved God and his regulations supremely, and his neighbor as himself, there would have been no friction in such an arrangement.

Thus seen, the original design of the Creator for earth's government was a Republic in form, a government in which each individual would share; in which every man would be a sovereign, amply qualified in every particular to exercise the duties of his office for both his own and the general good.

This dominion of earth conferred upon man had but one contingency upon which its everlasting continuance depended; and that was that this divinely-conferred rulership be always exercised in harmony with the Supreme Ruler of the universe, whose one law, briefly stated, is Love. "Love is the fulfilling of the law." "Thou shalt love the Lord thy God with all thy heart, and with all thy soul, and with all

thy mind; . . . and thou shalt love thy neighbor as thyself."
Rom. 13:10; Matt. 22:37-40

Concerning this great favor conferred upon man, David,
praising God, says: "Thou madest him a little lower than the
angels; thou crownedst him with glory and honor; thou
madest him to have dominion over the works of thy hands."
(Psa. 8:5, 6) This dominion given to mankind in the person
of Adam was the first establishment of the Kingdom of God
on the earth. Man thus exercised dominion as God's
representative. But man's disobedience to the Supreme Ruler
forfeited not only his life, but also all his rights and privileges
as God's representative ruler of earth. He was thenceforth a
rebel, dethroned and condemned to death. Then speedily the
kingdom of God on earth ceased, and has not since been
established, except for a short time, in a typical manner, in
Israel. Although in Eden man lost his right to life and
dominion, neither was taken from him suddenly; and while
the condemned life lasts man is permitted to exercise the
dominion of earth according to his own ideas and ability, until
God's due time for him whose right it is to take the dominion
which he purchased.

Our Lord's death redeemed or purchased not only man,
but also all his original inheritance, including the dominion of
earth. Having purchased it, the title is now in him: he is now the
rightful heir, and in due time, and shortly, he will take possession
of his purchase. (Eph. 1:14) But as he bought man not for the
sake of holding him as his slave, but that he might restore him
to his former estate, so with the dominion of earth: he purchased
it and all of man's original blessings for the purpose of restoring
them when man is again made capable of exercising them in
harmony with the will of God. Hence the reign of Messiah on
earth will not be everlasting. It will continue only until, by his
strong iron rule, he will have put down all rebellion and
insubordination, and restored the fallen race to the original

perfection, when they will be fully capable of rightly exercising the dominion of earth as originally designed. When thus restored, it will again be the Kingdom of God on earth, under man, God's appointed representative.

During the Jewish age God organized the people of Israel as his kingdom, under Moses and the Judges—a sort of Republic—but it was typical only. And the more despotic rule afterward established, especially under David and Solomon, was in some respects typical of the kingdom promised, when Messiah should reign. Unlike the surrounding nations, Israel had Jehovah for their King, and their rulers nominally served under him, as we learn from Psa. 78:70, 71. This is quite definitely stated in 2 Chron. 13:8 and 1 Chron. 29:23, where Israel is called "the Kingdom of the Lord," and where it is said that Solomon "sat on the THRONE OF THE LORD, instead of David his father," who sat upon or exercised the rule of the same throne for the forty years previous, following Saul, the first king.

When the people of Israel transgressed against the Lord, he chastised them repeatedly, until finally he took away their kingdom entirely. In the days of Zedekiah, the last who reigned of the line of David, the scepter of royal power was removed. There the typical kingdom of God was overthrown.

God's decision relative to the matter is expressed in the words, "Thou profane, wicked prince of Israel, whose day is come, when iniquity shall have an end, Thus saith the Lord God: Remove the diadem, and take off the crown: this shall not be the same. . . . I will overturn, overturn, overturn it; and it shall be NO MORE, *until* he come, whose right it is; and I will give it him." (Ezek. 21:25-27) In fulfilment of this prophecy the king of Babylon came against Israel, took the people captive and removed their king. Though afterward restored to national existence by Cyrus the Persian, they were subjects and tribute payers to the successive empires of Medo-Persia, Greece, and Rome, down to the final destruction of their nationality, A.D. 70, since which time they have been scattered among all nations.

The kingdom of Israel is the only one, since the fall, which God ever recognized as in any way representing his government, laws, etc. There had been many nations before theirs, but no other could rightfully claim God as its founder, or that its rulers were God's representatives. When the diadem was taken from Zedekiah and the kingdom of Israel was overturned, it was decreed that it should remain overturned until Christ, the rightful heir of the world, should come to claim it. Thus, inferentially, all other kingdoms in power until the re-establishment of God's kingdom are branded "kingdoms of this world," under the "prince of this world"; and hence any claims put forth by any of them to being kingdoms of God are spurious. Nor was this Kingdom of God "SET UP" at the first advent of Christ. (Luke 19:12) Then and since then God has been selecting from the world those who shall be accounted worthy to reign with Christ as joint-heirs of that throne. Not until his second advent will Christ take the kingdom, the power and the glory, and reign Lord of all.

All other kingdoms than that of Israel are Scripturally called heathen or Gentile kingdoms—"the kingdoms of this world," under the "prince of this world"—Satan. The removal of God's kingdom in the days of Zedekiah left the world without any government of which God could approve, or whose laws or affairs he specially supervised. The Gentile governments God recognized indirectly, in that he publicly declares his decree (Luke 21:24) that during the interregnum the control of Jerusalem and the world should be exercised by Gentile governments.

This interregnum, or intervening period of time between

the removal of God's scepter and government and the restoration of the same in greater power and glory in Christ, is Scripturally termed "The Times of the Gentiles." And these "times" or years, during which the "kingdoms of this world" are permitted to rule, are fixed and limited, and the time for the re-establishment of God's Kingdom under Messiah is equally fixed and marked in Scripture.

Evil as these Gentile governments have been, they were permitted or "ordained of God" for a wise purpose. (Rom. 13:1) Their imperfection and misrule form a part of the general lesson on the exceeding sinfulness of sin, and prove the inability of fallen man to govern himself, even to his own satisfaction. God permits them, in the main, to carry out their own purposes as they may be able, overruling them only when they would interfere with his plans. He designs that eventually all shall work for good, and that finally even the "wrath of man shall praise him." The remainder, that would work no good, serve no purpose or teach no lesson, he restrains. Psa. 76:10

Man's inability to establish a perfect government is attributable to his own weaknesses in his fallen, depraved condition. These weaknesses, which of themselves would thwart human efforts to produce a perfect government, have also been taken advantage of by Satan, who first tempted man to disloyalty to the Supreme Ruler. Satan has continually taken advantage of man's weaknesses, made good to appear evil, and evil to appear good; and he has misrepresented God's character and plans and blinded men to the truth. Thus working in the hearts of the children of disobedience (Eph. 2:2), he has led them captive at his will and made himself what our Lord and the apostles call him—the prince or ruler of this world. (John 14:30; 12:31) He is not the prince of this world by right, but by usurpation; through fraud and deception and control of fallen

men. It is because he is a usurper that he will be summarily
deposed. Had he a real title as prince of this world, he would
not thus be dealt with.

Thus it will be seen that the dominion of earth, as at
present exercised, has both an invisible and a visible phase.
The former is the spiritual, the latter the human phase—the
visible earthly kingdoms measurably under the control of a
spiritual prince, Satan. It was because Satan possessed such
control that he could offer to make our Lord the supreme
visible sovereign of the earth under his direction. (Matt. 4:9)
When the Times of the Gentiles expire, both phases of the
present dominion will terminate: Satan will be bound and
the kingdoms of this world will be overthrown.

The fallen, blinded, groaning creation has for centuries
plodded along its weary way, defeated at every step, even its
best endeavors proving fruitless, yet ever hoping that the
golden age dreamed of by its philosophers was at hand. It
knows not that a still greater deliverance than that for which
it hopes and groans is to come through the despised
Nazarene and his followers, who as the Sons of God will
shortly be manifested in kingdom power for its deliverance.
Rom. 8:22, 19

In order that his children should not be in darkness
relative to his permission of present evil governments and
concerning his ultimate design to bring in a better
government when these kingdoms, under his overruling
providence, shall have served the purpose for which they
were permitted, God has given us, through his prophets,
several grand panoramic views of the "kingdoms of this
world," each time showing, for our encouragement, their
overthrow by the establishment of his own righteous and
everlasting kingdom under the Messiah, the Prince of Peace.

That man's present effort to exercise dominion is not in
successful defiance of Jehovah's will and power, but by his

permission, is shown by God's message to Nebuchadnezzar, wherein God gives *permission* to rule, until the time for the setting up of Christ's kingdom, to the four great empires, Babylon, Medo-Persia, Greece and Rome. (Dan. 2:37-43) This shows where this lease of the dominion will end.

As we now glance at these prophetic views, let us remember that they begin with Babylon at the time of the overthrow of the kingdom of Israel, the typical kingdom of the Lord.

Nebuchadnezzar's Vision of Earth's Governments

Among those things "written aforetime for our edification," that we, who are commanded to be subject to the powers that be, might through patience and comfort of the Scriptures have hope (Rom. 15:4; 13:1), is the dream of Nebuchadnezzar and its divine interpretation through the Prophet. Dan. 2:31-45

Daniel explained the dream, saying: "Thou, O king, sawest, and behold a great image. This great image, whose brightness was excellent, stood before thee; and the form thereof was terrible. This image's head was of fine gold, his breast and his arms of silver, his belly and his thighs of brass, his legs of iron, his feet part of iron and part of clay. Thou sawest till that a stone was cut out without hands, which smote the image upon his feet that were of iron and clay, and brake them to pieces.

"Then was the iron, the clay, the brass, the silver and the gold broken to pieces together, and became like the chaff of the summer threshing-floors; and the wind carried them away, that no place was found for them; and the stone that smote the image became a great mountain and filled the whole earth.

"This is the dream, and we will tell the interpretation thereof before the king. Thou, O king, art a king of kings:

for *the God of heaven hath given* thee a kingdom, power, and strength, and glory. [There the Gentile kingdoms, or powers that be, were ordained of God.] And wheresoever the children of men dwell, the beasts of the field and the fowls of the heaven hath he given into thine hand, and hath made thee ruler over them all. Thou art this head of gold.

"And after thee shall arise another kingdom inferior to thee [silver], and another third kingdom of brass, which shall bear rule over all the earth. And the fourth kingdom shall be strong as iron: forasmuch as iron breaketh in pieces and subdueth all things; and as iron that breaketh all these, shall it break in pieces and bruise. And whereas thou sawest the feet and toes, part of potter's clay and part of iron, the kingdom shall be mixed; but there shall be in it of the strength of the iron: forasmuch as thou sawest the iron mixed with the miry clay. And as the toes of the feet were part of iron and part of clay, so the kingdom shall be partly strong and partly brittle."

The student of history can readily trace, among the many smaller empires of earth which have arisen, the four above described by Daniel. These are termed UNIVERSAL EMPIRES—Babylon, first, the head of gold (verse 38); Medo-Persia, conqueror of Babylon, second, the breast of silver; Greece, conqueror of Medo-Persia, third, the belly of brass; and Rome, fourth, the strong kingdom, the iron legs and clay-mixed feet. Three of these empires had passed away, and the fourth, the Roman, held universal sway, at the time of our Lord's birth, as we read, "There went out a decree from Caesar Augustus that *all the world* should be taxed." Luke 2:1

The iron empire, Rome, was by far the strongest, and endured longer than its predecessors. In fact, the Roman Empire still continues, as represented in the nations of Europe. This division is represented in the ten toes of the image. The clay element blended with the iron in the feet represents the mixture of church and state. This mixture is in the Scriptures termed "Babylon"—confusion. As we shall presently see, *stone* is the symbol of the true Kingdom of God, and Babylon substituted an imitation of stone—clay—which it has united with the fragmentary remains of the [iron] Roman Empire. And this mixed system—church and state—the Church nominal wedded to the kingdoms of this world, which the Lord calls Babylon, confusion, presumes to call itself Christendom—Christ's Kingdom. Daniel explains: "Whereas thou sawest iron mixed with miry clay, they shall mingle themselves with the seed of men [church and world blend—Babylon], but they shall not cleave one to another, even as iron is not mixed with clay." They cannot thoroughly amalgamate. "And in the days of these kings [the kingdoms represented by the toes, the so-called "Christian kingdoms" or "Christendom"] shall the God of heaven set up a kingdom which shall never be destroyed; and the kingdom shall not be left to other people, but it shall break in pieces and consume all these kingdoms; and it shall stand forever." Dan. 2:43, 44

Daniel does not here state the time for the end of these Gentile governments: that we find elsewhere; but every foretold circumstance indicates that today the end is nigh, even at the doors. The Papal system has long claimed that it is the kingdom which the God of heaven here promised to set up, and that, in fulfilment of this prophecy, it did break in pieces and consume all other kingdoms. The truth, however, is that the nominal Church merely united with earthly empires as the clay with the iron, and that Papacy never was the true Kingdom of God, but merely a counterfeit of it. One of the best evidences that Papacy did not destroy and consume these earthly kingdoms is that they still exist. And now that the miry clay has become dry and "brittle," it is losing its adhesive power, and the iron and clay show signs of dissolution, and will quickly crumble when smitten by the "stone," the true Kingdom.

Continuing his interpretation, Daniel states: "Forasmuch as thou sawest that the stone was cut out of the mountain without hands, and that it brake in pieces the iron, the brass, the clay, the silver and the gold, the great God hath made known to the king what shall come to pass hereafter; and the dream is certain and the interpretation thereof sure." Verse 45

The stone cut out of the mountain without hands, which smites and scatters the Gentile powers, represents the true Church, the Kingdom of God. During the Gospel age this "stone" kingdom is being formed, "cut out," carved and shaped for its future position and greatness—not by human hands, but by the power or spirit of the truth, the invisible power of Jehovah. When complete, when entirely cut out, it will smite and destroy the kingdoms of this world. Not the people, but the governments, are symbolized by the image, and these are to be destroyed that the people may be delivered. Our Lord Jesus came not to destroy men's lives, but to save them. John 3:17

The stone, during its preparation, while being cut out, might be called an embryo mountain, in view of its future destiny; so, too, the Church could be, and sometimes is, called the Kingdom of God. In fact, however, the stone does not become the mountain until it has smitten the image; and so the Church, in the full sense, will become the Kingdom to fill the whole earth when "the day of the Lord," the "day of wrath upon the nations" or "time of trouble," will be over, and when it will be established and all other dominions have become subservient to it.

Call to mind now the promise made by our Lord to the overcomers of the Christian Church: "To him that overcometh will I grant to sit with me in my throne"—"and he that overcometh and keepeth my works unto the end, to him will I give power over the nations; and he shall rule them with a rod of iron; as the vessels of a potter shall *they* be broken to shivers, even as I received of my Father." (Rev. 3:21; 2:26, 27; Psa. 2:8-12) When the iron rod has accomplished the work of destruction, then will the hand that smote be turned to heal, and *the people* will return to the Lord, and he shall heal them (Isa. 19:22; Jer. 3:22, 23; Hos. 6:1; 14:4; Isa. 2:3), giving them beauty for ashes, the oil of joy for mourning and the garment of praise for the spirit of heaviness.

Daniel's Vision of Earthly Governments

In Nebuchadnezzar's vision we see the empires of earth, as viewed from the world's standpoint, to be an exhibition of human glory, grandeur, and power; though in it we also see an intimation of their decay and final destruction, as expressed in the deterioration from gold to iron and clay.

The stone class, the true Church, during its selection or taking out of the mountain, has been esteemed by the world as of no value. It has been despised and rejected of men. They see no beauty in it that they should desire it. The world loves, admires, praises and defends the rulers and governments represented in this great image, though it has been continually disappointed, deceived, wounded and oppressed by them. The world extols, in prose and verse, the great and successful agents of this image, its Alexanders, Caesars, Bonapartes and others, whose greatness showed itself in the slaughter of their fellowmen, and who, in their lust for power, made millions of widows and orphans. And such is still the spirit which exists in the "ten toes" of the image, as we see it exhibited today in their marshaled hosts of more than twelve millions of men armed with every fiendish device of modern ingenuity, to slaughter one another at the command of "the powers that be."

The proud are now called happy; yea, they that work wickedness are set up in power. (Mal. 3:15) Can we not see, then, that the destruction of this great image by the smiting of the stone, and the establishment of God's kingdom, mean the liberating of the oppressed and the blessing of all? Though for a time the change will cause disaster and trouble, it will finally yield the peaceable fruits of righteousness.

But now, calling to mind the difference of standpoint, let us look at the same four universal empires of earth from the standpoint of God and those in harmony with him, as portrayed in vision to the beloved prophet Daniel. As to us these kingdoms appear inglorious and beastly, so to him these four universal empires were shown as four great and ravenous wild beasts. And to his view the coming Kingdom of God (the stone) was proportionally grander than as seen by Nebuchadnezzar. Daniel says: "I saw in my vision by night, and behold the four winds of heaven strove upon the great sea. And four great beasts came up from the sea, diverse one from another. The first was like a lion and had eagle's wings; . . . and behold another beast, a second, like a bear; . . . and lo another, like a leopard. . . . After this I saw in the night visions, and behold a fourth beast, dreadful and terrible, and strong exceedingly; and it had great iron teeth. It devoured and brake in pieces, and stamped the residue with the feet of it; and it was diverse from all the beasts that were before it, and it had ten horns." Dan. 7:2-7

The details relative to the first three beasts (Babylon the lion, Medo-Persia the bear, and Greece the leopard), with their heads, feet, wings, etc., all of which are symbolic, we pass by, as of less importance in our present examination than the details of the fourth beast, Rome.

Of the fourth beast, Rome, Daniel says: "After this I saw in the night visions, and behold a fourth beast, dreadful and terrible, and strong exceedingly; . . . and it had ten horns. I considered the horns, and, behold, there came up among them another little horn, before whom there were three of the first horns plucked up by the roots; and, behold, in this horn were eyes, like the eyes of man, and a mouth speaking great things." Dan. 7:7, 8

Here the Roman Empire is shown; and the divisions of its power are shown in the ten horns, a horn being a symbol of power. The little horn which arose among these, and which appropriated the power of three of them to itself, and ruled among the others, represents the small beginning and gradual rise to power of the Church of Rome, the Papal power or horn. As it rose in influence, three of the divisions, horns or powers of the Roman Empire (the Heruli, the Eastern Exarchate and the Ostrogoths) were plucked out of the way to make room for its establishment as a civil power or horn. This last specially notable horn, Papacy, is remarkable for its eyes, representing intelligence, and for its mouth—its utterances, its claims, etc.

To this fourth beast, representing Rome, Daniel gives no descriptive name. While the others are described as lion-like, bear-like and leopard-like, the fourth was so ferocious and hideous that none of the beasts of earth could be compared with it. John the Revelator, seeing in vision the same symbolic beast (government), was also at a loss for a name by which to describe it, and finally gives it several. Among others, he called it "the Devil." (Rev. 12:9) He certainly chose an appropriate name; for Rome, when viewed in the light of its bloody persecutions, certainly has been the most devilish of all earthly governments. Even in its change from Rome Pagan to Rome Papal it illustrated one of Satan's chief characteristics; for he also transforms himself to appear *as* an angel of light (2 Cor. 11:14), as Rome transformed itself from heathenism and claimed to be Christian—the Kingdom of Christ.*

After giving some details regarding this last or Roman beast, and especially of its peculiar or Papal horn, the Prophet states that judgment against this horn would be rendered, and it would begin to lose its dominion, which would be *consumed* by gradual process until the *beast* should be destroyed.

This beast or Roman Empire in its horns or divisions still exists, and will be slain by the rising of the masses of the people, and the overthrow of governments, in the "Day of the Lord," preparatory to the recognition of the heavenly rulership. This is clearly shown from other scriptures yet to be examined. However, the *consuming* of the Papal horn comes first. Its power and influence began to consume when Napoleon took the Pope prisoner to France. Then, when neither the curses of the Popes nor their prayers delivered them from Bonaparte's power, it became evident to the nations that the divine authority and power claimed by the Papacy were without foundation. After that, the temporal power of the Papacy waned rapidly until, in September, 1870, it lost the last vestige of its temporal power at the hands of Victor Emmanuel.

Nevertheless, during all that time in which it was being "consumed," it kept uttering its great swelling words of blasphemy, its last great utterance being in 1870, when, but a few months before its overthrow, it made the declaration of the *infallibility* of the Popes. All this is noted in the

---

*The fact that Rome is called "the Devil" by no means disproves a *personal* devil: rather the reverse. It is because there are such beasts as lions, bears and leopards, with known characteristics, that governments were likened to them: and so, it is because there is a Devil, with known characteristics, that the fourth empire is likened to him.

prophecy: "I beheld *then* [*i.e., after* the decree against this 'horn,' after its consumption had begun] because of the voice of the GREAT WORDS which the horn spake." Dan. 7:11

Thus we are brought down in history to our own day, and made to see that the thing to be expected, so far as the empires of the earth are concerned, is their utter destruction. The next thing in order is described by the words, "I beheld even till the beast was slain and his body destroyed and given to the burning flame." The slaying and burning are symbols, as well as the beast itself, and signify the utter and hopeless destruction of present organized government. In verse 12 the prophet notes a difference between the end of this fourth beast and its predecessors. They three successively (Babylon, Persia and Greece) had their *dominion* taken from them; they ceased to hold the ruling power of earth; but their lives as nations did not cease immediately. Greece and Persia still have some life, though it is long centuries since universal dominion passed from their grasp. Not so, however, with the Roman Empire, the fourth and last of these beasts. It will lose dominion and life at once, and go into utter destruction; and with it the others will pass away also. Daniel 2:35

No matter what may be the means or instrumentality used, the *cause* of this fall will be the establishment of the Fifth Universal Empire of earth, the Kingdom of God, under Christ, whose right it is to take the dominion. The transfer of the kingdom from the fourth beast, which for its appointed time was "ordained of God," to the fifth kingdom, under the Messiah, when its appointed season has come, is described by the Prophet in these words: "And behold, one like the Son of man came with the clouds of heaven, and came to the Ancient of days, and they brought him near before him. And there was given unto him [the Christ—head and body complete] dominion, and glory, and a kingdom, that all people, nations and languages should serve him. His dominion is an everlasting dominion which shall not pass away, and his kingdom that which shall not be destroyed." This the angel interpreted to mean that "the kingdom and dominion, and the greatness of the kingdom under the whole heaven, shall be given to the people of the saints of the Most High, whose kingdom is an everlasting kingdom; and all dominions shall serve and obey him." Dan. 7:13, 27

Thus seen, the dominion of earth is to be placed in the hands of Christ by Jehovah ("the Ancient of days"), who shall "put all things under his feet." (1 Cor. 15:27) Thus enthroned over God's kingdom, he must reign until he shall have put down all authority and power in conflict with the will and law of Jehovah. To the accomplishment of this great mission, the overthrow of these Gentile governments is first necessary; for the "kingdoms of this world," like the "prince of this world," will not surrender peaceably, but must be bound and restrained by force. And thus it is written, "To bind their kings with chains and their nobles with fetters of iron; to execute upon them the judgment written; this honor have all his saints." Psa. 149:8, 9

As we thus view present governments from the standpoint of our Lord and of the Prophet Daniel, and realize their ferocious, destructive, beastly and selfish character, our hearts long for the end of Gentile governments and joyfully look forward to that blessed time when the overcomers of the present age will be enthroned with their Head, to rule, bless and restore the groaning creation. Surely all of God's children can heartily pray with their Lord—"THY KINGDOM COME, thy will be done on earth as it is in heaven."

Each of these governments represented in the image and by the beasts existed before it came into power as the universal empire. So, too, with the true Kingdom of God: it has long existed separate from the world, not attempting rulership, but awaiting its time—the time appointed by the Ancient of days. And, like the others, it must receive its appointment and must come into authority or be "set up" *before* it can exercise its power in the smiting and slaying of the beast or kingdom preceding it. Hence the appropriateness of the statement, "In the days of these kings [while they still have power] shall the God of heaven set up [establish in power and authority] a kingdom." And after it is set up, "it shall break in pieces and consume all these kingdoms, and it shall stand forever." (Dan. 2:44) Hence, however we may look for it, we must expect God's Kingdom to be inaugurated *before* the fall of the kingdoms of this world, and that its power and smiting will bring their overthrow.

Present Governments from Another Standpoint

Supreme right and authority to rule the world are and ever will be vested in the Creator, Jehovah, no matter whom he may permit or authorize to have subordinate control. Under the imperfections and weaknesses resulting from his disloyalty to the King of kings, Adam soon grew weak and helpless. As a monarch he began to lose the power by which, at first, he commanded and held the obedience of the lower animals by the strength of his will. He lost control of himself also, so that when he would do good his weaknesses interfered and evil was present with him; and the good he even would do he did not do, and the evil which he would not, he did.

Hence, while making no attempt to excuse our rebel race, we can sympathize with its vain efforts to govern itself and to arrange for its own well-being. And something can be said of the success of the world in this direction; for, while recognizing the real character of these beastly governments, corrupt though they have been, they have been vastly superior to none—much better than lawlessness and anarchy. Though anarchy would probably have been quite acceptable to the "prince of this world," it was not so to his subjects, and his power is not absolute: it is limited to the extent of his ability to operate through mankind; and his policy must conform in great measure to the ideas, passions, and prejudices of men. Man's idea was self-government independent of God; and when God permitted him to try the experiment, Satan embraced the opportunity to extend his influence and dominion. Thus it was by wishing to forget God (Rom. 1:28) that man exposed himself to the influence of this wily and powerful though unseen foe; and therefore he has ever since been obliged to work against Satan's machinations, as well as his own personal weaknesses.

This being the case, let us again glance at the kingdoms of this world, viewing them now as the effort of fallen humanity to govern itself independent of God. Though individual corruption and selfishness have turned aside the course of justice, so that full justice has seldom been meted out to any under the kingdoms of this world, yet the ostensible object of all governments ever organized among men has been to promote justice and the well-being of all the people.

To what extent that object has been attained is another question; but such has been the claim of all governments, and such the object of the people governed in submitting to and supporting them. And where the ends of justice have been greatly ignored, either the masses have been blinded and deceived with reference to them, or wars, commotions and revolutions have been the result.

The dark deeds of base tyrants, who gained positions of power in the governments of the world, did not represent the laws and institutions of those governments, but in usurping authority and turning it to base ends they gave to those governments their beastly character. Every government has had a majority of wise, just and good laws—laws for the protection of life and property, for the protection of domestic and commercial interests, for the punishment of crime, etc. They have also had courts of appeal in matters of dispute, where justice is meted out to some extent, at least; and however imperfect those in office may be, the advantage and necessity for such institutions is apparent. Poor as these governments have been, without them the baser element of society would, by force of numbers, have overcome the juster, better element.

While, therefore, we recognize the beastly character of these governments, as rendered so by the exaltation to power of a majority of unrighteous rulers, through the intrigues and deceptions of Satan, operating through man's weaknesses and depraved tastes and ideas, yet we recognize them as the best efforts of poor, fallen humanity at governing itself. Century after century God has allowed them to make the effort, and to see the results. But after centuries of experiment, the results are as far from satisfactory today as at any period of the world's history. In fact, the dissatisfaction is more general and widespread than ever before; not because there is more oppression and injustice than ever, but because, under God's arrangement, men's eyes are being opened by the increase of knowledge.

The various governments which have been established from time to time have exhibited the *average ability* of the people represented by them to govern themselves. Even where despotic governments have existed, the fact that they have been tolerated by the masses proved that as a people they were not capable of establishing and supporting a better government, though many individuals were always, doubtless, far in advance of the average standing.

As we compare the condition of the world today with its condition at any former period, we find a marked difference in the sentiments of the masses. The spirit of independence is now abroad, and men are not so easily blindfolded, deceived and led by rulers and politicians, and therefore they will not submit to the yokes of former days. This change of public sentiment has not been a gradual one from the very beginning of man's effort to govern himself, but clearly marked only as far back as the sixteenth century; and its progress has been most rapid within the last fifty years. This change, therefore, is not the result of the experience of past ages, but is the natural result of the recent increase and general diffusion of knowledge among the masses of mankind. The preparation for this general diffusion of knowledge began with the invention of printing, about 1440 A.D., and the consequent multiplication of books and news periodicals. The influence of this invention in the general public enlightenment began to be felt about the sixteenth century; and the progressive steps since that time all are acquainted with. The general education of the masses has become popular, and inventions and discoveries are becoming everyday occurrences. This increase of knowledge among men, which is of God's appointment, and comes to pass in his own due time, is one of the mighty influences which are now at work binding Satan—curtailing his influence and circumscribing his power in this "Day of *Preparation*" for the setting up of God's kingdom in the earth.

The increase of knowledge in every direction awakens a feeling of self-respect among men, and a realization of their natural and inalienable rights, which they will not long permit to be ignored or despised; rather, they will go to an opposite extreme. Glance back along the centuries and see how the nations have written the history of their discontent in blood. And the prophets declare that because of the increase of knowledge a still more general and widespread dissatisfaction will finally express itself in a world-wide revolution, in the overthrow of all law and order; that anarchy and distress upon all classes will be the result; but that in the midst of this confusion the God of heaven will SET UP his Kingdom, which will satisfy the desires of all nations. Wearied and disheartened with their own failures, and finding their last and greatest efforts resulting in anarchy, men will gladly welcome and bow before the heavenly authority, and recognize its strong and just government. Thus man's extremity will become God's opportunity, and "the desire of all nations shall come"—the Kingdom of God, in power and great glory. Hag. 2:7

Knowing this to be the purpose of God, neither Jesus nor the apostles interfered with earthly rulers in any way. On the contrary, they taught the Church to submit to these powers, even though they often suffered under their abuse of power. They taught the Church to obey the laws, and to respect those in authority because of their office, even if they were not personally worthy of esteem; to pay their appointed taxes, and, except where they conflicted with God's laws (Acts 4:19; 5:29), to offer no resistance to any established law. (Rom. 13:1-7; Matt. 22:21) The Lord Jesus and the apostles and the early Church were all law-abiding, though they were separate from, and took no share in, the governments of this world.

Though the powers that be, the governments of this world, were ordained or arranged for by God, that mankind might gain a needed experience under them, yet the Church, the consecrated ones who aspire to office in the coming Kingdom of God, should neither covet the honors and the emoluments of office in the kingdoms of this world, nor should they oppose these powers. They are fellow citizens and heirs of the heavenly kingdom (Eph. 2:19), and as such should claim only such rights and privileges under the kingdoms of this world as are accorded to *aliens*. Their mission is not to help the world to improve its present condition, nor to have anything to do with its affairs at present. To attempt to do so would be but a waste of effort; for the world's course and its termination are both clearly defined in the Scriptures and are fully under the control of him who in his own time will *give us* the kingdom. The influence of the *true* Church is now and always has been small—so small as to count practically nothing politically; but however great it might appear, we should follow the example and teaching of our Lord and the apostles. Knowing that the purpose of God is to let the world fully test its own ability to govern itself, the true Church should not, while in it, be *of* the world. The saints may influence the world only by their separateness from it, by letting *their light* shine; and thus through their lives the spirit of truth REPROVES the world. Thus—as peaceable, orderly obeyers and commenders of every righteous law, reprovers of lawlessness and sin, and pointers forward to the promised Kingdom of God and the blessings to be expected under it, and not by the method commonly adopted of mingling in politics and scheming with the world for power, and thus being drawn into wars and sins and the general degradation—in glorious chastity should the prospective Bride of the Prince of Peace be a power for good, as her Lord's representative in the world.

The Church of God should give its *entire attention* and effort to preaching the Kingdom of God, and to the advancement of the interests of that Kingdom according to the plan laid down in the Scriptures. If this is faithfully done, there will be no time nor disposition to dabble in the politics of present governments. The Lord had no time for it; the apostles had no time for it; nor have any of the saints who are following their example.

The early Church, shortly after the death of the apostles, fell a prey to this very temptation. The preaching of the coming Kingdom of God, which would displace all earthly kingdoms, and of the crucified Christ as the heir of that Kingdom, was unpopular, and brought with it persecution, scorn and contempt. But some thought to improve on God's plan, and, instead of suffering, to get the Church into a position of favor with the world. By a combination with earthly powers they succeeded. As a result Papacy was developed, and in time became the mistress and queen of nations. Rev. 17:3-5; 18:7

By this policy everything was changed: instead of suffering, came honor; instead of humility, came pride; instead of truth, came error; and instead of being persecuted, she became the persecutor of all who condemned her new and illegal honors. Soon she began to invent new theories and sophistries to justify her course, first deceiving herself, and then the nations, into the belief that the promised millennial reign of Christ HAD COME, and that Christ the King was represented by her popes, who reigned over the kings of the earth as his vicegerents. Her claims were successful in deceiving the whole world. "She made all nations *drunk*" with her erroneous doctrines (Rev. 17:2), intimidating them by teaching that eternal torment awaited all who resisted her claims. Soon the kings of Europe were crowned or deposed by her edict, and under her supposed authority.

Thus it comes that the kingdoms of Europe today claim to be Christian kingdoms, and announce that sovereigns reign "by the grace of God," i.e., through appointment of either Papacy or some of the Protestant sects. For though the Reformers abandoned many of Papacy's claims to ecclesiastical jurisdiction, etc., they held to this honor which the kings of earth had come to attach to Christianity. And thus the Reformers fell into the same error, and exercised the authority of monarchs in appointing and sanctioning governments and kings, and denominating such "Christian kingdoms," or kingdoms of Christ. So we hear much today of that strange enigma, "*The Christian World*"—an enigma indeed, when viewed in the light of the true principles of the Gospel. Our Lord said of his disciples, "They are not of the world, even as I am not of the world." And Paul exhorts us, saying, "Be not conformed to this world." John 17:16; Rom. 12:2

God never approved of calling these kingdoms by the name of Christ. Deceived by the Church nominal, these nations are sailing under false colors, claiming to be what they are not. Their only title, aside from the vote of the people, is in God's *limited* grant, spoken to Nebuchadnezzar—until he come whose right the dominion is.

The claim that these imperfect kingdoms, with their imperfect laws and often selfish and vicious rulers, are the "kingdoms of our Lord and his Anointed" is a gross libel upon the true Kingdom of Christ, before which they must shortly fall, and upon its "Prince of Peace" and righteous rulers. Isa. 32:1

Another serious injury resulting from that error is that the attention of the children of God has thereby been attracted away from the promised heavenly kingdom; and they have been led to an improper recognition of and intimacy with earthly kingdoms, and to almost fruitless attempts to engraft upon these wild, worldly stocks the graces and morals of Christianity, to the neglect of the gospel concerning the true Kingdom and the hopes centering in it. Under this deception, some are at present very solicitous that the name of God should be incorporated into the

Constitution of the United States, that *thereby* this may become a Christian nation. The Reformed Presbyterians have for years refused to vote or hold office under this government, *because* it is not Christ's Kingdom. Thus they recognize the impropriety of Christians sharing in any other. We have great sympathy with this sentiment, but not with the conclusion, that if God's *name* were mentioned in the Constitution, that fact would transform this government from a kingdom of this world to a kingdom of Christ, and give them liberty to vote and to hold office under it. O, how foolish! How great the deception by which the "Mother of harlots" has made all nations drunk (Rev. 17:2); for in a similar manner it is claimed that the kingdoms of Europe were transferred from Satan to Christ, and became "Christian nations."

Let it be seen that the best and the worst of earth's nations are but "kingdoms of this world," whose lease of power from God is now about expired, that they may give place to their ordained successor, the Kingdom of Messiah, the Fifth Universal Empire of earth (Dan. 2:44; 7:14,17, 27)—this view will do much to establish truth and to overthrow error.

But as it is, the actions of Papacy in this regard, sanctioned by the Protestant Reformers, go unquestioned among Christian people. And since they should uphold the Kingdom of Christ, they feel themselves bound to champion the present falling kingdoms of so-called Christendom, whose time is fast expiring; and thus their sympathies are often forced to the side of oppression, rather than to the side of right and freedom—to the side of the kingdoms of this world, and the prince of this world, rather than to the side of the coming true Kingdom of Christ. Rev. 17:14; 19:11-19

The world is fast coming to realize that the "kingdoms

of this world" are not Christlike, and that their claim to be of Christ's appointment is not unquestionable. Men are beginning to use their reasoning powers on this and similar questions; and they will act out their convictions so much more violently, as they come to realize that a deception has been practiced upon them in the name of the God of Justice and the Prince of Peace. In fact, the tendency with many is to conclude that Christianity itself is an imposition without foundation, and that, leagued with civil rulers, its aim is merely to hold in check the liberties of the masses.

O that men were wise, that they would apply their hearts to understand the work and plan of the Lord! Then would the present kingdoms melt down gradually—reform would swiftly follow reform, and liberty follow liberty, and justice and truth would prevail until righteousness would be established in the earth. But they will not do this, nor can they in their present fallen state; and so, armed with selfishness, each will strive for mastery, and the kingdoms of this world will pass away with a great time of trouble, such as was not since there was a nation. Of those who will be vainly trying to hold to a dominion which has passed away, when the dominion is given to him whose right it is, the Lord speaks, urging that they are fighting against him—a conflict in which they are sure to fail. He says:

"Why do the nations tumultuously assemble, and the people meditate a vain thing? The kings of the earth set themselves, and the rulers take counsel together against the Lord, and against his Anointed, saying, Let us break their bands asunder, and cast away their cords from us. He that sitteth in the heavens shall laugh: the Lord shall have them in derision. Then shall he speak unto them in his wrath, and vex them in his sore displeasure [saying], *I have anointed my king* upon my holy hill of Zion. . . . Be wise now, therefore, O ye kings: be instructed, ye judges of the earth. Serve the

Lord with fear and rejoice with trembling. Kiss [make friends with] the Son [God's Anointed] lest he be angry, and ye perish in the way; for his wrath may soon be kindled. Blessed are all they that take refuge in him." Psa. 2:1-6,10-12

The Kingdom Near

"Watchman, tell us of the night—
    What its signs of promise are.
Traveler, o'er yon mountain's height,
    See that glory-beaming star!
Watchman, does its beauteous ray
    Aught of hope or joy foretell?
Traveler, yes, it brings the day—
    Promised day of Israel.

"Watchman, tell us of the night—
    Higher yet that star ascends.
Traveler, blessedness and light,
    Peace and truth its course portends.
Watchman, will its beams alone
    Gild the spot that gave them birth?
Traveler, ages are its own;
    See, its glory fills the earth.

"Watchman, tell us, does the morning
    Of fair Zion's glory dawn?
Have the signs that mark its coming
    Yet upon thy pathway shone?
Traveler, yes: arise! look round thee!
    Light is breaking in the skies!
Gird thy bridal robes around thee!
    Morning dawns! arise! arise!"

STUDY XIV
THE KINGDOM OF GOD

ANY who have not carefully examined this subject, with concordance and Bible in hand, will be surprised, on doing so, to find its prominence in the Scriptures. The Old Testament abounds with promises and prophecies in which the Kingdom of God and its King, Messiah, figure as the very center. It was the hope of every Israelite (Luke 3:15) that as a people God would exalt their nation under Messiah; and when the Lord came to them, it was as their King, to establish the long promised Kingdom of God upon the earth.

John, the forerunner and herald of our Lord Jesus, opened his mission with the announcement, "Repent ye; for the Kingdom of Heaven is at hand." (Matt. 3:2) The Lord commenced his ministry with the same announcement exactly (Matt. 4:17); and the apostles were sent forth to preach the same message. (Matt. 10:7; Luke 9:2) Not only was the kingdom the topic with which the Lord began his public ministry, but it was really the main topic of all

273

his preaching (Luke 8:1; 4:43; 19:11), other subjects being mentioned merely in connection with or in explanation of this one subject. The majority of his parables were either illustrations of the kingdom from various standpoints, and in different features, or else served to point out entire consecration to God as essential to a share in the kingdom, and to correct the Jewish misapprehension that they were sure of the kingdom because natural children of Abraham, and hence natural heirs to the promises.

Our Lord Jesus in his talks with his followers strengthened and encouraged their expectations of a coming kingdom, saying to them, "I appoint unto you a kingdom as my Father hath appointed unto me, that ye may eat and drink at my table in my kingdom, and sit on thrones, judging [ruling] the twelve tribes of Israel." (Luke 22:29, 30) And, again, "Fear not, little flock; it is your Father's good pleasure to give you the kingdom." (Luke 12:32) And when, instead of being crowned and enthroned, their recognized king was crucified, his disciples were sorely disappointed. As two of them expressed it to the supposed stranger on their way to Emmaus after his resurrection, they *had* "*trusted* that it had been he which should have redeemed Israel"— delivering them from the Roman yoke, and making of Israel the Kingdom of God in power and glory. But they were sadly disappointed by the changes of the few days previous. Then Jesus opened their understanding by showing them from the Scriptures that his *sacrifice* was needful first of all before the kingdom could be established. Luke 24:21, 25-27

God could have given to Jesus the dominion of earth without redeeming man; for "The Most High ruleth over the kingdom of men, and giveth it to whomsoever he pleaseth." (Dan. 4:32) But God had a grander design than could have been accomplished by such a plan. Such a kingdom could have brought blessings which, however good, could have been of only a temporary character, since all of mankind were under condemnation to death. To make the blessings of his kingdom everlasting and complete, the race had first to be ransomed from death and thus legally released from the condemnation which passed upon all in Adam.

That in explaining the prophecies Jesus revived the disciples' hope of a coming kingdom is evident from the fact that afterward, as he was leaving them, they inquired, "Lord, wilt thou at *this time* restore the kingdom to Israel?" His answer, though not explicit, did not contradict their hopes. He said, "It is not for *you* to know the *times and seasons* which the Father hath put in his own power." Acts 1:6, 7

True, the disciples at first, in common with the entire Jewish nation, had an imperfect conception of the Kingdom of God in supposing it to be exclusively an earthly kingdom, even as many today err in an opposite direction in supposing it to be exclusively a heavenly kingdom. And many of the parables and dark sayings of our Lord Jesus were intended in due time to correct these misconceptions. But he always held forth the idea of a kingdom, a government, to be established *in the earth* and to rule among men. And he not only inspired in them a hope for a share in the kingdom, but he also taught them to pray for its establishment—"Thy kingdom *come*; thy will be done ON EARTH as it is in heaven."

To the worldly-wise among the Jews, our Lord seemed an impostor and fanatic; and they considered his disciples mere dupes. His wisdom and tact, and his miracles, they could not well gainsay, nor reasonably account for; yet, from their standpoint of unbelief, his claim that he was the heir of the world, and would establish the promised kingdom which should rule the world, and that his followers, all of them from the humbler walks of life, would be joint-rulers with him in that kingdom, seemed too absurd for consideration. Rome, with its disciplined warriors, its able generals and immense wealth, was the master of the world, and was daily growing more powerful. Who, then, was this Nazarene? and who were these fishermen, without money or influence, and with but a meager following among the common people? Who were these that they should talk about establishing the kingdom long promised to be the grandest and mightiest earth had ever known?

The Pharisees, hoping to expose the supposed weakness of our Lord's claims, and thereby to undeceive his followers, demanded of him—When will this kingdom which you preach begin to make its *appearance?*—when will your soldiers arrive?—when will this Kingdom of God appear? (Luke 17:20-30) Our Lord's answer would have given them a new thought had they not been prejudiced against him and blinded by their own supposed wisdom. He answered that his kingdom would never appear in the manner in which they expected it. The kingdom which he preached, and in which he invited his followers to joint-heirship, was an invisible kingdom, and they must not expect to see it. "He answered them, and said, The Kingdom of God cometh not with *observation* [outward manifestation]; neither shall they say, Lo here! or, lo there! for the Kingdom of God is [to be] in your midst."* In a word, he showed that when his kingdom should come, it would be everywhere present and everywhere powerful, yet nowhere visible.

---

*The Diaglott and Rotherham's translation render this "among you," which is synonymous with "in your midst." It certainly would agree with no theory to insist that the kingdom which Jesus claimed to be about to establish would be within the hearts of the Pharisees, whom he styled hypocrites and whited sepulchres. But this kingdom, when established, will be "*in the midst of*" or "*among*" all classes, ruling and judging all.

Thus he gave them an idea of the spiritual kingdom which he preached; but they were unprepared and received it not. There was a measure of truth in the Jewish expectation concerning the promised kingdom, which will in due time be realized, as will be shown; but our Lord's reference here is to that spiritual phase of the kingdom, which will be invisible. And as this phase of the kingdom will be *first* set up, its presence will be unseen, and for a time unrecognized. The privilege of heirship in this spiritual phase of the Kingdom of God was the only offer then being made, and has been the one hope of our high calling during the entire Gospel age, which then began. Hence Jesus referred to it exclusively. (Luke 16:16) This will be more clearly seen as we proceed.

It was probably because of this adverse public sentiment, especially among the Pharisees, that Nicodemus came to Jesus by night, being anxious to solve the mystery, yet apparently ashamed to acknowledge publicly that such claims had any weight upon his mind. The conversation between the Lord and Nicodemus (John 3), though but partially recorded, gives a somewhat further insight into the character of the Kingdom of God. Evidently the main points of the conversation are mentioned that from these we may readily gather the drift of the whole, which we may reasonably paraphrase as follows:

Nicodemus—"Rabbi, we know that thou art a teacher come from God; for no man can do these miracles that thou doest, except God be with him." Yet some of your statements seem very inconsistent to me, and I come to ask an explanation. For instance, you and your disciples go about proclaiming, "The kingdom of heaven is at hand"; but you have neither an army, nor wealth, nor influence, and to all appearance this claim is untrue; and in this you seem to be deceiving the people. The Pharisees generally regard you as an impostor, but I am sure there must be some truth in your teachings, "for no man can do these miracles that thou doest, except God be with him." The object of my visit is to inquire of what sort, when and whence is this kingdom you proclaim? and when and how is it to be established?

Jesus—Your request to have a full understanding concerning the kingdom of heaven cannot now be answered to your satisfaction; not that I do not know about it fully, but that in your present condition you could not understand or appreciate it, if I would fully explain. "Except a man be *begotten** from above, he cannot *see* [Greek, *eidon*,+ know, or be acquainted with] the kingdom of God."

Even my disciples have as yet very indistinct ideas of the character of the kingdom they are proclaiming. I cannot tell them, for the same reason that I cannot tell you; and

---

*The Greek word *gennao* and its derivatives, sometimes translated *begotten* and sometimes *born*, really contains both ideas, and should be translated by either one of these two English words, according to the sense of the passage in which it occurs. The two ideas, begetting and birth, are always in the word, so that if the one is stated, the other is always implied, as birth is the natural consequence of begetting, and begetting the natural antecedent to birth. When the active agent with which *gennao* is associated is a male, it should be translated *begotten*; when a female, *born*. Thus in 1 John 2:29; 3:9; 4:7; 5:1,18, *gennao* should be *begotten*, because God (masculine) is the active agent.

Sometimes, however, the translation is dependent on the nature of the act, whether masculine or feminine. Thus used in conjunction with *ek*, signifying *from* or *out of*, it should be translated *born*. So in John 3:5,6, *gennao* should be translated *born*, as indicated by the word *ek*—"*out of* water," "*out of* flesh," "*out of* spirit."

+This same Greek word is translated *consider* in Acts 15:6. "The apostles and elders came together for to *consider* [know or understand] this matter." The same word is rendered *behold* in Rom. 11:22. "*Behold* [consider, understand] therefore, the goodness and severity of God"; also in 1 John 3:1—"*Behold* [consider, know, understand] what manner of love the Father hath bestowed upon us."

they could not understand, for the same reason. But, Nicodemus, one peculiarity of God's dealings is that he requires obedience to the light already possessed before more light is given; and in the selection of those who shall be accounted worthy to share the kingdom, a manifestation of faith is required. They must be such as are willing to follow God's leading, step by step, often seeing only the one advance step clearly. They walk by faith and not by sight.

Nicodemus—But I do not understand you. What do you mean? "How can a man be begotten when he is old? can he enter a second time into his mother's womb, and be born?" Or do you mean that the repentance preached by "John the Immerser," and signified by baptism in water, is somehow a symbolic *birth*? I notice that your disciples preach and baptize similarly. Is this the new birth necessary to those who would see or enter your kingdom?

Jesus—Our nation is a consecrated nation, a covenant people. They were all baptized into Moses in the sea and in the cloud when they left Egypt. God accepted them in Moses, the mediator of their covenant, at Sinai; but they have forgotten their covenant, some are openly living as publicans and sinners, and many others are self-righteous hypocrites; hence John's preaching and that of my disciples is *repentance*—a return to God and to a recognition of the covenant made; and the baptism of John signifies this repentance and reformation of heart and life, and *not the new birth*. But unless you have more than this you will never see the Kingdom. Except in addition to the reformation symbolized by John's baptism you receive a begetting and birth of the spirit, you cannot see my Kingdom. Repentance will bring you back to a justified condition; in that condition you will be able readily to recognize me as Messiah, the antitype of Moses; and thus consecrating to me you will be *begotten* of the Father to a new life and the divine nature, which, if it develop and become quickened, will insure your being *born* a new creature, a spirit being, in the first resurrection; and as such you shall not only see but share the Kingdom.

The change to be wrought by this new birth of the Spirit is truly great, Nicodemus; for that which is born of the flesh is flesh, but that which is born of the Spirit is spirit. Wonder not, then, at my first statement, that you must be *begotten* from above ere you can understand, know and appreciate the things of which you inquire. "Marvel not that I said unto thee, Ye must be born again." The difference between your present condition, born of the flesh, and the condition of those born of the Spirit, who shall enter into or constitute the kingdom I am preaching, is very great. Let me give you an illustration by which you will gain some idea of the beings who, when born of the Spirit, will constitute this kingdom: "The wind bloweth where it listeth, and thou hearest the sound thereof, but canst not tell whence it cometh and whither it goeth—so is every one that is born of the Spirit." As the wind blows here and there, you cannot see it, though it exerts an influence all about you. You know not whence it comes nor where it goes. This is as good an illustration as I can give you of those born of the Spirit in the resurrection, those who will "enter into" or constitute the Kingdom which I am now preaching. They will all be as invisible as the wind, and men, not born of the Spirit, will neither know whence they came nor whither they go.

Nicodemus—How can this be?—invisible beings!

Jesus—"Art thou a master in Israel, and knowest not these things?"—that spirit beings can be present, yet invisible? Have you, who attempt to teach others, never read about Elisha and his servant, or about Balaam's ass? and the many instances in the Scriptures which illustrate this principle, that spirit beings can be present among men, yet invisible? Furthermore, you are of the Pharisees, who professedly believe in angels as spirit beings. But this illustrates what I told you at first: Except a man be begotten from above, he cannot see [know, become acquainted with, or understand as reasonable] the Kingdom of God and the various things connected with it.

If you would enter into and become a joint-heir with me of that kingdom which I am announcing, you must follow the light, step by step. As you do so, more light will come, and this as rapidly as you will be prepared for it. I have been preaching these things now due which you can understand, and performing miracles, and you acknowledge me to be a teacher come from God, but you have not acted out your faith and openly become my disciple and follower. You must not expect to see more, until you live up to all you do see; then God will give you more light and evidence for the next step. "Verily, verily, I say unto thee, we speak that *we do know*, and testify that we have seen, and ye [Pharisees] receive not our witness. If I have told you earthly things, and ye believe not, how shall ye believe if I tell you of heavenly things?" It would be useless for me to attempt to tell you of heavenly things, for you would not be convinced and my preaching would seem the more foolish to you. If what I have taught, which has been of an earthly character, or illustrated by earthly things, which you could and do understand, has not brought conviction enough to your mind to lead you openly to become my disciple and follower, it would be no more convincing to you if I were to tell you of heavenly things, of which you know nothing; for no man has ever ascended into heaven, hence none could corroborate my testimony. I, who descended from heaven, alone understand heavenly things. "No man hath ascended up to heaven, but he that came down from heaven, even the Son of man."* A knowledge of the heavenly things can be received only after the begetting of the Spirit; and the heavenly things themselves, when born of the spirit, spirit beings.

Thus it required patience on the Lord's part, in declaring the nature of the kingdom to those whose prejudices and education hindered their seeing anything except distorted views of the earthly phase of it. Nevertheless the selection of a proper class to share Messiah's kingdom proceeded, though but a few were selected from Israel, to whom exclusively it was offered for seven years. As God had foreseen, through their unreadiness for it, and their failure to grasp and comply with the conditions presented, the privilege of sharing in Messiah's kingdom passed from them as a people, only a remnant of whom received it, and came to the Gentiles to take out of them also "a people for his name." And among these also only a remnant, a "little flock," appreciate the privilege and are counted worthy of joint-heirship in his kingdom and glory.

Serious has been the error introduced into the nominal Christian Church, which misinterprets this promised kingdom to mean merely the Church nominal in its present condition, and its work merely a work of grace in the hearts of believers; and to such an extreme has this error been carried that the present unholy alliance and reign of the Church nominal with the world is believed by many to be the reign of the Kingdom of God on the earth. True, there is a sense in which the Church is now the Kingdom of God, and a work of grace is now going on in the hearts of believers; but to consider this all, and to deny a veritable future Kingdom

---

*The words *"which is in heaven"* (John 3:13) are not found in the most ancient and reliable MSS.

of God yet to be established under the whole heavens, in which the will of God will be done as it is in heaven, is to make void and meaningless the strongest and most pointed promises recorded by our Lord and the apostles and prophets, for our encouragement and help in overcoming the world.

In the parables of our Lord, the Church is frequently called the kingdom; and the Apostle speaks of it as the kingdom over which Christ now reigns, saying that God hath translated us out of the kingdom of darkness into the kingdom of his dear Son. We who accept of Christ now recognize his purchased right of dominion, and render him grateful and voluntary obedience before he forcibly establishes it in the world. We recognize the difference between the laws of righteousness, which he will enforce, and the kingdom of darkness supported by the usurper, at present the prince of this world. Faith in God's promises thus changes our allegiance, and we reckon ourselves subjects of the new prince, and, by his favor, joint-heirs with him in that kingdom yet to be set up in power and great glory.

But this fact by no means disannuls the promises that ultimately Christ's kingdom shall be "from sea to sea, and from the river to the ends of the earth" (Psa. 72:8); that all nations shall serve and obey him; and that unto him every knee shall bow, of things both in heaven and on earth. (Dan. 7:27; Phil. 2:10) Rather, on the contrary, the selection now of the "little flock" confirms those promises.

When the parables of our Lord are carefully examined, it will be found that they clearly teach that the coming or setting up of the Kingdom of God in power is future; and, as a matter of course, not until the King comes. Thus the parable of the young nobleman going into a far country to receive a kingdom and to return, etc. (Luke 19:11-15), clearly locates the establishment of the Kingdom at the return of

Christ. And the message sent by the Lord to the Church long years afterward was, "Be thou faithful unto death, and I *will give* thee a crown of life." (Rev. 2:10) From this it is evident that the kings who will reign with him will not be crowned nor reign as kings in *this* life.

The Church at present, therefore, is not the Kingdom of God set up in power and glory, but in its incipient, embryo condition. And so, indeed, all the expressions of the New Testament with reference to it teach. The kingdom of heaven now suffers violence at the hands of the world; the King was maltreated and crucified; and whosoever will follow in his footsteps shall suffer persecution and violence in some form. This, it will be observed, is true only of the *real* Church, and not of the nominal one. But the promise is held out that if now we (the Church, the embryo kingdom) suffer with Christ, we also, in due time, when he takes to himself his great power and reigns, shall be glorified and shall reign with him.

James (2:5), in harmony with our Lord's teaching, tells us that God has chosen the poor and despised according to this world's standards, not to reign now, but as "*heirs* of the kingdom which he hath *promised*." The Lord says, "How hardly shall they that have riches enter into the Kingdom of God." (Mark 10:23) It is evident that he does not mean the nominal Church, which is now reigning with the world; for the rich are pressed into it. Peter exhorts the heirs of the kingdom to patience, perseverance, virtue and faith, saying: "Brethren, give diligence to make your calling and election sure; for if ye do these things ye shall never fall; for so an entrance shall be ministered unto you abundantly into the everlasting kingdom of our Lord and Savior, Jesus Christ." 2 Peter 1:10, 11

Paul's statement in Romans 14:17 is supposed by some to refer to a *figurative* kingdom; but when examined in the light of the context, it is evident that the passage means simply this: We, brethren, translated now into the kingdom of God's dear Son, have certain liberties as to our food, etc., which we had not as Jews under the law (verse 14); yet let us rather not use this liberty if it cause brethren who do not yet realize it to stumble and violate their consciences. Let us not, by our liberty as to our food, ruin our brother for whom Christ died; but let us remember that the privileges of the kingdom, both now and in the future, consist of much greater blessings than liberty as to food; namely, in our liberty as to right-doing, our peace toward God through Christ, and our joy in participating in the holy Spirit of God. These liberties of the kingdom (now and ever) are so great that the minor liberty as to food may well be sacrificed, for the present, for our brother's good.

Thus, no matter from what scripture standpoint we look, the idea that the kingdom promises are mythical deceptions, or that our present conditions fulfil these promises, is contradicted.

With the early Church, the promises of kingdom honor and joint-heirship with the Master were strong incentives to faithfulness under present trials and persecutions, which they had been forewarned to expect; and in all the words of comfort and encouragement in the Apocalypse, given to the seven churches, none shine out more clearly and forcibly than those which declare, "To him that overcometh will I grant to sit with me in my throne, even as I also overcame and am set down with my Father in his throne"; and, "To him that overcometh will I give power over the nations."

These are promises which could not reasonably be misconstrued to apply to a present work of grace in the heart, nor yet to a reign over the nations in the present life; since they who would overcome must do so by *death* in the service, and thus gain the kingdom honors. Rev. 20:6

But human nature seeks to avoid suffering and is ever ready to grasp honor and power; hence we find that even in the apostles' day some in the Church were disposed to appropriate the promises of future honor and power to the present life, and were beginning to act as though they thought the time had already come for the world to honor and even to obey the Church. The Apostle Paul writes, correcting this error, knowing that such ideas would have an injurious effect upon the Church by cultivating pride and leading away from sacrifice. He says to them, ironically, "Now ye are full, now ye are rich; ye have reigned as kings without us." And then he adds, earnestly, "I would to God ye did reign, that we [persecuted apostles] also might reign with you." (1 Cor. 4:8) They were enjoying their Christianity by trying to get out of it and with it as much honor as possible; and the Apostle well knew that if they were *faithful* as followers of the Lord they would be in no such condition. Hence he reminds them that if indeed the long-looked-for reign had begun, *he* also would be reigning no less than they, and of the fact that he by faithfulness was a sufferer for the truth's sake, which was a proof that *their reign* was premature, and a snare rather than a glory. Then, with a touch of irony, he adds, "We [apostles and faithful servants] are fools for Christ's sake, but ye are wise in Christ; we are weak, but ye are strong; ye are honorable, but we are despised." I do not write these things merely to shame you: I have a better and a nobler object—TO WARN YOU; for the path of present honor leads not to the glory and honor *to be* revealed; but present suffering and self-denial are the narrow path to glory, honor, immortality and joint-heirship in the kingdom. Wherefore, I beseech you, be ye *followers of me.* Suffer and be reviled and persecuted now, that you may share with me the crown of life, which the Lord, the righteous judge, will give me at *that day*; and not to me only, but unto all those that love his appearing. 1 Cor. 4:10-17; 2 Tim. 4:8

But, after a great deal of persecution had been faithfully endured by the early Church, theories began to spread to the effect that the mission of the Church was to conquer the world, establish the kingdom of heaven on earth and reign over the nations *before* the Lord's second advent. This laid the foundation for worldly intrigue, pomp and pride, ostentatious show and ceremony in the Church, which was designed to impress, captivate and overawe the world, and which led step by step to the great claims of Papacy that as God's kingdom on earth it had a right to command the respect and obedience to its laws and officers of every kindred, nation, and people. Under this false claim (and they seemingly deceived themselves as well as others) Papacy for a time crowned and uncrowned the kings of Europe, and still claims the authority which it is now unable to enforce.

The same idea through Papacy has come down to Protestantism, which also claims, though more vaguely, that somehow the *reign* of the Church is in progress; and like the Corinthians its adherents are "full" and "rich," and reign "as kings," as graphically described by our Lord. (Rev. 3:17, 18) Thus it has come to pass that the merely nominal members of the Church—those not really converted, not really wheat, but tares, mere imitations of the wheat—far outnumber the true disciples of Christ. And these are much opposed to every real sacrifice and self-denial, do not suffer persecution for righteousness' [truth's] sake, and at most hold to only a form of fastings, etc., instead. They are really reigning with the world and are not in the line of preparation for sharing in the real kingdom which is to be set up by our Lord at his second presence.

To any careful observer, there is a manifest incongruity between this view and the teaching of Jesus and the apostles. They taught that there can be no kingdom until the King comes. (Rev. 20:6; 3:21; 2 Tim. 2:12) Consequently the kingdom of heaven must suffer violence *until* that time, when it shall be set up in glory and power.

Two Phases of the Kingdom of God

While it is true, as stated by our Lord, that the Kingdom of God *cometh not*—does not make its first appearance—with outward show, in due time it is to be made manifest to all by outward, visible and unmistakable signs. When fully set up, the Kingdom of God will be of two parts, a spiritual or heavenly phase and an earthly or human phase. The spiritual will always be invisible to men, as those composing it will be of the divine, spiritual nature, which no man hath seen nor can see (1 Tim. 6:16; John 1:18); yet its presence and power will be mightily manifested, chiefly through its human representatives, who will constitute the earthly phase of the Kingdom of God.

Those who will constitute the spiritual phase of the kingdom are the overcoming saints of the Gospel age—the Christ, head and body—glorified. Their resurrection and exaltation to power precedes that of all others, because through this class all others are to be blessed. (Heb. 11:39,40) Theirs is the *first resurrection*. (Rev. 20:5*) The great work before this glorious anointed company—the Christ—

---

*In this verse the words *"But the rest of the dead lived not again until the thousand years were finished"* are spurious. They are not found in the oldest and most reliable Greek MSS, the Sinaitic, Vatican Nos. 1209 and 1160, nor the Syriac MS. We must remember that many passages found in the modern copies are *additions* which do not properly belong to the Bible. Since commanded not to add to the Word of God, it is our duty to repudiate such additions as soon as their spurious character is established. The words indicated probably crept into the text by accident, in the fifth century; for no MS of earlier date (either Greek or Syriac) contains this clause. It was probably at first merely a *marginal comment* made by a reader, expressive necessitates their exaltation to the divine nature: no other than divine power could accomplish it. Theirs is a work pertaining not only to this world, but to all things *in heaven and in earth*—among spiritual as well as among human beings. Matt. 28:18; Col. 1:20; Eph. 1:10; Phil. 2:10; 1 Cor. 6:3

The work of the earthly phase of the Kingdom of God will be confined to this world and to humanity. And those so highly honored as to have a share in it will be the most exalted and honored of God among men. These are the class referred to in Chapter VIII (page 145), whose judgment

---

of his thought upon the text, and copied into the body of the text by some subsequent transcriber who failed to distinguish between the text and the comment.

However, the repudiation of this clause is not essential to the "Plan" as herein set forth; for the rest of the dead—the world at large—will not *live* again in the full sense, in the perfect sense that Adam *lived* before he sinned and came under the sentence "*dying* thou shalt die." Perfect life without weakness or dying is the only sense in which God recognizes the word *life*. From his standpoint all the world has already lost life, is dying, and might now be more properly described as *dead* than as *alive*. 2 Cor. 5:14; Matt. 8:22

The word *resurrection* (Greek, *anastasis*) signifies *raising up*. As related to man, it signifies *raising up* man to that condition from which he fell, to full perfection of manhood—the thing lost through Adam. The perfection *from which* our race fell is the perfection *to which* they will gradually rise, during the Millennial age of restitution or resurrection (raising up). The Millennial age is not only the age of trial, but also the age of blessing, and through resurrection or restitution to *life* all that *was lost* is to be restored to all who, when they know and have opportunity, gladly obey. The process of resurrection will be a gradual one, requiring the entire age for its full accomplishment; though the mere awakening to a measure of life and consciousness, as at present enjoyed, will of course be a momentary work. Consequently it will not be until the thousand years are finished that the race will have fully attained the complete measure of life lost in Adam. And since anything short of perfect life is a condition of partial death, it follows that, although the above words are no part of the inspired record, it would be strictly true to say that the rest of *the dead will not live* again (will not regain the fulness of life lost) until the thousand years of restitution and blessing are complete.

day was previous to the Gospel age. Having been tried and found faithful, in the awakening they will not be brought forth to judgment again, but will at once receive the reward of their faithfulness—an instantaneous resurrection to perfection as *men*. (Others than these and the spiritual class will be *gradually* raised to perfection during that Millennial age.) Thus this class will be ready at once for the great work before it as the human agents of the Christ in restoring and blessing the remainder of mankind. As the spiritual nature is necessary to the accomplishment of the work of Christ, so perfect human nature is appropriate for the future accomplishment of the work to be done among men. These will minister among and be seen of men, while the glory of their perfection will be a constant example and an incentive to other men to strive to attain the same perfection. And that these ancient worthies will be in the human phase of the kingdom and seen of mankind is fully attested by Jesus' words to the unbelieving Jews who were rejecting him. He said, "Ye shall see Abraham, Isaac, and Jacob, and all the prophets, in the Kingdom of God." It should be noticed also, that the Master does not mention that he or the apostles will be visible with Abraham. As a matter of fact, men will see and mingle with the earthly phase of the kingdom, but not with the spiritual; and some will, no doubt, be sorely vexed to find that they rejected so great an honor.

We are not given explicit information as to the exact manner in which these two phases of the heavenly kingdom will harmoniously operate; but we have an illustration of the manner in which they *may* operate, in God's dealings with Israel through their representatives, Moses, Aaron, Joshua, the prophets, etc.—though the coming manifestations of divine power will far exceed those of that typical age; for the work of the coming age comprises the awakening of all the dead and the restoration of *the obedient* to perfection. This work will necessitate the establishment of a perfect government among men, with perfect men in positions of control, that they may rightly order the affairs of state. It will necessitate the appointment of proper educational facilities of every character, as well as philanthropic measures of various kinds. And this noble work of thus elevating the race by sure and steady steps (under the direction of the unseen spiritual members of the same kingdom) is the high honor to which the ancient worthies are appointed, and for which they will come forth prepared soon after the final wreck of the kingdoms of this world and the binding of Satan, their prince. And as the divinely honored representatives of the heavenly kingdom, they will soon receive the honor and cooperation of all men.

To gain a place in the earthly phase of the kingdom of God will be to find the gratification of every desire and ambition of the perfect human heart. It will be a glorious and satisfying portion from the first entrance into it, and yet the glory will accumulate as time advances and the blessed work progresses. And when, at the end of a thousand years, the great work of restitution is accomplished by the Christ (in great measure through the agency of these noble human co-workers); when the whole human race (except the incorrigible—Matt. 25:46; Rev. 20:9) stands approved, without spot, or wrinkle, or any such thing, in the presence of Jehovah, these who were instrumental in the work will shine among their fellowmen and before God and Christ and the angels, as "the stars forever and ever." (Dan. 12:3) Their work and labor of love will never be forgotten by their grateful fellowmen. They will be held in everlasting remembrance. Psa. 112:6

But great as will be the accumulating glory of those perfect men who will constitute the earthly phase of the kingdom, the glory of the heavenly will be the glory that excelleth. While the former will shine as the stars forever, the latter will shine as the brightness of the firmament—as the sun. (Dan. 12:3) The honors of heaven as well as of earth shall be laid at the feet of the Christ. The human mind can approximate, but cannot clearly conceive, the glory to be revealed in the Christ through the countless ages of eternity. Rom. 8:18; Eph. 2:7-12

It is through these two phases of the kingdom that the promise to Abraham is to be verified—"In thee and in thy seed shall all the families of the earth be blessed." "Thy seed shall be as the sand of the sea, *and* as the stars of heaven"— an earthly and a heavenly seed, both God's instruments of blessing to the world. Both phases of the promises were clearly seen and intended by God from the beginning, but only the earthly was seen by Abraham. And though God selected from the natural seed the chief of the spiritual class (the apostles and others), and proffered the chief blessing, the spiritual, to all of that nation living in the due time for that heavenly call, this was just so much beyond what Abraham ever saw in the covenant—favor upon favor.

Paul (Rom. 11:17) speaks of the Abrahamic covenant as a root out of which fleshly Israel grew *naturally*, but into which the Gentile believers were *grafted* when the natural branches were cut off because of unbelief. This proves the double fulfilment of the promise in the development of the *two seeds*, earthly (human) and heavenly (spiritual), which will constitute the two phases of the kingdom. This root-covenant bears these two distinct kinds of branches, each of which in the resurrection will bear its own distinct kind of perfect fruitage—the human and spiritual classes in kingdom power. In order of development it was first the natural (earthly), afterward the heavenly rulers; but in order of grandeur of position and time of instalment, it will be first the spiritual, afterward the natural; and so there are last which shall be first, and first which shall be last. Matt. 19:30; Luke 16:16

The promise made to Abraham, to which Stephen refers (Acts 7:5), and in which Israel trusted, was earthly: it related to the *land*. God "promised that he would give it to him for a possession," said Stephen. And God said to Abraham, "Lift up now thine eyes, and look from the place where thou art, northward and southward and eastward and westward; for all the *land* which thou seest, to thee will I give it, and to thy seed forever. And I will make thy seed as the dust of the earth, so that if a man can number the dust of the earth, then shall thy seed be numbered. Arise, walk through the land, in the length of it and in the breadth of it; for I will give it unto thee." (Gen. 13:14-17) Stephen shows that this promise *must yet* be fulfilled; for he declares that God gave Abraham "none inheritance in it [in the land], no, not so much as to set his foot on."

The Apostle, writing of this same class of ancient worthies—Abraham among others—agrees with Stephen's statement that the promise to Abraham has not yet been fulfilled; and he goes further and shows that those earthly promises cannot and will not be fulfilled until the still higher heavenly promises concerning the Christ (Head and body) are fulfilled. He says of them: These all died in faith, not [i.e., without] having received [the fulfilment of] the promise, God having provided some better thing for us [the Christ], that *they* without *us* should not be made perfect. (Heb. 11:13, 39, 40) Thus is shown again that the Redeemer and Restorer is spiritual, having given up the human a sacrifice for all, and that from this spiritual class when highly exalted all blessings must proceed, whoever may be honored as its instruments or agents. Rom. 12:1; Gal. 3:29

The earthly phase of the kingdom is thus seen to be Israelitish; and around this fact cluster those many prophecies which relate to the prominence of that nation in God's plan for the future blessing of the world, when their tabernacle, fallen in the dust, shall be restored, and Jerusalem shall be a praise in the whole earth. We find statements by both prophets and apostles which clearly indicate that in the times of restitution Israel as a nation will be the first among the nations to come into harmony with the new order of things; that the earthly Jerusalem will be rebuilt upon her old heaps; and that their polity will be restored as in the beginning under princes or judges. (Isa. 1:26; Psa. 45:16; Jer. 30:18) And what could be more reasonably expected than that Israel should first of all rejoice to recognize the prophets and patriarchs? and that their acquaintance with and long discipline under the law should have prepared them for tractability and obedience under the authority of the kingdom? And while Israel will be the first of the nations to be recognized and blessed, it is written also of Israel that "The Lord shall save the tents of Judah first."

We do not deem it of importance to enter into a discussion as to where the "lost tribes" of Israel are to be sought. It may or may not be true, as some claim, that those "lost tribes" are traceable to certain civilized nations of the present day. But though some of the suggested proofs are not unreasonable, yet, as a whole, it is largely inference and guess-work. But should it yet be clearly demonstrated that some of the civilized nations are descendants of the lost tribes, it would prove *no advantage* to them under the "heavenly" "high calling," which, since their national rejection, knows no difference between Jew and Greek, bond and free. Should such evidence ever become clear (which as yet it is not), it would be in perfect harmony with the prophecies and promises relating to that nation yet awaiting fulfilment in and under the earthly phase of the kingdom.

Natural attachment, as well as a still surviving measure of trust in the long unfulfilled promises, and all their natural prejudices, will be favorable to Israel's general and speedy acceptance of the new rulers; while their habits of measurable obedience to the law will also be favorable to their speedy harmony with the principles of the new government.

As Jerusalem was the seat of empire under the typical Kingdom of God, it will again occupy the same position, and be "the city of the Great King." (Psa. 48:2; Matt. 5:35) A city is a symbol of a kingdom or dominion, and so God's Kingdom is symbolized by the New Jerusalem, the new dominion coming from heaven to earth. At first it will consist of only the spiritual class, the Bride of Christ, which, as seen by John, will gradually come down to earth; that is, it will gradually come into power as the present empires break in pieces, during the Day of the Lord. In due time, however, the earthly phase of this city or government will be established, parts or members of which will be the ancient worthies. There will not be two cities (governments), but one city, one heavenly government, the one for which Abraham looked, "a city which hath foundations"—a government established in righteousness, being founded upon the sure rock foundation of the righteousness of Christ the Redeemer, the value of man's ransom which he gave, and the firmness of divine justice, which can no more condemn the redeemed than it could previously excuse the guilty. Rom. 8:31-34; 1 Cor. 3:11

Glorious City of Peace! whose walls signify salvation, protection and blessing to all who enter it, whose foundations laid in justice can never be moved, and whose builder and designer is God! It is in the light which will shine from this glorious city (kingdom) of God that the nations (people) will walk on the highway of holiness, up to perfection and to full harmony with God. Rev. 21:24*

When mankind reaches perfection at the close of the Millennial age, as already shown, they will be admitted into membership in the Kingdom of God and given the entire control of earth as at first designed—each man a sovereign, a king. This is clearly shown in the symbolic prophecy of John (Rev. 21:24-26); for in vision he not only saw the people walk in the light of it, but he saw the *kings* enter it in glory; yet none could enter who would defile it. None can become identified with that city (kingdom) who has not first been thoroughly tested; none who would work, or love to work, deceit and unrighteousness; only those whom the Lamb will write as worthy of life everlasting, and to whom he will say, "Come, ye blessed of my Father, inherit the kingdom prepared for you."

It should be remembered, then, that though undoubtedly the literal city of Jerusalem will be rebuilt, and though probably it will become the capital of the world, yet many prophecies which mention Jerusalem and its future glories refer, under that as a symbol, to the Kingdom of God to be established in great splendor.

Concerning the future glory of the earthly phase of the kingdom as represented in Jerusalem, the prophets speak in glowing terms, saying: "Break forth into joy, sing together, ye waste places of Jerusalem; for the Lord hath comforted

---

*The following words are omitted from this verse by the most authentic ancient manuscripts, viz., "*of them which are saved*," also "*and honor*." The latter words are also lacking from verse 26.[1]

[1]Recent research in ancient manuscripts and textual authorities concerning the words "and honor" in Rev. 21:26 support retaining these two words.

his people, he hath redeemed Jerusalem." "Behold, I create
Jerusalem a rejoicing, and her people a joy." "Rejoice ye with
Jerusalem and be glad with her, . . . that ye may be delighted
with the abundance of her glory; for saith the Lord, Behold, I
will extend peace to her like a river, and the glory of the Gentiles
like a flowing stream." "At that time they shall call Jerusalem
the throne of the Lord, and all nations shall be gathered unto
it." "And many people shall go and say, Come ye, and let us go
up to the mountain [kingdom] of the Lord, to the house of the
God of Jacob; and he will teach us of his ways, and we will walk
in his paths; for out of Zion [the spiritual phase] shall go forth
the law, and the word of the Lord from Jerusalem"—the earthly
phase. Isa. 52:9; 65:18; 66:10-12; Jer. 3:17; Isa. 2:3

When considering the many precious promises of future
blessing made to Israel, and expecting an accurate fulfilment of
them to that people, it is proper that we should remember that
as a people they are typical, as well as actual. In one aspect they
are typical of the whole world of mankind; and their Law
Covenant, of obedience and life, was typical of the New
Covenant to be established with the world during the Millennial
and future ages.

The blood of atonement under their typical covenant,
and the priesthood which applied it to that nation, typified
the blood of the New Covenant and the Royal Priesthood
which will, during the Millennium, apply its cleansings and
blessings to the whole world. Thus their priesthood typified
the Christ, and that nation typified all for whom the real
sacrifice was made, and to whom the real blessings will
come—"every man," "the whole world."

Then let us remember that though the future blessings,
like the past, will be to the Jew first, and also to the Gentile,
it will be in the matter of time only that the Jews will have
the precedence to divine favor; and this we have shown
would be a natural consequence of their training under the

Law, which in due time will serve its purpose to bring them to Christ. Though it brought only a remnant of them at the first advent, it will bring them as a people at the second advent, and as a people they will be a first-fruit among the nations. Ultimately every blessing promised to Israel, except those pertaining to the elected classes, will have, not only its actual fulfilment in that people, but also its antitypical fulfilment in all the families of the earth. Under that government "God will render to every man according to his deeds—glory, honor, and peace to every man that worketh good, to the Jew first, and also to the Gentile; for there is no respect of persons with God." Rom. 2:6, 10, 11

The Apostle Paul calls our attention specially to the sureness of God's promises to Israel in the future, and shows what favors they lost by unbelief, and what favors are still sure. He says that it was because of pride, hardness of heart and unbelief that Israel as a people had *not obtained* that for which they sought—the chief place in divine favor and service. Paul's reference here is not to all the generations of Israel, from Abraham down, but to those generations living at the time of the first advent; and his words would apply to all their generations which have lived during the Gospel age, the age wherein the chief favor has been offered—the high calling to the divine nature and joint-heirship with Jesus. This favor Israel as a people has failed to recognize and lay hold of. And though God visited the Gentiles and called many of them through the gospel, they, like fleshly Israel, will fail to obtain the heavenly prize. Nevertheless, a class, a remnant, a little flock from among all the called ones, heeds the call, and, by obedience and self-sacrifice, makes its calling and election sure. Thus what Israel as a people failed to obtain, and what the nominal Christian Church also fails to obtain, is given to the elect or selected class, the faithful—"body of Christ"—elect or chosen (according to the foreknowledge of God) through sanctification of the spirit and belief of the truth. 2 Thess. 2:13; 1 Pet. 1:2

But though, through the rejection of Messiah, Israel did lose all this special favor, yet Paul shows that this did not prove them entirely cut off from favor; for they still had the same privilege of being grafted into Christ and the spiritual favors which the rest of mankind enjoyed, if, during the time that call was being made, they accepted in faith; for, argues Paul, God is as able to graft them in again as to graft in wild branches, and as willing, if they continue not in unbelief. Rom. 11:23, 24

Moreover, Paul argues that though Israel lost the chief blessing, "which he seeketh for," the chief place in God's kingdom, yet it remains that great promises are still due to be fulfilled toward that people; for, he reasons, God's gifts, callings, covenants and promises are not to be turned aside unfulfilled. God knew the end from the beginning; he knew that Israel would reject Messiah; and his unequivocal promises to them in view of this knowledge give us assurance that Israel is yet to be used of the Lord in service, as his agency in blessing the world, though "Israel hath not obtained that which he seeketh for"—the chief favor. Paul then proceeds to show that God's covenant promises to Israel were of such a nature as to leave it open and indefinite whether as a people they would be the heavenly or the earthly seed—whether they would inherit and fulfil the higher or the lower service mentioned in the promises. God kept secret the higher spiritual favor until due time, and the promises made to them mentioned the earthly favor only, though He favored them by the first offer of the spiritual favors also, and so offered them more than he had ever promised. In a word, the heavenly promises were hidden in the earthly. These promises, says Paul, cannot fail, and the offering of the hidden favor first, and Israel's blind rejection of it, in no way invalidates or disannuls the other feature of the promise. Hence he declares that though Israel as a nation is cast off from favor during the time the Bride of Christ is being selected from both Jews and Gentiles, yet the time will come when, the Deliverer (Christ, Head and body) being complete, divine favor will return to fleshly Israel, and the glorious Deliverer will turn away ungodliness from Jacob,* and so all Israel will be saved [recovered to favor], as it is written by the prophet. The Apostle's words are:

"Brethren, that you may not be conceited with yourselves, I wish you not to be ignorant of this secret, that hardness in some measure has happened to Israel *until* the fulness of the Gentiles may come in [until the full number selected from the Gentiles has been completed]. And then all Israel will be saved, as it has been written, 'The Deliverer [Christ, Head and body] shall come out of Zion and shall turn away ungodliness from Jacob.' And 'This is the covenant with them from me, when I shall take away their sins.' In relation to the GLAD TIDINGS, indeed, they are enemies on your account; but in regard to the election they are [still] beloved on account of the fathers, because the gracious gifts and calling of God are not things to be repented of. Besides, as you [Gentiles] were once disobedient to God, but have now obtained mercy by their disobedience; so also, now, these have disobeyed so that they may obtain mercy through *your* mercy [at the hands of the glorified Church]. For God shut up together all, for disobedience, that he might have mercy on all. [Compare Rom. 5:17-19.] O the depth of the riches and wisdom and knowledge of God." Rom. 11:25-33

---

*Spiritual Israel is never called "Jacob."

Heirs of the Kingdom

"Who shall ascend into the hill [literally *mountain*, symbol of kingdom] of Jehovah? or who shall stand in his holy place [temple]? He that hath clean hands and a pure heart." Psa. 24:3, 4

The city of Jerusalem was built upon a mountain top—a double top; for it was separated by the valley Tyropoeon into two parts. Still it was one city, surrounded by one wall, with bridges connecting the two divisions. On one of these mountain tops the Temple was built. This might be understood to symbolize the union of the kingly and the priestly qualities in the glorified Church; or, the one Kingdom of God with its two phases—the spiritual temple, not of earthly origin, but of a new, heavenly or spiritual nature (Heb. 9:11), separate from, yet united with, the earthly phase.

David appears to refer to the two places. It was an honor to be of the city at all, and a still greater honor to ascend into the holy temple, into the sacred precincts of which only the priests were permitted to enter. And David shows that purity of life and honesty of heart are necessary to any who would attain either honor. They that would be of the Royal Priesthood are exhorted to purity, even as the high priest of our profession is pure, if they would be accounted worthy of joint-heirship with him. And he that hath this hope in him purifieth himself, even as he is pure. This, as already shown, is a purity of *intent*, reckoned to us as absolute or actual purity, Christ's imputed purity supplying our unavoidable deficiency, and compensating for our unavoidable weaknesses, while we walk *after* the spirit and not *after* the flesh.

But let it not be forgotten that purity, sincerity, and entire consecration to God are essential to all those who would enter the Kingdom of God in either phase. It was thus with those ancient worthies who will inherit the earthly phase of the kingdom under Christ. They loved righteousness and hated iniquity, and were deeply grieved and penitent when overtaken by a fault, or stumbled by a weakness or besetment. So, too, it has been with the faithful of the Gospel age; and so it will be with all in the Millennial age, when the spirit of God, the spirit of truth, is poured upon all flesh. The overcomers of that age will also need to strive for purity of heart and life, if they would have a right under God's arrangement to enter into the city—the kingdom prepared for them from the foundation of the world—the original dominion restored.

The Iron Rule

Many erroneously suppose that when Christ's Millennial Kingdom is inaugurated every one will be pleased with its ruling. But not so. Its regulations will be far more exacting than those of any previous government, and the liberties of the people will be restricted to a degree that will be galling indeed to many now clamoring for an increase of liberty. Liberty to deceive, to misrepresent, to overreach and to defraud others, will be entirely cut off. Liberty to abuse themselves or others in food or in drink, or in any way to corrupt good manners, will be totally denied to all. Liberty or license to do wrong of any sort will not be granted to any. The only liberty that will be granted to any will be the true and glorious liberty of the sons of God—liberty to do good to themselves and others in any and in every way; but nothing will be allowed to injure or destroy in all that Holy Kingdom. (Isa. 11:9; Rom. 8:21) That rule will consequently be felt by many to be a severe one, breaking up all their former habits and customs, as well as breaking up present institutions founded upon these false habits and false ideas of liberty. Because of its firmness and vigor, it is symbolically called an iron rule—"He shall rule them with a rod of iron." (Compare Rev. 2:26, 27; Psa. 2:8-12 and 49:14.) Thus will be fulfilled the statement, "Judgment will I lay to the line and righteousness to the plummet. And the hail [righteous judgment] shall sweep away the refuge of lies, and the waters [truth] shall overflow the hiding place," and every hidden thing shall be revealed. Isa. 28:17; Matt. 10:26

Many will feel rebellious against that perfect and equitable rule because accustomed in the past, under the rule of the present prince, to lord it over their fellow mortals, and to live wholly at the expense of others without rendering compensating service. And many and severe will be the stripes which a present life of self-indulgence and gratification will *naturally* demand and receive under that reign, before such will learn the lessons of that kingdom—equity, justice, righteousness. (Psa. 89:32; Luke 12:47, 48) The lesson on this subject comes first to the living generation, and is near at hand. James 5

But, blessed thought! when the Prince of Life has put in force the laws of righteousness and equity with an iron rule, the masses of mankind will learn that "Righteousness exalteth a nation, but sin is a reproach to any people." They will learn that God's plan and laws are best in the end for all concerned, and ultimately they will learn to *love* righteousness and hate iniquity. (Psa. 45:7; Heb. 1:9) All who under that reign have not learned to love the right will be counted unworthy of lasting life and will be cut off from among the people. Acts 3:23; Rev. 20:9; Psa. 11:5-7

The Kingdom Everlasting

"Jehovah shall be King over all the earth in that day." (Zech. 14:9) The kingdom which Jehovah will establish in the hands of Christ during the Millennium will be Jehovah's kingdom, but it will be under the direct control of

Christ, as his vicegerent, in much the same manner as the Southern States were dealt with after the Rebellion by the United States government. The Southern States for a while were not permitted to govern themselves by electing their own officers, lest they should not conform to the Constitutional laws of the Union; but governors, with full power to act, were placed in control for the purpose of reconstructing those state governments and bringing them back into full harmony with the central government. Thus the special reign of Christ over the affairs of earth is for a limited time and for a particular purpose, and it will terminate with the accomplishment of that purpose. Man, through rebellion, forfeited his God-given rights—among others, self-government in harmony with Jehovah's laws. God, through Christ, redeems all those rights, and secures the right for man not only to return personally to his former estate, but also to return to his former office as king of earth. But to bring man back, as God designs, in the way best suited to impress the lesson of present experience—namely, by requiring him to put forth effort toward his own recovery—will require a strong, a perfect government. And this honor of completing man's recovery, the right to which he died to secure, is conferred upon Christ; and "he must reign *until* he hath put all enemies under his feet"—until none exist who do not recognize, honor and obey him. Then, having accomplished his mission as regards the reconstruction or restitution of mankind, he will deliver up the kingdom to God, even the Father, and mankind will deal directly, as at first, with Jehovah—the mediation of the man Christ Jesus having accomplished fully and completely the grand work of reconciliation. 1 Cor. 15:25-28

The kingdom, when delivered up to the Father, will still be the Kingdom of God, and the laws will always be the same. All mankind, then perfectly restored, will be capable of rendering perfect obedience, in letter as well as in spirit; while now, the spirit of obedience or endeavor to observe God's law is all of which men are capable. The full letter of that perfect law would condemn them at once to death. (2 Cor. 3:6) Our acceptableness now is only through Christ's ransom.

Until actually perfect, "It is a fearful thing to fall into the hands of the living God." (Heb. 10:31) Now, and until actually perfect, none could stand before the law of exact justice: all need the mercy provided freely under Christ's merit and sacrifice. But when Christ delivers up the kingdom to the Father, he will present them *faultless* before him, fit and able to enjoy everlasting blessedness under Jehovah's perfect law. All fearfulness will then be gone, and Jehovah and his restored creatures will be in perfect harmony, as at first.

When, in the end of the Millennial age, Christ delivers up the dominion of earth to the Father, he does so by delivering it to mankind as the Father's representatives, who were designed from the first to have this honor. (1 Cor. 15:24; Matt. 25:34) Thus the Kingdom of God lasts forever. And so we read in our Lord's words: "Then shall the King say to them on his right hand [those who, during the Millennial reign, will have attained the position of favor by harmony and obedience], Come, ye blessed of my Father [you whom my Father designs thus to bless], inherit the kingdom *prepared* FOR YOU from the foundation of the world."

This kingdom and honor prepared for man should not be confounded with that still higher kingdom and honor prepared for the Christ, which were "ordained *before* the world unto *our* glory" (1 Cor. 2:7), and to which we were chosen in Christ *before* the foundation of the world. And though the *special* intervention and reign of the Christ over earth will close, as foreshown, we must not conclude that Christ's glory and dominion and power will then cease. Nay, Christ is associated forever with all the divine glory and power at the right hand of Jehovah's favor; and his Bride and joint-heir will forever share his increasing glory. What wondrous works in other worlds await the power of this highly exalted agent of Jehovah, we will not here surmise, further than to suggest the infinitude and activity of divine power, and the boundlessness of the universe.

Truly, then, in whatever phase of the kingdom our interest centers, it is "the desire of all nations"; for under it all will be blessed. Hence, all may earnestly long for that time; and all may well pray, "Thy Kingdom come, thy will be done on earth as it is in heaven." It is for this that ignorantly the whole creation has long been groaning and waiting—waiting for the manifestation of the Sons of God, the kingdom which will crush out evil and bless and heal all nations. Rom. 8:19; 16:20

STUDY XV
THE DAY OF JEHOVAH

THE "DAY OF JEHOVAH," THE "DAY OF VENGEANCE," THE "DAY OF WRATH"—A TIME
OF GREAT TROUBLE—ITS CAUSE—THE BIBLE'S TESTIMONY REGARDING IT—ITS
FIRE AND STORM, ITS SHAKING AND MELTING, SHOWN TO BE SYMBOLIC—DAVID'S
TESTIMONY—THE REVELATOR'S TESTIMONY—THE PRESENT SITUATION AND THE
FUTURE OUTLOOK AS VIEWED BY THE OPPOSING PARTIES, CAPITALISTS AND WAGE-
WORKERS—A REMEDY WHICH WILL NOT SUCCEED—THE VEIL LIFTED AND LIGHT
ADMITTED JUST IN DUE TIME—THE PROOF OF THIS—THE CONDITION OF THE
SAINTS DURING THE TROUBLE, AND THEIR PROPER ATTITUDE TOWARD IT.

THE "Day of Jehovah" is the name of that period of time
in which God's kingdom, under Christ, is to be gradually
"set up" in the earth, while the kingdoms of this world are
passing away and Satan's power and influence over men are
being bound. It is everywhere described as a dark day of
intense trouble and distress and perplexity upon mankind.
And what wonder that a revolution of such proportions, and
necessitating such great changes, should cause trouble.
Small revolutions have caused trouble in every age; and this,
so much greater than any previous revolution, is to be a time
of trouble such as never was since there was a nation—no,
nor ever shall be. Dan. 12:1; Matt. 24:21, 22

It is called the "Day of Jehovah" because, though Christ,
with royal title and power, will be present as Jehovah's
representative, taking charge of all the affairs during this day
of trouble, it is more as the General of Jehovah, subduing
all things, than as the Prince of Peace, blessing all.
Meantime, as false and imperfect views and systems fall, the
standard of the new King will rise, and eventually he shall

307

be recognized and owned by all as King of kings. Thus it is presented by the prophets as Jehovah's work to *set up* Christ's dominion: "*I will give* thee the Gentiles for thine inheritance, and the uttermost parts of the earth for thy possession." (Psa. 2:8) "In the days of these kings shall the God of heaven set up a kingdom." (Dan. 2:44) The Ancient of days did sit, and there was brought before him one like unto a son of man, and there *was given him* a dominion, that all kingdoms should serve and obey him. (Dan. 7:9, 13, 14, 22, 27) Added to these is Paul's statement that, when Christ shall accomplish the object of his reign, "then shall the Son also himself be subject unto him [the Father] that PUT ALL THINGS UNDER HIM." 1 Cor. 15:28

This period is called the "Day of Vengeance of our God," and a "Day of Wrath." (Isa. 61:2; 63:1-4; Psa. 110:5) And yet the mind that grasps only the idea of anger, or supposes divine malice, seriously errs. God has established certain laws, in harmony with which he operates, and those who from any cause come into conflict with these reap the penalty or wrath of their own course. God's counsel to mankind has been continually rejected, except by the few; and, as we have shown, he permitted them to have their own way and to drop him and his counsels from their hearts. (Rom. 1:28) He then confined his special care to Abraham and his seed, who professed to desire his way and his service. Their hardness of heart as a people, and the insincerity of their hearts toward God, not only naturally prevented them from receiving Messiah, but just as naturally prepared them for and led them into the trouble which terminated their national existence.

And so the light borne in the world during the Gospel age by the true Church of Christ (the class whose names are written in heaven) has borne witness to the civilized world of the difference between right and wrong, good and evil, and of a coming time in which the one will be rewarded and the other punished. (John 16:8-11; Acts 24:25) This would have had a wide influence upon men had they heeded the Lord's instruction, but, willful as ever, they have profited little by the advice of the Scriptures, and the trouble of the Day of the Lord will come as a consequence of the neglect. Again, it may be said to be the wrath of God inasmuch as it comes through disregard of his counsels, and as a reward of unrighteousness. Nevertheless, viewed in another light, the trouble coming upon the world is the natural or legitimate result of sin, which God foresaw, and against which his counsels would have protected them, had they been followed.

While God's message to the Church has been, "Present your bodies a living sacrifice" (Rom. 12:1), his message to the world has been, "Keep thy tongue from evil, and thy lips from speaking guile; depart from evil and do good; seek peace and pursue it." (Psa. 34:13, 14) Few have heeded either message. Only a little flock sacrificed; and as for the world, though it nailed up the motto, "Honesty is the best policy," it has neglected in general to practice it. It heeded rather the voice of avarice—Get all you can of riches and honor and power in this world, no matter what the method by which you obtain it, and no matter who loses by your gain. In a word, the trouble of this Day of the Lord would not come, could not come, if the principles of God's law were observed to any considerable extent. That law briefly summed up is—Thou shalt love the Lord thy God with all thy heart, and thy neighbor as thyself. (Matt. 22:37-39) It is because the depraved or carnal mind is opposed to this law of God, and is not subject to it, that, as a natural consequence, the trouble will come, as reaping after sowing.

The carnal or depraved mind, so far from loving its neighbor as itself, has always been selfish and grasping—often leading even to violence and murder to get for self the things possessed by others. However exercised, the selfish principle is always the same, except as governed by circumstances of birth, education and surroundings. It has been the same in every age of the world, and will be, until, by the *force* of the iron rule of Messiah, not might nor greed, but love, will decide what is RIGHT, and *enforce* it, until all may have opportunity to learn the superior benefits of the rule of righteousness and love as compared with that of selfishness and might; until, under the influence of the sunlight of truth and righteousness, the selfish, stony heart of man will become once more as when God pronounced it "very good"—a heart of flesh. Ezek. 36:26

Looking back, we can see without difficulty how the change from Godlike love and kindness to hard selfishness came about. The circumstances tending to promote selfishness were encountered as soon as man, through disobedience, lost the divine favor and was exiled from his Eden home, where his every want had been bountifully supplied. As our condemned parents went forth and began the battle of life, seeking to prolong existence to its farthest limit, they were met at once with thorns and briers and thistles and sterile ground; and the contending with these produced weariness and the sweat of face which the Lord had declared. Gradually the mental and moral qualities began to dwarf from lack of exercise, while the lower qualities retained fuller scope from constant exercise. Sustenance became the principal aim and interest of life; and its cost in labor became the standard by which all other interests were estimated, and Mammon became master of men. Can we wonder that under such circumstances mankind became selfish, greedy and grasping, each striving for most—first of the necessities, and secondly of the honors and luxuries bestowed by Mammon? It is but the natural tendency of which Satan has taken great advantage.

During past ages, under various influences (among others, ignorance, race prejudices, and national pride), the great wealth of the world has generally been in the hands of the few—the rulers—to whom the masses rendered slavish obedience as to their national representatives, in whose wealth they felt a pride and an interest as their own representatively. But as the time drew near in which Jehovah designed to bless the world through a Restitution at the hands of Messiah, he began to lift up the veil of ignorance and superstition, through modern facilities and inventions; and with these came the general elevation of the people and the decreasing power of earthly rulers. No longer is the wealth of the world in the hands of its kings, but chiefly among the people.

Though wealth brings many evils, it also brings some blessings: the wealthy obtain better educations—but thus they are lifted intellectually above the poorer people and become more or less associated with royalty. Hence an aristocracy exists which has both money and education to back it, and to assist in its avaricious struggle to get all it can and to keep self in the front rank at any cost.

But, as intelligence spreads, as the people take advantage of educational facilities, now so abundant, they begin to *think* for themselves; and with the self-esteem and selfishness in them led on by *a little* learning—sometimes a dangerous thing—they fancy that they see ways and means by which the interests and circumstances of all men, and especially their own, can be promoted at the cost of the fewer numbers in whose hands the wealth now lies. Many of these, doubtless, honestly believe that the conflicting interests of Mammon's worshipers (themselves on one side, and the wealthy on the other) could be easily and fairly adjusted; and no doubt they feel that were they wealthy they would be very benevolent, and quite willing to love their neighbors as themselves. But they evidently deceive themselves; for in their present condition very few indeed manifest such a spirit, and he that would not be faithful in the use of a little of this world's goods would not be faithful if he had greater riches. In fact, circumstances prove this; for some of the hardest hearted and most selfish among the wealthy are those who have risen suddenly from the humble walks of life.

On the contrary, while by no means excusing but reproving covetousness and grasping selfishness on the part of all classes, it is but proper to notice that the provision made for the sick and helpless and poor, in the way of asylums, hospitals, poor-houses, public libraries, schools and various other enterprises for the good and comfort of the masses, rather than of the wealthy, is maintained mainly by taxes and donations from the rich. These institutions almost always owe their existence to the kindhearted and benevolent among the rich, and are matters which the poorer classes have neither the time, nor generally the necessary education or interest, to bring into successful operation.

Nevertheless, today sees a growing opposition between the wealthy and laboring classes—a growing bitterness on the part of labor, and a growing feeling among the wealthy that nothing but the strong arm of the law will protect what they believe to be *their rights*. Hence, the wealthy are drawn closer to the governments; and the wage-working masses, beginning to think that laws and governments were designed to aid the wealthy and to restrain the poor, are drawn toward Communism and Anarchy, thinking that their interests would best be served thereby, and not realizing that the worst government, and the most expensive, is vastly better than no government at all.

Many scriptures clearly show that this will be the character of the trouble under which present civil, social and religious systems will pass away; that this is the way in which increase of knowledge and liberty will result, because of man's imperfection, mental, moral and physical. These scriptures will be referred to in due course; but here we can only call attention to a few of the many, advising our readers meanwhile that in many of the prophecies of the Old Testament in which Egypt, Babylon and Israel figure so largely, not only was there a literal fulfilment intended, but also a secondary and larger one. Thus, for instance, the predictions regarding the fall of Babylon, etc., must be considered extravagant beyond measure, did we not recognize a symbolic and antitypical as well as a literal Babylon. The book of Revelation contains predictions recorded long after literal Babylon was in ruins, and hence evidently applicable only to symbolic Babylon; yet the close resemblance of the words of the prophets, apparently directly addressed to literal Babylon, are thus shown to belong in an especial sense to symbolic Babylon. In this larger fulfilment, Egypt represents the world; Babylon represents the nominal Church, called Christendom; while, as already shown, Israel often represents the whole world in its *justified* condition, as it will be—its glorious Royal Priesthood, its holy Levites and its believing and worshiping people, justified by the sacrifice of the Atonement, and brought into a condition of reconciliation with God. To Israel the blessings are promised, to Egypt the plagues, and to strong Babylon a wonderful, complete and everlasting overthrow, "as a great millstone cast into the sea" (Rev. 18:21), never to be recovered, but to be held in everlasting odium.

The Apostle James points out this day of trouble, and tells of its being the result of differences between capital and labor. He says: "Come now, ye wealthy! wail ye, howling at your hardships that are coming upon you. Your wealth has rotted [lost its value], and your garments have become moth-eaten: your gold and silver have become rusted out, and their rust for a witness to you shall be, and shall eat your flesh as fire. Ye treasured it up in the last days. Behold! the wages of the workers who cut down your fields—that which has been kept back by reason of you [of your hoarding] is crying out; and the outcries of those who reaped, into the ears of the Lord of the whole people have entered." (Jas. 5:1-4) He adds that the class coming into trouble has been used to luxury, obtained largely at the cost of others, among whom were some of the righteous, and out of them, because they resisted not, the very life had been crushed. The Apostle urges the "brethren" to bear patiently whatever their part may be, looking beyond, and expecting deliverance through the Lord. This very condition of things can now be seen approaching; and in the world, among those who are awake, "men's hearts are failing them for looking after the things that are coming on the earth." All know that the constant tendency of our times is toward lower wages for labor, unless where the prices are artificially sustained or advanced by labor combinations, strikes, etc.; and with the present sentiment of the masses, all can see that it is but a question of time when the lowest point of endurance will be reached, and a revolt will surely result. This will alarm capital, which will be withdrawn from business and manufacturing channels and hoarded in vaults and treasuries, to eat itself up with charges for its protection in idleness, to the great annoyance of its owners. This in turn will certainly produce bankruptcy, financial panic and business prostration, because all business of magnitude is now conducted largely on credit. The natural result of all this will be to throw out of employment tens of thousands who are dependent on their wages for daily bread, and to fill the world with tramps and persons whose necessities will defy all law. Then it will be as described by the prophet (Ezek. 7:10-19), when the buyer need not rejoice, nor the seller mourn; for trouble will be upon the entire multitude and there will be no security of property. Then all hands will be feeble and helpless to turn aside the trouble. They will cast their silver in the streets, and their gold will be removed. Their silver and their gold will not be able to deliver them in the day of the Lord's wrath.

It should not be forgotten that though the last forty years of the existence of Israel as a nation was a day of trouble, a "day of vengeance" upon that people, ending in the complete overthrow of their nation, yet their day of wrath was but a shadow or type of a still greater and more extensive trouble upon nominal Christendom, even as their past history as a people during their age of favor was typical of the Gospel age, as will be conclusively shown hereafter. All then will see why these prophecies concerning the Day of the Lord should be, and are, addressed to Israel and Jerusalem more or less directly, though the connections show clearly that all mankind is included in the complete fulfilments.

Take another prophetic testimony (Zeph. 1:7-9, 14-18). "The Lord hath prepared a slaughter, he hath bid his guests. [Compare Rev. 19:17.] And it shall come to pass in the day of the Lord's slaughter that I will punish the princes and the king's children, and all such as are clothed in imported clothing. And I will inflict punishment [also] on all those [marauders] who leap over the threshold on that day, who fill their masters' houses with violence and deceit. [This shows not only that there will be a great overthrow of wealth and power in this time of trouble, but that those who will for the time be the instruments of heaven in breaking down present systems will also be punished for their equally unjust and unrighteous course; for the coming trouble will involve all classes, and bring distress upon all the multitude.]

"Nigh is the great Day of the Lord: it is nigh. Nearer and louder comes the uproar of the Day of the Lord. There the mighty shall shriek bitterly! That day is a day of wrath, a day of distress and anxiety, a day of wasting and desolation, a day of darkness and obscurity [uncertainty and foreboding, as well as present distress], a day of clouds [trouble] and tempestuous gloom, a day of the trumpet [the seventh *symbolic* trumpet, which sounds throughout this day of trouble—also called the trump of God, because connected with the *events* of this Day of the Lord] and shouting against the fenced cities and the high battlements [clamorous and conflicting denunciations of strong and well-intrenched governments]. And I will bring distress upon men, and they shall walk about as blind men [groping in uncertainty, not knowing what course to pursue], because they have sinned against Jehovah. Their blood shall be poured out as the dust, and their flesh shall be as dung. Neither their silver nor their gold shall be able to deliver them in the day of the Lord's wrath [though previously wealth could furnish ease and every luxury], but the whole land shall be devoured by the FIRE of his *zeal*; for destruction, yea, quite sudden, will he prepare for all them [the wealthy] that dwell in the land." This destruction will destroy many of the wealthy in the sense that they will cease to be wealthy, though doubtless it will also involve the loss of many lives of all classes.

We shall not attempt to follow the prophets in their details, from various standpoints, of the trouble of that day, but shall follow briefly the thought last suggested by the prophet above, namely, the *devouring* of the whole earth with the FIRE of God's zeal. This prophet refers to the same fire, etc., again (Zeph. 3:8, 9), saying: "Wait ye upon me, saith Jehovah, until the day that I rise up to the prey; for my decision is to gather the nations [peoples], to draw together the kingdoms, to pour upon them [the kingdoms] my indignation, even all my fierce anger. [The gathering of the peoples of all nations in common interest in opposition to present governments is growing; and the result will be a uniting of the kingdoms for common safety, so that the trouble will be upon all kingdoms, and all will fall.] For all the earth shall be devoured with the *fire* of my zeal. Yea [*then*, after this destruction of kingdoms, after this destruction of the present social order in the fire of trouble], then will I turn unto the people a pure language [the pure Word—uncontaminated by human tradition], that they may call upon the name of the Lord, to serve him with one accord."

This fire of God's zeal is a symbol, and a forcible one, representing the intensity of the trouble and the destruction which will envelop the whole earth. That it is not a literal fire, as some suppose, is evident from the fact that *the people* remain after it, and are blessed. That the people who remain are not saints, as some would suggest, is evident from the fact that they are then *turned* to serve the Lord, whereas the saints are turned (converted) already.*

---

*We mention this as an offset to the argument of some who regard the fire as literal, and who claim that the literal earth is to be melted, etc. These, to fit their theory, claim that "*the people*," here mentioned, are the saints, who, after the earth has melted and cooled off, will return to earth and build houses and inhabit them, plant vineyards and eat the fruit of them, and long enjoy the work of their hands. They consider the present few years as a training or preparation for inheriting, and forget that it would be completely lost in the *aerial* experiences of the thousand or more years of waiting for the earth to cool off—according to their theory. This is a serious mistake, and results from too literal an interpretation of the figures, parables, symbols and dark sayings of our Lord and the apostles and

Throughout the Scriptures, *earth*, when used symbolically, represents society; *mountains* represent kingdoms; *heavens*, the powers of spiritual control; *seas*, the restless, turbulent, dissatisfied masses of the world. *Fire* represents the destruction of whatever is burned—tares, dross, earth (social organization), or whatever it may be. And when *brimstone* is added to *fire* in the symbol, it intensifies the thought of destruction; for nothing is more deadly to all forms of life than the fumes of sulphur.

With this thought in mind, if we turn to Peter's symbolic prophecy of the Day of Wrath, we find it in perfect accord with the above testimony of the prophets. He says: "The world that was, being overflowed with water, perished. [Not the literal earth and literal heavens ceased there, but that dispensation or arrangement of things, existing before the flood, passed away.] But the heavens and the earth which are now [the present dispensation] by the same word [of divine authority] are kept in store, reserved unto fire." The fact that the water was literal leads some to believe that the fire also must be literal, but this by no means follows. The temple of God once was of literal stones, but that does not set aside the fact that the Church, which is the true temple, is built up a spiritual building, a holy temple, not of earthly material. Noah's ark was literal, too, but it typified Christ and the power in him which will replenish and reorganize society.

"The Day of the Lord will come as a thief in the night [unobservedly], in the which the heavens [present powers of the air, of which Satan is the chief or prince] shall pass away with a great [hissing] noise, and the elements shall melt

---

prophets. Following up the same error, these claim that there will be no mountains and seas after this fire, failing to see that all these, as well as the fire, are symbols.

with fervent heat; the earth [social organization] also, and the works that are therein [pride, rank, aristocracy, royalty], shall be burned up. The heavens being on fire shall be dissolved and the elements shall melt with fervent heat. Nevertheless we, according to his promise, look for new heavens [the new spiritual power—Christ's kingdom] and a new earth" [earthly society organized on a new basis—on the basis of love and justice, rather than of might and oppression]. 2 Peter 3:6, 7, 10-13

It should be remembered that some of the apostles were prophets as well—notably Peter, John and Paul. And while as apostles they were God's mouthpieces to expound the utterances of preceding prophets for the benefit of the Church, they were also used of God as prophets to predict things to come, which, as they become due to be fulfilled, become meat in due season for the household of faith, to dispense which, God in his own time raises up suitable servants or expounders. (See our Lord's statement of this fact—Matt. 24:45, 46.) The apostles as prophets were moved upon to write things which, not being *due* in their day, they could but imperfectly appreciate, even as it was with the Old Testament prophets (1 Pet. 1:12, 13), though, like them, their words were specially guided and directed so that they have a depth of meaning of which they were not aware when using them. Thus emphatically the Church is ever guided and fed by God himself, whoever may be his mouthpieces or channels of communication. A realization of this must lead to greater confidence and trust in God's Word, notwithstanding the imperfections of some of his mouthpieces.

The Prophet Malachi (4:1) tells of this Day of the Lord under the same symbol. He says: "The day cometh that shall burn as an oven; and all the *proud*, yea, and all that do wickedly, shall be stubble; and the day that cometh shall burn them up . . . that it shall leave them neither root nor branch." Pride, and every other cause from which haughtiness and oppression could again spring forth, will be entirely consumed by the great trouble of the Day of the Lord and by the after disciplines of the Millennial age—the last of which is described in Rev. 20:9.

But, while pride (in all its forms sinful and detestable) is to be utterly rooted out, and all the proud and wicked are to be utterly destroyed, it does not follow that there is no hope for a reformation in this class. No, thank God: while this fire of God's just indignation will be burning, the Judge will grant opportunity for *pulling some out of the consuming fire* (Jude 23); and those only who refuse the aid will perish with their pride; because they have made it part of their character, and refuse to reform.

The same prophet gives another description of this day (Mal. 3:1-3), in which again, under the figure of fire, he shows how *the Lord's children* will be purified and blessed and brought nigh to him by having the dross of error *destroyed*: "The Messenger of the Covenant, whom ye delight in: behold, he shall come, saith the Lord of hosts. But who may abide the day of his coming? and who shall *stand* [the test] when he appeareth? for he is as a refiner's fire: . . . and he shall sit as a refiner and purifier of silver: and he shall purify the sons of Levi [typical of believers, of whom the chief are the Royal Priesthood] and purge them as gold and silver, that they may offer unto the Lord an offering in righteousness."

Paul refers to this same fire, and this refining process affecting believers in the Day of the Lord (1 Cor. 3:12-15), and in such a manner as to leave it beyond all question that the symbolic fire will *destroy* every error, and thus effect purification of faith. After declaring that he refers only to those building their faith upon the only recognized foundation,

Christ Jesus' finished work of redemption, he says: "Now if any man build [character] upon *this* foundation, gold, silver, precious stones [divine truths and corresponding character, or] wood, hay, stubble [traditional errors and corresponding unstable characters], every man's work shall be made manifest; for THE DAY shall declare it, because it shall be revealed by FIRE; and so every one's work [2 Pet. 1:5-11], whatever it is, the same fire will prove." Surely even the most prejudiced will concede that the fire which tries a spiritual work is not literal fire; fire is an appropriate symbol to represent the utter destruction of conditions represented here by wood, hay and stubble. This fire will be powerless to destroy the faith-and-character structure built with the gold, silver and precious stones of divine truth, and founded upon the rock of Christ's ransom-sacrifice.

The Apostle shows this, saying: "If any man's work abide which he hath built thereupon [upon Christ] he shall receive a *reward*. [His reward will be in proportion to his faithfulness in building, making use of the truth in the development of true character—putting on the whole armor of God.] If any man's work shall be consumed, he shall suffer loss [loss of the reward, because of unfaithfulness], but he himself shall be preserved so as through a fire"—singed, scorched and alarmed. All who build on the rock foundation of Christ's ransom are sure: none that trust in his righteousness as their covering will ever be utterly confounded. But those who *wilfully* reject him and his work, after coming to a clear, full knowledge thereof, will be subject to the second death. Heb. 6:4-8; 10:26-31

In yet another way is this trouble of the Day of the Lord symbolically described. The Apostle shows (Heb. 12:26-29) that the inauguration of the Law Covenant at Sinai was typical of the introduction of the New Covenant to the world at the opening of the Millennial age, or reign of

Christ's kingdom. He says that in the type God's voice shook the literal earth, but now he hath promised, saying, "Yet once for all [finally], I will shake not only the earth, but the heaven also." Concerning this the Apostle explains, saying, "Now this [statement], Yet once for all, denotes the removal of the things shaken, because they are fabricated [false, made up, not the true], so that the unshaken things [true, righteous things, only] may remain. Wherefore, seeing that we are to receive a kingdom which cannot be shaken, let us hold fast the favor through which we may serve God acceptably with reverence and piety; for [as it is written], Our God is a consuming fire." Thus we see this apostle uses a storm to symbolize the trouble of this Day of the Lord, which he and others elsewhere refer to under the symbol of fire. The same events are here noted that are described under the fire symbol, namely, the sweeping away of all falsities, both from believers and from the world—errors regarding God's plan and character and Word, and also errors as to social and civil affairs in the world. It will be good indeed for all to be rid of these fabrications, which came to man largely through his own depraved desires, as well as by the cunning craftiness of Satan, the wily foe of righteousness; but it will be at great cost to all concerned that they will be swept away. It will be a terribly hot fire, a fearful storm, a dark night of trouble, which will precede the glorious brightness of that Kingdom of Righteousness which can never be shaken, that Millennial day in which the Sun of Righteousness will shine forth in splendor and power, blessing and healing the sick and dying but redeemed world. Compare Mal. 4:2 and Matt. 13:43.

David, the prophet through whose Psalms God was pleased to foretell so much concerning our Lord at his first advent, gives some vivid descriptions of this Day of Trouble by which his glorious reign will be introduced; and he uses these various symbols—fire, storm and darkness—alternately and interchangeably, in his descriptions. Thus, for instance, he says (Psa. 50:3): "Our God shall come, and shall not keep silence: a fire shall devour before him, and it shall be very tempestuous round about him." In Psa. 97:2-6: "Clouds and darkness are round about him: righteousness and justice are the support of his throne. A fire goeth before him and burneth up his enemies round about. His lightnings give light to the world; the earth seeth it and trembleth. The mountains melt away like wax at the presence of the Lord, at the presence of the Lord of the whole earth. The [new] heavens [then] tell of his righteousness, and all the people see his glory." Psa. 46:6: "The peoples raged, the kingdoms were moved: he uttered his voice, the earth melted." Again (Psa. 110:2-6), "Rule thou in the midst of thine enemies. . . . The Lord at thy right hand shall crush kings in the day of his wrath. He will judge among the nations—there shall be a fulness of corpses. He crusheth the heads [rulers] over many countries." Again (46:1-5), "God is *our* protection; . . . therefore *we* will not fear when the earth [society] is transformed, and when the mountains [kingdoms] are swept into the midst of the sea [swallowed up by the turbulent masses], when the waters thereof roar and are troubled [infuriated], when the mountains shake with the swelling thereof. . . . God will help her [the Bride, the faithful "little flock"] at the dawning of the morning." And in the same Psalm, verses 6-10, the same story is restated in other symbols: "The peoples rage, kingdoms are displaced: he letteth his voice be heard, the earth [society] melteth. Jehovah of hosts is with *us*, a Tower for us is the God of Jacob." Then, viewing the results of that time of trouble from beyond it, he adds: "Come ye, behold the deeds of the Lord—what desolations he hath made in the earth. . . . Desist [from your former ways, O people] and know [come to the knowledge] that I am God. I will be exalted among the peoples, I will be exalted in the earth." The "new earth" or new order and arrangement of society will exalt God and his law, as over and controlling all.

Another testimony in proof of the fact that the Day of the Lord will be a great day of trouble and of destruction to every form of evil (yet *not* a time of literal burning of the earth) is furnished in the last symbolic prophecy of the Bible. Referring to this time when the Lord will take his great power to reign, the *storm* and *fire* are thus described— "And the nations were enraged and thy wrath came." (Rev. 11:17, 18) And again, "And out of his mouth proceeded a two-edged broadsword, that with it he should smite the nations: and he shall rule them with a rod of iron: and he treadeth the winepress of the fierceness of the wrath of Almighty God. . . . And I saw the beast [symbolic], and the kings of the earth and their armies, gathered together to make war against him that sat on the horse, and against his army. And the beast was taken, and with him the false prophet. . . . These were cast alive into a lake of fire burning with brimstone." Rev. 19:15, 19

We cannot here digress to examine these symbols— "beast," "false prophet," "image," "lake of fire," "horse," etc., etc. For this the reader is referred to a succeeding volume. Now we would have you notice that the great symbolic BATTLE, and the harvesting of the vine of the earth here described as closing the present age and opening up the Millennial age (Rev. 20:1-3), are but other symbols covering the same great and troublous events elsewhere symbolically called fire, storm, shaking, etc. In connection with the battle and winepress figures of Revelation, note the striking harmony of Joel 2:9-16 and Isa. 13:1-11, in describing the same events by similar figures. The variety of symbolic figures used helps us to appreciate more fully all the features of that great and notable Day of the Lord.

The Present Situation

We here leave the prophetic statements regarding that day, to mark more particularly the present aspect of affairs in the world, as we now see them shaping themselves for the rapidly approaching conflict—a conflict which, when its terrible climax is reached, must necessarily be a short one, else the race would be exterminated. The two rival parties to this battle are already visible. Wealth, arrogance and pride are on one side, and widely-prevailing poverty, ignorance, bigotry and a keen sense of injustice are on the other. Both, impelled by selfish motives, are now organizing their forces all over the civilized world. With our eyes anointed with truth, wherever we look we can see that the sea and the waves are already roaring and lashing and foaming out against the mountains, as represented in the threats and attempts of anarchists and discontents whose numbers are constantly increasing. We can see, too, that the *friction* between the various factions or elements of society is rapidly getting to the point described by the prophets, when the earth (society) will be on fire, and the elements will melt and disintegrate with the mutually generated heat.

It is of course, difficult for people, on whichever side of this controversy they may be, to see contrary to their own interests, habits and education. The wealthy feel that they have a right to more than their proportional share of this world's goods; a right to purchase labor and every commodity as low as they can; a right to the fruit of their efforts; and a right to use their intelligence so to run their business as to make profit for themselves and to increase their hoarded wealth, no matter who else may be compelled by force of circumstances to drag through life with few of its comforts, even if with all of its necessities. They reason thus: It is the inevitable; the law of supply and demand must govern; rich and poor have always been in the world; and if the wealth were evenly divided in the morning, some would, through dissipation or improvidence, be poor before night, while others, more careful and prudent, would be rich. Besides, they will argue with effect, Can it be expected that men of greater brain power will undertake vast enterprises, employing thousands of men, with the risks of large losses, unless there be hopes of gain and some advantage?

The artisan and the laborer, on the contrary, will say: We see that while labor enjoys many advantages today above any other day, while it is better paid, and can therefore procure greater comforts, yet it is in this enjoying only its right, from which it has long been debarred to some extent; and it is thus properly deriving a share of the advantages of the inventions, discoveries, increasing knowledge, etc., of our time. We recognize labor as honorable, and that, when accompanied with good sense, education, honesty and principle, it is as honorable, and has as many rights, as any profession. And, on the contrary, we esteem idleness a discredit and disgrace to all men, whatever their talent or occupation in life. All, to be valued and appreciated, should be useful to others in some respect. But though realizing our present improvement and advancement, intellectually, socially and financially, we realize this to be more the result of circumstances than of human design on the part of either ourselves or our employers. We see our improved condition, and that of all men, to be the result of the great increase of intelligence, invention, etc., of the past fifty years particularly. These came up so rapidly that labor as well as capital got a lift from the tidal wave, and was carried to a higher level; and if we could see a prospect that the flood tide would continue to rise, and to benefit all, we would feel satisfied; but we are anxious and restless now because we see that this is not the case. We see that the flood tide is beginning to turn, and that whereas many have been lifted high in wealth by it, and are firmly and securely fixed upon the shore of ease, luxury and opulence, yet the masses are not thus settled and secured, but are in danger of being carried as low as ever, or lower, by the undercurrent of the now ebbing tide. Hence it is that we are disposed to grasp hold of something to insure our present state and our further advancement before it is too late.

To state the matter in other words, we (artisans and laborers) see that while all mankind has largely shared the blessings of the day, yet those who by reason of greater talent for business, or by inheritance, or by fraud and dishonesty, have become possessors of tens of thousands and millions of dollars, have not only *this* advantage over all others, but, aided by the mechanical inventions, etc., they are in a position to continue the ratio of their increase in wealth, in proportion to the decrease in the wage-workers' salaries. We see that unless we take some steps toward the protection of the increasing number of artisans against the increasing power of monopoly, combined with labor-saving machinery, etc., the cold-blooded law of supply and demand will swallow us up completely. It is against this impending disaster, rather than against *present conditions*, that we organize and seek protective arrangements. Each day adds largely to our numbers by natural increase and by immigration; and each day adds to the labor-saving machinery. Each day, therefore, increases the number seeking employment and decreases the demand for their service. The natural law of supply and demand, therefore, if permitted to go on uninterruptedly, will soon bring labor back where it was a century ago, and leave all the advantages of our day in the hands of capital. It is *this* that we seek to avert.

This ultimate tendency of many real blessings to work injury, unless restrained by wise and equitable laws, was long since seen; but the *rapidity* with which one invention has followed another, and the consequent increased demand for labor in providing this labor-saving machinery, has been so great that the ultimate result has been delayed, and instead, the world has had a "boom"—an inflation of values, wages, wealth, credits (debts) and ideas—from which the reaction is now commencing gradually to take place.

In the last few years there have been produced in vast quantities agricultural implements of every description which enable one man to accomplish as much as five could formerly. This has a two-fold effect: first, three times as many acres are worked, giving employment to three out of the five laborers, thus setting two adrift to compete for other labor; secondly, the three who remain can, by the use of the machinery, produce as great a crop as fifteen would have done without it. The same or greater changes are wrought in other departments by similar agencies; for instance, in iron and steel making. Its growth has been so enormous that the number of employees has greatly increased, notwithstanding the fact that machinery has enabled one man at present to accomplish about as much as twelve did formerly. One of the results will be that very shortly the capacity of these extensive works will more than meet the present enormous demands, and the demands, instead of continuing to increase, will probably decrease; for the world is fast being supplied with railroads beyond present needs, and the yearly repairs on these could probably be supplied by less than one-half the present number of establishments.

Thus we are brought in contact with the peculiar condition

in which there is an over-production, causing idleness occasionally to both capital and labor, while at the same time some lack the employment which would enable them to procure necessities and luxuries and thus in a measure cure the over-production. And the tendency toward both over-production and lack of employment is on the increase, and calls for a remedy of some kind which society's physicians are seeking, but of which the patient will not make use.

While, therefore (continues the wage-worker), we realize that as the supply begins to exceed the demand, competition is greatly reducing the profits of capital and machinery, and throughout the world is distressing the rich by curtailing their profits, and in some cases causing them actual loss instead of profit, yet we believe that the class which benefited most by the "boom" and inflation *should* suffer most in the reaction, rather than that the masses should suffer from it. To this end, and for these reasons, wage-workers are moving to obtain the following results—by legislation if possible, or by force and lawlessness in countries where, for any cause, the voice of the masses is not heard, and the interests of the masses are not conserved:

It is proposed that the hours of labor be shortened in proportion to the skill or severity of the labor, without a reduction of wages, in order thus to employ a greater number of persons without increasing the products, and thus to equalize the coming over-production by providing a larger number with the means of purchasing. It is proposed to fix and limit the rate of interest on money at much less than the present rates, and thus compel a *leniency* of the lenders toward the borrowers or poorer class, or else an idleness or rusting of their capital. It is proposed that railroads shall either be the property of the people, operated by their servants, government officials, or that legislation shall restrict their liberties, charges, etc., and compel their operation in such a manner as to serve the public better. As it is, railroads built during a period of inflated values, instead of curtailing their capital to conform to the general shrinkage of values experienced in every other department of trade, have multiplied their originally large capital stocks two or three times (commonly called *watering* their stocks), without real value being added. Thus it comes that great railroad systems are endeavoring to pay interest and dividends upon stocks and bonded debts which on an average are four times as great as these railroads would actually cost today *new*. As a consequence the public suffers. Farmers are charged heavily for freights, and sometimes find it profitable to burn their grain for fuel; and thus the cost of food to the people is greater without being to the farmer's advantage. It is proposed to remedy this matter, so that railroads shall pay to their stockholders about four per cent on their present actual value, and not four to eight per cent, on three or four times their present value, as many of them now do, by preventing competition through pooling arrangements.

We well know, says the artisan, that in the eyes of those who hold watered railroad stocks, and other stocks, this reduction of profits on their invested capital will seem terrible, and will come like drawing teeth, and that they will feel that their *rights* (?) to use their franchises granted by the people, to squeeze from them immense profits, based upon fictitious valuations, are being grievously outraged, and that they will resist it all they know how. But we feel that they should be thankful that the public is so lenient, and that they are not required to make restitution of millions of dollars already thus obtained. We feel that the time has come for the masses of the people to share more evenly the blessings of this day of blessings, and to do this it is necessary so to legislate that all greedy corporations, fat with money and power derived from the public, shall be restrained, and *compelled* by law to serve the public at reasonable rates. In no other way can these blessings of Providence be secured to the masses. Hence, while great corporations, representing capital, are to a large extent a blessing and a benefit, we are seeing daily that they have passed the point of benefit and are becoming masters of the people, and if unchecked will soon reduce wage-workers to penury and slavery. Corporations, composed of numbers of people all more or less wealthy, are rapidly coming to occupy the same relation to the general public of America that the Lords of Great Britain and all Europe occupy toward the masses there, only that the corporations are more powerful.

To accomplish our ends, continue the wage-workers, we need organization. We must have the cooperation of the masses or we can never accomplish anything against such immense power and influence. And though we are organized into unions, etc., it must not be understood that our aim is anarchy or injustice toward any class. We, the masses of the people, simply desire to protect our own rights, and those of our children, by putting reasonable bounds upon those whose wealth and power might otherwise crush us—which wealth and power, properly used and limited, may be a more general blessing to all. In a word, they conclude, we would *enforce* the golden rule—"Do unto others as you would that they should do to you."

Happy would it be for all concerned if such moderate and reasonable means would succeed; if the rich would rest with their present acquirements and cooperate with the great mass of the people in the general and permanent improvement of the condition of all classes; if the wage-workers would content themselves with reasonable demands; if the golden rule of love and justice could thus be put in practice. But men in their present condition will not observe this rule without compulsion. Though there be some among the artisans of the world who would be thus moderate and just in their ideas, the majority are not so, but will be extreme, unjust and arrogant in their ideas and demands, beyond all reason. Each concession on the part of capitalists will but add to such demands and ideas; and all having experience know that the arrogance and rule of the ignorant poor are doubly severe. And so among those of wealth—some are fully in sympathy with the laboring classes, and would be glad to act out their sympathy by making such arrangements as would gradually effect the needed reforms; but they are greatly in the minority and wholly powerless in the operating of corporations and to a great extent in their private business. If they be merchants or manufacturers, they cannot shorten the hours of labor or increase the wages of their employees; for competitors would then undersell them, and financial disaster to themselves, their creditors and their employees would follow.

Thus we see the natural cause of the great trouble of this "Day of Jehovah." Selfishness, and blindness to all except their own interests, will control the majority on both sides of the question. Wage-workers will organize and unify their interests, but selfishness will destroy the union; and each, being actuated mainly by that principle, will scheme and conspire in that direction. The majority, ignorant and arrogant, will gain control, and the better class will be powerless to hold in check that which their intelligence organized. Capitalists will become convinced that the more they yield the more will be demanded, and will soon determine to resist all demands. Insurrection will result; and in the general alarm and distrust capital will be withdrawn from public and private enterprises, and business depression and financial panic will follow. Thousands of men thrown out of employment in this way will finally become desperate. Then law and order will be swept away—the mountains will be swallowed up in that stormy sea. Thus the social earth will melt, and the governmental heavens (church and state) will pass away; and all the proud, and all who do wickedly, will be as stubble. Then the mighty men will weep bitterly, the rich will howl, and fear and distress will be upon all the multitude. Even now, wise, far-seeing men find their hearts failing them as they look forward to those things coming upon the world, even as our Lord predicted. (Luke 21:26) The Scriptures show us that in this general rupture the nominal church (including all denominations) will be gradually drawn more and more to the side of the governments and the wealthy, will lose much of its influence over the people, and will finally fall with the governments. Thus the heavens [ecclesiastical rule], being on fire, will pass away with a great hissing.

All this trouble will but prepare the world to realize that though men may plan and arrange ever so well and wisely, all their plans will prove futile as long as ignorance and selfishness are in the saddle and have the control. It will convince all that the only feasible way of correcting the difficulty is by the setting up of a strong and righteous government, which will subdue all classes, and enforce principles of righteousness, until gradually the stony-heartedness of men will, under favorable influences, give place to the original image of God. And this is just what God has promised to accomplish for all, by and through the Millennial Reign of Christ, which Jehovah introduces by the chastisements and lessons of this day of trouble. Ezek. 11:19; 36:25, 36; Jer. 31:29-34; Zeph. 3:9; Psa. 46:8-10

Though this day of trouble comes as a natural and unavoidable result of man's fallen, selfish condition, and was fully foreseen and declared by the Lord, who foresaw that his laws and instructions would be disregarded by all but the few until experience and compulsion force obedience, yet all who realize the state of things coming should set themselves and their affairs in order accordingly. Thus we say to all the *meek*—the humble of the world, as well as the body of Christ: Seek ye the Lord, ye meek of the earth which have wrought his judgment [his will]; seek righteousness; seek meekness, that ye may be partially hidden in the day of the Lord's anger. (Zeph. 2:3) None will entirely escape the trouble, but those seeking righteousness and rejoicing in meekness will have many advantages over others. Their manner of life, their habits of thought and action, as well as their sympathies for the right, which will enable them to grasp the situation of affairs, and also to appreciate the Bible account of this trouble and its outcome, will all conspire to make them suffer less than others— especially from harassing fears and forebodings.

The trend of events in this Day of the Lord will be very deceptive to those not Scripturally informed. It will come suddenly, as fire consuming chaff (Zeph. 2:2), in comparison to the long ages past and their slow operation; but not suddenly as a flash of lightning from a clear sky, as some erroneously expect who anticipate that all things written concerning the Day of the Lord will be fulfilled in a twenty-four hour day. It will come as "a thief in the night," in the sense that its approach will be stealthy and unobserved by the world in general. The trouble of this day will be in spasms. It will be a series of convulsions more frequent and severe as the day draws on, until the final one. The Apostle so indicates when he says—"*as travail* upon a woman." (1 Thess. 5:2, 3) The relief will come only with the birth of the NEW ORDER of things—a new heavens (the spiritual control of Christ) and a new earth (reorganized society) wherein dwelleth righteousness (2 Pet. 3:10,13)—in which justice and love, instead of power and selfishness, will be the law.

Each time these labor pangs of the new era come upon the present body politic, her strength and courage will be found less, and the pains severer. All that society's physicians (political economists) can do for her relief will be to help, and wisely direct the course of the inevitable birth—to prepare gradually the way for the event. They cannot avert it if they would; for God has decreed that it shall come to pass. Many of society's physicians will, however, be totally ignorant of the real ailment and of the necessities and urgency of the case. These will undertake repressive measures; and as each paroxysm of trouble passes away, they will take advantage of it to fortify the resistive appliances, and will thereby increase the anguish; and while they will not long delay the birth, their malpractice will hasten the death of their patient; for the old order of things will die in the labor of bringing forth the new.

To lay aside the forcible figure suggested by the Apostle, and speak plainly: The efforts of the masses for deliverance from the grasp of Capital and machinery will be *immature*; plans and arrangements will be incomplete and insufficient, as time after time they attempt to force their way and burst the bands and limits of "supply and demand" which are growing too small for them. Each unsuccessful attempt will increase the confidence of Capital in its ability to keep the new order of things within its present limits, until at length the present restraining power of organizations and governments will reach its extreme limit, the cord of social organism will snap asunder, law and order will be gone, and widespread anarchy will bring *all* that the prophets have foretold of the trouble "such as was not since there was a nation"—and, thank God for the assurance added—"nor ever shall be" afterward.

The deliverance of Israel from Egypt and from the plagues which came upon the Egyptians seems to illustrate the coming emancipation of the world, at the hands of the greater than Moses, whom he typified. It will be a deliverance from Satan and every agency he has devised for man's bondage to sin and error. And as the plagues upon Egypt had a hardening effect as soon as removed, so the temporary relief from the pains of this Day of the Lord will tend to harden some, and they will say to the poor, as did the Egyptians to Israel, "Ye are idle," and therefore dissatisfied! and will probably, like them, attempt to increase the burden. (Exod. 5:4-23) But in the end such will wish, as did Pharaoh in the midnight of his last plague, that they had dealt more leniently and wisely long ago. (Exod. 12:30-33) To mark further the similarity, call to mind that the troubles of this Day of the Lord are called "seven vials of wrath," or "seven last plagues," and that it is not until the last of these that the *great earthquake* (revolution) occurs, in which every mountain (kingdom) will disappear. Rev. 16:17-20

Another thought with reference to this Day of Trouble is that it has come just in *due* time—God's due time. In the next volume of this work, evidence is adduced from the testimony of the Law and the Prophets of the Old Testament, as well as from Jesus and the apostolic prophets of the New Testament, which shows clearly and unmistakably that this Day of Trouble is located chronologically in the beginning of the glorious Millennial reign of Messiah. It is this necessary preparation for the coming work of restitution in the Millennial age that precipitates the trouble.

During the six thousand years interim of evil, and until the appointed time for the establishment of the righteous and powerful government of Christ, it would have been a positive injury to fallen men had they been afforded much idle time, through an earlier development of present labor-saving machinery, or otherwise. Experience has given rise to the proverb that "Idleness is the mother of vice," thus approving the wisdom of God's decree, "In the sweat of thy face shalt thou eat bread till thou return unto the dust." Like all God's arrangements, this is benevolent and wise, and for the ultimate good of his creatures. The trouble of the Day of the Lord, which we already see gathering, confirms the wisdom of God's arrangement; for, as we have seen, it comes about as the result of over-production by labor-saving machinery, and an inability on the part of the various elements of society to adjust themselves to the new circumstances, because of selfishness on the part of each.

An unanswerable argument, proving that this is God's due time for the introduction of the new order of things, is that he is lifting the veil of ignorance and gradually letting in the light of intelligence and invention upon mankind, just as foretold, when foretold, and with the results predicted. (Dan. 12:4, 1) Had the knowledge come sooner, the trouble would have come sooner; and though society might have reorganized after its storm and melting, it would have been *not* a new earth [social arrangement] wherein righteousness would prevail and dwell, but a new earth or arrangement in which sin and vice would have much more abounded than now. The equitable division of the benefits of labor-saving machinery would in time have brought shorter and shorter hours of labor; and thus, released from the original safeguard, fallen man, with his perverted tastes, would not have used his liberty and time for mental, moral and physical improvement, but, as the history of the past proves, the tendency would have been toward licentiousness and vice.

The partial lifting of the veil *now* prepares thousands of conveniences for mankind, and thus furnishes, from the outstart of the age of restitution, time for education and moral and physical development, as well as for preparation for the feeding and clothing of the companies who will from time to time be awakened from the tomb. And furthermore, it locates the time of trouble just where it will be of benefit to mankind, in that it will give them the lesson of their own inability to govern themselves, just at the Millennial dawn, when, by the Lord's appointment, he who redeemed all is to begin to bless them with the strong rule of the iron rod, and with full knowledge and assistance whereby they may be restored to original perfection and everlasting life.

Duty and Privilege of the Saints

An important question arises regarding the duty of the saints during this trouble, and their proper attitude toward the two opposing classes now coming into prominence. That some of the saints will still be in the flesh during at least part of this burning time seems possible. Their position in it, however, will differ from that of others, not so much in that they will be miraculously preserved (though it is distinctly promised that their bread and water shall be sure), but in the fact that, being instructed from God's Word, they will not feel the same anxiety and hopeless dread that will overspread the world. They will recognize the trouble as the preparation, according to God's plan, for blessing the whole world, and they will be cheered and comforted through it all. This is forcibly stated in Psa. 91; Isa. 33:2-14, 15-24.

Thus comforted and blessed by the divine assurance, the first duty of the saints is to let the world see that in the midst of all the prevailing trouble and discontent, and even while they share the trouble and suffer under it, they are hopeful, cheerful and always rejoicing in view of the glorious outcome foretold in God's Word.

The Apostle has written that "Godliness with *contentment* is great gain"; and though this has always been true, it will have double force in this Day of the Lord, when discontent is the chief ailment among all worldly classes. To these the saints should be a notable exception. There never was a time when dissatisfaction was so widespread; and yet there never was a time when men enjoyed so many favors and blessings. Wherever we look, whether into the palaces of the rich, replete with conveniences and splendors of which Solomon in all his glory knew almost nothing, or whether we look into the comfortable home of the thrifty and temperate wage-worker, with its evidences of taste, comfort, art and luxury, we see that in every way the present exceeds in bountiful supply every other period since the creation, many-fold; and yet the people are *unhappy* and discontented. The fact is that the desires of a selfish, depraved heart know no bounds. Selfishness has so taken possession of all, that, as we look out, we see the whole world madly pushing and driving and clutching after wealth. A few only being successful, the remainder are envious and soured because they are not the fortunate ones, and all are discontented and miserable— more so than in any former time.

But the saint should take no part in that struggle. His consecration vow was that he would strive and grasp and run for a higher, a heavenly prize, and hence he is weaned from earthly ambitions, and labors not for earthly things, except to provide things *decent* and *needful*; for he is giving heed to the course and example of the Master and the apostles.

Therefore they have *contentment* with their godliness, not because they have no ambition, but because their ambition is turned heavenward and absorbed in the effort to lay up treasure in heaven and to be rich toward God; in view of which, and of their knowledge of God's plans revealed in his Word, they are content with whatever of an earthly sort God may provide. These can joyfully sing:

> "Content, whatever lot I see,
> Since 'tis God's hand that leadeth me."

But alas! not all of God's children occupy this position. Many have fallen into the discontent prevalent in the world, and are robbing themselves of the enjoyments of life because they have left the Lord's footsteps and are casting their lot and taking their portion with the world—*seeking* earthly things whether attaining them or not, sharing the world's discontent, and failing to realize the contentment and peace which the world can neither give nor take away.

We urge the saints, therefore, to abandon the strife of greed and vainglory and its discontent, and to strive for the higher riches and the peace they do afford. We would remind them of the Apostle's words:

"Godliness with contentment is great gain; for we brought nothing into this world, and it is certain we can carry nothing out. And having [*needful*] food and raiment, let us therewith be content. But they that will [to] be rich [whether they succeed or not] fall into temptation and a snare, and into many foolish and hurtful lusts which *drown* [sink] men in ruin and destruction. For a root of all vices is the love of money [whether in rich or poor], which some being *eager for* were led away from the faith and pierced themselves through with many pangs. But thou, O man of God, flee from these, and be pursuing righteousness, godliness, faith, love, endurance, meekness; be contesting in the *noble contest* of the faith, lay hold on everlasting life, unto which thou wast called and didst make a noble covenant." 1 Tim. 6:6-12

If the example of the saints is thus one of contentment and joyful anticipation, and a cheerful submission to present trials in sure hope of the good time coming, such living examples alone are valuable lessons for the world. And in addition to the example, the counsel of the saints to those about them should be in harmony with their faith. It should be of the nature of ointment and healing balm. Advantage should be taken of circumstances to point the world to the good time coming, to preach to them the coming Kingdom of God, and to show the real cause of present troubles, and the only remedy. Luke 3:14; Heb. 13:5; Phil. 4:11

The poor world groans, not only under its real, but also under its fancied ills, and especially under the discontent of selfishness, pride and ambitions which fret and worry men because they cannot fully satisfy them. Hence, while we can see both sides of the question, let us counsel those willing to hear to contentment with what they have, and to patient waiting until God in his due time and way brings to them the many blessings which his love and wisdom have provided.

By probing and inflaming either real or fancied wounds and wrongs, we would do injury to those we should be helping and blessing, thus spreading their discontent, and hence their trouble. But by fulfilling our mission, preaching the good tidings of the *ransom* given for ALL, and the consequent *blessings* to come to ALL, we shall be true heralds of the kingdom—its ambassadors of peace. Thus it is written, "How beautiful upon the mountains [kingdoms] are the feet of him [the last members of the body of Christ] that bringeth good tidings, that publisheth peace, that bringeth good tidings of good." Isa. 52:7

The troubles of this "Day of Jehovah" will give opportunity for preaching the good tidings of coming good, such as is seldom afforded, and blessed are they who will follow the footsteps of the Master, and be the good Samaritans binding up the wounds and pouring in the oil and wine of comfort and cheer. The assurance given such is that their labor is not in vain; for when the judgments of the Lord are in the earth, the inhabitants of the world *will learn* righteousness. Isa. 26:9

The sympathy of the Lord's children, like that of their heavenly Father, must be largely in harmony with the groaning creation, striving for any deliverance from bondage; although they should, like him, remember and sympathize with those of the opposing classes whose desires are to be just and generous, but whose efforts are beset and hindered, not only by the weaknesses of their fallen nature, but also by their surroundings in life, and their association with and dependence upon others. But the Lord's children should have no sympathy with the arrogant, insatiate desires and endeavors of any class. Their utterances should be calm and moderate, and always for peace where principle is not at stake. They should remember that this is the Lord's battle, and that so far as politics or social questions are concerned, they have no real solution other than that predicted in the Word of God. The duty of the consecrated, therefore, is first of all to see that they are not in the way of Jehovah's chariot, and then to "stand still and see the salvation of God," in the sense of realizing that it is no part of their work to share in the struggle, but that it is the Lord's doing, through other agencies. Regardless of all such things, they should press along the line of their own mission, proclaiming the heavenly kingdom at hand as the only remedy for all classes, and their only hope.

STUDY XVI
CONCLUDING THOUGHTS

OUR DUTY TOWARD THE TRUTH—ITS COST, ITS VALUE, ITS PROFIT.

IN THE preceding chapters we have seen that both the light of nature and that of revelation clearly demonstrate the fact that an intelligent, wise, almighty and righteous God is the Creator of all things, and that he is the supreme and rightful Lord of all; that all things animate and inanimate are subject to his control; and that the Bible is the revelation of his character and plans so far as he is pleased to disclose them to men. From it we have learned that though evil now predominates among some of his creatures, it exists for only a limited time and to a limited extent, and by his permission, for wise ends which he has in view. We have also learned that though darkness now covers the earth, and gross darkness the people, yet God's light will in due time dispel all the darkness, and the whole earth will be filled with his glory.

We have seen that his great plan is one that has required ages for its accomplishment thus far, and that yet another age will be required to complete it; and that during all the dark ages of the past, when God seemed to have almost forgotten his creatures, his plan for their future blessing has been silently but grandly working out, though during all those ages the mysteries of his plan have been wisely hidden from men. We have also seen that the day or age which is now about to dawn upon the world is to be the day of the world's judgment or trial, and that all previous preparation

343

has been for the purpose of giving mankind in general as favorable an opportunity as possible, when, *as individuals*, they will be placed on trial for eternal life. The long period of six thousand years has greatly multiplied the race, and their buffetings and sufferings under the dominion of evil have given them an experience which will be greatly to their advantage when they are brought to judgment. And though the race as a whole has been permitted thus to suffer for six thousand years, yet as individuals they have run their course in a few brief years.

We have seen that while the race was undergoing this necessary discipline, in due time God sent his Son to redeem them; and that while the mass of mankind did not recognize the Redeemer in his humiliation, and would not believe that the Lord's Anointed would *thus* come to their rescue, yet from among those whose hearts were toward God, and who believed his promises, God has been, during these ages past, selecting two companies to receive the honors of his kingdom—the honors of sharing in the execution of the divine plan. These two select companies, we have seen, are to constitute the two phases of the Kingdom of God. And from the prophets we learn that this kingdom is soon to be established in the earth; that under its wise and just administration all the families of the earth will be blessed with a most favorable opportunity to prove themselves worthy of everlasting life; that as the result of their redemption by the precious blood of Christ, a grand highway of holiness will be cast up; that the ransomed of the Lord (all mankind—Heb. 2:9) may walk in it; that it will be a public thoroughfare made comparatively easy for all who earnestly desire to become pure, holy; and that all the stumbling-stones will be gathered out, and all the snares, allurements and pitfalls removed, and blessed will all those be who go up thereon to perfection and everlasting life.

It is manifest that this judgment, or rulership, cannot begin until Christ, whom Jehovah hath appointed to be the Judge or Ruler of the world, has come again—not again in humiliation, but in power and great glory: not again to redeem the world, but to judge [rule] the world in righteousness. A trial can in no case proceed until the judge is on the bench and the court is in session at the appointed time, though before that time there may be a great preparatory work. Then shall the King sit upon the throne of his glory, and before him shall be gathered all nations, and he shall judge them during that age by their works, opening to them the books of the Scriptures and filling the earth with the knowledge of the Lord. And by their conduct under all that favor and assistance, he shall decide who of them are worthy of life everlasting in the ages of glory and joy to follow. Matt. 25:31; Rev. 20:11-13

Thus we have seen that the second advent of Messiah, to set up his kingdom in the earth, is an event in which all classes of men may have hope, an event which, when fully understood, will bring joy and gladness to all hearts. It is the day when the Lord's "little flock" of consecrated saints has the greatest cause for rejoicing. It is the glad day when the espoused virgin Church with joy becomes the Bride, the Lamb's wife; when she comes up out of the wilderness leaning upon the arm of her Beloved, and enters into his glorious inheritance. It is the day when the true Church, glorified with its Head, will be endued with divine authority and power, and will begin the great work for the world, the result of which will be the complete restitution of all things. And it will be a glad day for the world when the great adversary is bound, when the fetters that have held the race for six thousand years are broken, and when the knowledge of the Lord fills the whole earth as the waters cover the sea.

A knowledge of these things, and the evidences that they are nigh, even at the door, should have a powerful influence upon all, but especially upon the consecrated children of God, who are seeking the prize of the divine nature. We urge such, while they lift up their heads and rejoice, knowing that their redemption draweth nigh, to lay aside every weight and hindrance, and to run patiently the race in which they have started. Look away from self and its unavoidable weaknesses and imperfections, knowing that all such weaknesses are covered fully by the merits of the ransom given by Christ Jesus our Lord, and that your sacrifices and self-denials are acceptable to God through our Redeemer and Lord—and thus only. Let us remember that the strength sufficient which God has promised us, and by use of which we can be "overcomers," is provided in his Word. It is a strength derived from a *knowledge* of his character and plans, and of the conditions upon which we may share in them. Thus Peter expresses it, saying, "Grace and peace be multiplied unto you *through the knowledge* of God, and of Jesus Christ our Lord, according as his divine power hath given unto us all things that pertain unto life and godliness, *through the knowledge* of him who hath called us to glory and virtue; whereby are given unto us exceeding great and precious promises, that BY THESE ye might be partakers of the divine nature." 2 Pet. 1:2-4

But to obtain this knowledge and this strength, which God thus proposes to supply to each runner for the heavenly prize, will surely test the sincerity of your consecration vows. You have consecrated all your time, all your talents, to the Lord; now the question is, How much of it are you giving? Are you still willing, according to your covenant of consecration, to give up all?—to give up your own plans and methods, and the theories of yourselves and others, to accept of God's plan and way and time of doing his great work? Are you willing to do this at the cost of earthly friendships and social ties? And are you willing to give up time from other things for the investigation of these glorious themes so heart-cheering to the truly consecrated, with the certain knowledge that it will cost you this self-denial? If all is not consecrated, or if you only half meant it when you gave all to the Lord, then you will begrudge the time and effort needful to search his Word as for hid treasure, to obtain thus the strength needful for all the trials of faith incident to the present (the dawn of the Millennium) above other times.

But think not that the giving will end with the giving of the needful time and energy to this study: it will not. The sincerity of your sacrifice of self will be tested in full, and will prove you either worthy or unworthy of membership in that "little flock," the overcoming Church, which will receive the honors of the kingdom. If you give diligence to the Word of God, and receive its truths into a good, honest, consecrated heart, it will beget in you such a love for God and his plan, and such a desire to tell the good tidings, to preach the gospel, that it will become the all-absorbing theme of life thereafter; and this will not only separate you from the world and from many nominal Christians, *in spirit*, but it will lead to separation from such entirely. They will think you peculiar and separate you from their company, and you will be despised and counted a fool for Christ's sake; because they know us not, even as they knew not the Lord. 2 Cor. 4:8-10; Luke 6:22; 1 John 3:1; 1 Cor. 3:18

Are you willing to follow on to know the Lord through evil and through good report? Are you willing to forsake all, to follow as he may lead you by his Word?—to ignore the wishes of friends, as well as your own desires? It is hoped that many of the consecrated who read this volume may by it be so quickened to fresh zeal and fervency of spirit, through a clearer apprehension of the divine plan, that they will be able to say, "By the grace of God, I will follow on to know and to serve the Lord, whatever may be the sacrifice involved." Like the noble Bereans (Acts 17:11), let such studiously set themselves to prove what has been presented in the foregoing pages. Prove it, not by the conflicting traditions and creeds of men, but by the only correct and divinely authorized standard—God's own Word. It is to facilitate such investigation that we have cited so many scriptures.

It will be useless to attempt to harmonize the divine plan herein set forth with many of the ideas previously held and supposed to be Scriptural, yet not proved so. It will be observed that the divine plan is complete and harmonious with itself in every part, and that it is in perfect harmony with the character which the Scriptures ascribe to its great Author. It is a marvelous display of wisdom, justice, love and power. It carries with it its own evidence of superhuman design, being beyond the power of human invention, and almost beyond the power of human comprehension.

Doubtless questions will arise on various points inquiring for solution according to the plan herein presented. Careful, thoughtful Bible study will settle many of these at once; and to all we can confidently say, No question which you can raise need go without a sufficient answer, fully in harmony with the views herein presented. Succeeding volumes elaborate the various branches of this one plan, disclosing at every step that matchless harmony of which the *truth* alone can boast. And be it known that no other system of theology even claims, or has ever attempted, to harmonize in itself *every* statement of the Bible; yet nothing short of this we can claim for these views. This harmony not only with the Bible, but with the divine character and with sanctified common sense, must have arrested the attention of the conscientious reader already, and filled him with awe, as well as with hope and confidence. It is marvelous indeed, yet just what we should expect of the TRUTH, and of God's infinitely wise and beneficent plan.

And while the Bible is thus opening up from this standpoint, and disclosing wondrous things (Psa. 119:18), the light of the present day upon the various creeds and traditions of men is affecting them in an opposite manner. They are being recognized even by their worshipers as imperfect and deformed, and hence they are being measurably ignored; and though still subscribed to, they are seldom elaborated, for very shame. And the shame attaching to these human creeds and traditions is spreading to the Bible, which is supposed to uphold these deformities of thought as of divine origin. Hence the freedom with which the various advanced thinkers, so-called, are beginning to deny various parts of the Bible not congenial to their views. How striking, then, the providence of God, which at this very time opens before his children this truly glorious and harmonious plan—a plan that rejects not one, but harmonizes every part and item of his Word. Truth, when due, becomes *meat* for the household of faith, that they may grow thereby. (Matt. 24:45) Whoever comes in contact with truth, realizing its character, has thereby a responsibility with reference to it. It must be either received and acted upon, or rejected and despised. To ignore it does not release from responsibility. If we accept it ourselves, we have a responsibility TOWARD IT also, because it is for ALL the household of faith; and each one receiving it becomes its debtor, and, if a faithful steward, must dispense it to the other members of the family of God. Let your light shine! If it again becomes darkness, how great will be the darkness. Lift up the light! Lift up a standard for the people!

The Divine Weaving

"See the mystic Weaver sitting
High in heaven—His loom below.
Up and down the treadles go.
Takes, for web, the world's dark ages,
Takes, for woof, the kings and sages.
Takes the nobles and their pages,
Takes all stations and all stages.
Thrones are bobbins in His shuttle.
Armies make them scud and scuttle—
Web into the woof must flow:
Up and down the nations go!
At the Weaver's *will* they go!

"Calmly see the mystic Weaver
Throw His shuttle to and fro;
'Mid the noise and wild confusion,
Well the Weaver seems to know
What each motion, and commotion,
What each fusion, and confusion,
In the grand result will show!

"Glorious wonder! What a weaving!
To the *dull*, beyond believing.
Such no fabled ages know.
Only faith can see the mystery,
How, along the aisles of history,
Where the feet of sages go,
Loveliest to the fairest eyes,
Grand the mystic tapet lies!
Soft and smooth, and ever spreading,
As if made for angels' treading—
Tufted circles touching ever:
Every figure has its plaidings,
Brighter forms and softer shadings,
Each illumined—what a riddle!
From a cross that gems the middle.

" 'Tis a saying—some reject it—
That its light is all reflected;
That the tapet's lines are given
By a Sun that shines in heaven!
'Tis believed—by all believing—
That great God, Himself, is weaving,
Bringing out the world's dark mystery,
In the light of faith and history;
And, as web and woof diminish,
Comes the grand and glorious finish,
When begin the Golden Ages,
Long foretold by seers and sages."

INDEX

TO

SCRIPTURE CITATIONS

OF

SCRIPTURE STUDIES, SERIES I

351

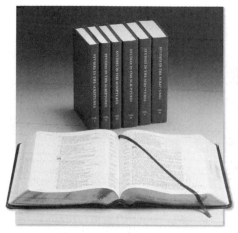

Studies in the Scriptures
The Most Comprehensive Bible Study Available!

Cloth bound pocket edition size books

The Divine Plan of the Ages—Gives an outline of the Divine Plan revealed in the Bible, Relating to man's Redemption, Restitution and the Object of the Lord's Return—*358 pages.*

The Time is at Hand—Studies deal with Bible chronology and time prophecies. Explains the Time and Manner of the Lord's Return; identifies the Antichrist—*371 pages.*

Thy Kingdom Come—Time Prophecies in Daniel, work of the Harvest of the Gospel Age, the setting up of the Kingdom of Christ; Great Pyramid of Egypt—*384 pages.*

The Battle of Armageddon—Explains the judgment and fall of the present order, discussing related prophecies such as Matthew 24, "The Lord's Great Prophecy"—*660 pages.*

The Atonement Between God and Man—A study of the facts and philosophy of Christ's providing the Ransom for All and his work of Atonement; the truth about hell and the operation of the holy Spirit—*498 pages.*

The New Creation—Studies in the Genesis account of Creation; also the laws, duties, privileges and hopes of consecrated followers of Christ—*738 pages.*

To order, contact Publisher:
Associated Bible Students
PO Box 92, Clawson, MI 48017 USA

—or order at www.bibletoday.com—

Most import.
Things about healing   relieved from
sin and
1st Peter 2:24   infirmities

Isaiah 53:4,5
Matt 8:17 (Isaiah) by

(1)   3 Witness
"It is God's will"   in plan of redemption
{ Not willing that any }
Believe it   (should perish)

(2) Sickness from Satan   Acts
     not from God   10:38 God anointed Jesus
Satan oppresses   Luke 13:16
Jesus delivers   (Satan bound)
     John 10:10

3) God deals with sickness in the
old and New testament

(4) Know there is more than one method
to heal (1) John 13:14
     ask   Jesus Name
James 5   Beyond helping themselves
Prayer faith (2) Prayer ask in Jesus name
heals the sick   Pray one for another

Mark 16:13 - the believing one
        signs shall follow them
(Gods Medicine)

5 you can initiate healing
        by your faith. said

John 5 - Jesus said rise

Luke 4:14 Jesus was annointed

6) Not always instantly
        John 9 - healing is a process

7. Gods method is spiritual and
        Can't be lost

Healing - one of the good things God
wants to give us

Luke 13:15,16 - Satan bound but Jesus
        loosed

Isiah 53
Matt 8:17
1st Peter 2:24